A Short Stay
on
Santa Cruz

A Short Stay
on
Santa Cruz

David Arathoon

With many thanks to Miles Bailey, Irene Wood and all the staff at the Choir Press.

First published in the United Kingdom in 2009
by Tumaiyek Publishing House

ISBN 978-0-9564471-0-4

Produced by
The Choir Press
www.thechoirpress.co.uk

Contents

Chapter 1	The Tropical Way	5
Chapter 2	Welcome to Lata	14
Chapter 3	Coconuts and Clams	22
Chapter 4	Spirits	32
Chapter 5	Bowels, Boats and Books	44
Chapter 6	Dozy Dogs and the Midday Sun	57
Chapter 7	Fun, Fire and Water	65
Chapter 8	Seized by Events (*Et tu* Cindrella)	76
Chapter 9	Gatherings, Greetings and Goodbyes	85
Chapter 10	Thrown: Up, Over, Along	95
Chapter 11	Working, Waiting and Wondering	113
Chapter 12	Beach ... Babes	125
Chapter 13	Tinakula	135
Chapter 14	Bikes, Boobies and Break-ins	148
Chapter 15	Laggards, Legs and Leave	156
Chapter 16	Food: Fish Guts, Foxes and Frights	166
Chapter 17	Holiday	175
Chapter 18	Canine Corpses and Contraception	188
Chapter 19	Nets and a Nitwit	197
Chapter 20	Anuta	207
End?		220
Note Quite ...		221

DAVID ARATHOON is of Armenian descent and was born in Kenya. After school in Wiltshire he qualified in medicine at St Bartholomew's Hospital. Since that time he has undertaken a trans-Africa photographic expedition, climbed three virgin peaks in the Chinese Pamirs and been elected a Fellow of the Royal Geographical Society. Having helped run the provincial health services in Temotu province of the Solomon Islands with his wife, he has learned his place, and now job shares with her in a small rural GP practice in Somerset.

For Sarah

In Memory of Wilson Lyno

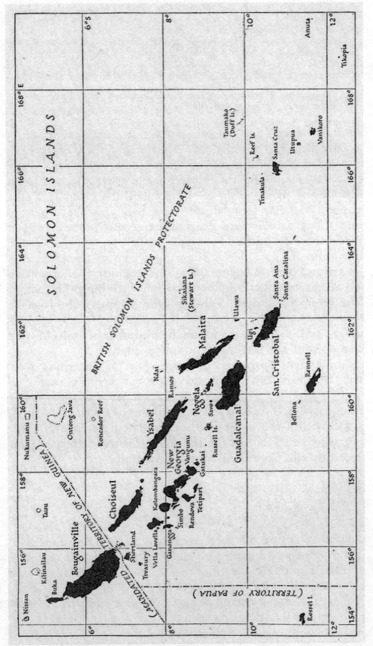

The Solomon Islands

In our two years we didn't see a single jet airliner. Not a sight, not a sound, not even a vapour trail. We lived in the most easterly and dispersed of the provinces in the Solomon Islands where we ran the health service for central government.

We had been offered medical posts out in this province of Temotu after a series of strange and occasionally bizarre coincidences and circumstances, including the miracle of the forwarding of a letter from Gizo Hospital (Western Province) to Geneva.

We set out as an ordinary little family of four, and came back a very changed family of five. Our perspectives altered entirely while we were in Lata, the provincial capital of Temotu. While there, the capital of the Solomons went from being a decrepit, filthy, rundown, slightly frightening place to a carefree, friendly, homely town in two years. Honiara hadn't changed, but we had.

I became a murdering dog-hater (actually I managed to do away with a wide variety of animal life – only a small minority of it human), having had a soft spot for canines before we left. Sarah, my wife, learnt to speak Pidgin fluently and made good friends with many locals, learning to understand their culture along the way. I made lots of friends, but apart from simple medical Pidgin I was hopeless. As for understanding their culture – I came away more bewildered than when I went.

Our eldest child, Meg, went to Lata at the age of four and came back at six. So one-third of her life was spent there. After an initial year of wariness she acted as if she had been born there. Her Pidgin was faultless and her attitudes became more and more Solomon. Barney, the boy, was four on his return, and had spent half his life in Lata. Because the UK had had a particularly benign paternal influence on their protectorate of the Solomons one of the consequences was that Barney as a white male child was spoilt by all and sundry, but luckily he didn't notice. Although Sarah and I spent a tiny proportion of our lives in the place it had a disproportionate effect on us.

As a family we found the transition into the Third World a piece of cake compared with the difficulties of our return to England. Even now, years later, I occasionally get nervous in Tesco's and daydream my way back to the lack of choice in Lata. The lack of choice and the relaxed way of life; the lack of rushing, and the time to read and swing in my hammock, and ... but no, looking round, Tesco's is the reality.

We had tropical rainstorms and droughts; cyclones and earthquakes; ships blown off course and canoes lost at sea; volcanoes erupting and spring tides closing the airstrip. Sharp-suited corrupt local politicians and ragged yet dignified local chiefs. We were only thirty years away from the last murderous inter-village dispute, but a lot further from our European predecessors who had come to the islands over the centuries. Mendana had set out from Spain in the sixteenth century promising to find a land overflowing with riches to enhance his king's power. He found our island instead and camped "down the bay" having inadvertently lost one of his three ships. He then lost the hearts of his crew soon before losing his life to the dreaded malarious mosquitoes. Not that they were dreaded in his time of course as most nasty fevers were blamed on the flux from the swamps. In the eighteenth century La Compte de la Perouse, a French gentleman explorer, was driven to the island of Vanikoro by a vicious cyclone, which threw him and his two ships onto the fringing reef. The cheerful locals couldn't believe their luck and ate quite a few of his crew. Many of the artefacts from his wrecked ships have been rescued from the enveloping coral and were brought to a tatty, damp, insecure storeroom in the Adult Education Centre in Lata.

We met and became friends with other expats, a strange bunch of whities most of whom we would have crossed the road to avoid back in the 'real' world. Many of them, like ourselves, were merely wisps passing through, but some had made a real difference for the local people.

Sarah and I went from the cosiness of general practice in the NHS to the wildness of medicine right on the edge. We were the only doctors in Temotu, a province of many thousands of square miles with severe communication problems; our 48-bed hospital on the island of Santa Cruz had seen better days, our drugs were old-fashioned and mostly time-expired. Our knowledge of tropical medicine was sketchy but we had to be all things: obstetricians, dermatologists, paediatricians, gynaecologists, surgeons, physicians and – probably the most difficult – managers of non-existent resources.

Our nearest help was in Honiara, three and a half hours flight away at the whim of the elements and the sudden tropical nights. And the telephones, which were often down. We felt naked and clinically rather isolated.

It was hot. The temperature hovered around 30° C day and night, week, month and year. The humidity heating index was always high at around 90%. We were uncomfortable. We sweated, we dripped and I think we smelt pretty ripe most of the time. Sarah hated the heat. I did not. Meg and Barney didn't notice.

This is the story of what happened to our family in those two years.

Chapter 1

The Tropical Way

Provincial Secretary
Lata   16/09/9#
Temotu Province.

WATER PROBLEM – LATA HOSPITAL

Once more due to the same Lata Hospital Out Patient Department and other
Laboratory services is closed for normal services.
For your informations nurses and other staff are now given time to go out to
fetch water and do their washing etc during official hours.

The situation as you are aware will be
disastreous if nothing is done immediately.

W. Lyno.
For: Director Provincial Health Services

TEMOTU PROVINCE.

Cc: DPHS/Temotu
cc: Para medics

We stepped off the plane at Henderson International Airport into what felt like warm soup and staggered over to the ramshackle, dripping, tin International terminal building herding our two very fractious children. We were suffering the worst of jet lag in the middle of the night.

The inside of the tin International terminal was hotter and even more humid than the soup outside; cockroaches abounded, geckoes darted and the screeching, rusty baggage conveyor could hardly be heard above the screeching of our children.

'Oh Mum ...'

'Come on Meg-peg, we'll be in bed soon ...' Lies, lies.

'Oh Mum ...' Arms straining upwards, face screwed up, pleading and tear stained.

'Don't worry ...' We just hoped we would be met, or spot a scrap of card with our name on it.

There were lots of people milling around on both sides of Customs: taxi-drivers, officials and who-knows-what moving to and fro, chatting and reverberating inside the terminal.

Finally our baggage appeared under the insect-flickering lights and we approached the first of many officials – pushing the unhappy children ahead as our forlorn hope.

'Hello sir, welcome to the Solomon Islands.' This from the large, fat, cheerful, very black and sweaty Immigration man from behind his narrow raised desk.'How long will you be staying in our Islands?'

'Well ... er ... shush Meg ... we're going to be working here for two years.'

'May I see your passports?' Still cheerful. 'Hmm, you don't seem to have work permits.' Not so cheerful ...

'Well, we are doctors and have contracts to work here for two years.'

'That's OK ... may I see your contracts? You haven't received them yet? Hmm – how about a letter from the Ministry of Health?'

'I'm sorry, we don't have any of those ...' He now looked even bigger, and much less happy. How had we allowed ourselves to come without a contract, or even a letter of authority? Why no work permits? Why had we paid for our own flights with only the promise of reimbursement? This was rather like the promises of pre-departure contracts, work permits and letters of authority ... Oh dear.

'Well we've been in touch with the Under-secretaries of State for Health,' hoping he would be as impressed by the title as we had been, but he wasn't, 'and ... er ... well, we are going to work in Lata Hospital on Santa Cruz.'

'Oh, Lata Hospital.' Very happy again, he leant back in his chair and said over his shoulder to one of the officials in the milling category: 'Hemi doctor, olketa by go lo' Lata for worka lo' hospital.' It wasn't the words that conveyed much meaning to us, more the tone. What was wrong with Lata? The official in charge of milling approached and they both looked at us miserable whities with huge sympathy. 'Tch ... Lata eh?' with benevolent and slightly amused shakes of the head.

The large official waved us through and the official of the milling category helped us carry our bags to the Customs area, all of three yards further through the International terminal.

Miller to Customs official: 'Dis fella man, hemi Doctor. Hem by go lo' Lata. By hemi worka lo' hospital lo' Lata.'

More sympathy and shaking of heads. However that dealt with Customs, and we were just beginning to wonder what was next when a tall, slim well-dressed chap approached and introduced himself as Ezekial Nakuru, one of the Under-secretaries of State for Health. All our bags were whipped away and loaded into the back of a pick-up which promptly disappeared into the darkness – we hoped they were heading to wherever we would be staying the night. Then we were led over the mud outside the tin terminal to a car. We were pleased to see that there were still a lot of whities wandering around looking lost.

What was wrong with Lata?

The car sped off with us along a dark road, which alternated between good and very poor, with the car's speed varying accordingly between 40 mph and 40 mph-with-bumps. We made very short shrift of a group of large crabs crossing the road from the sea to our right to the ... well we knew not what in the darkness to the left. They may have waved their claws in as threatening a manner as their tiny brains could conceive but we ran them over anyway, with the rather attractive crunching noise wafted in to us on the soup through the open windows.

Honiara is not a big place. Before we knew it, and in fact while waiting for it to develop into something a bit more like a capital city, we were through the other side and entering the western suburbs. Here was the Iron Bottom Sound Hotel where we collapsed, having been told by the correct Dr Nakuru to be ready by 9 am the next day so we could be taken to Central Hospital and to various Ministries. We had seen the all-colour adverts for the IBS

Hotel in the airline magazine – but it had failed to mention that the hotel wasn't quite finished. There was no reception desk but the air conditioning worked and soon dispersed the soup from our rooms. Next day we found out that the food was good ... and we also discovered that the Coral Sea was beginning to make inroads into the wall in front of our room, but we reckoned we would be long gone for when the brochure changed from 'Sea-view' to 'Sea'.

We had also learnt the meaning of 'Solomon Island time' by 11 o'clock when we were still waiting to be picked up. Unusually for me I was quite relaxed by this appalling demonstration of punctuality, and I spent a couple of useful hours down on the tiny beach with Meg and Barney examining the view across the glassy sea to Tulaghi, the coral, the hermit crabs and all the other bits and bobs to be found on a ten-foot-long tropical beach. We discovered that one of the best things to do was to sit still on the gently sloping shore for a few minutes until the tiny hermit crabs reckoned that the giant-crab-eating-monsters must, by definition, have gone away ... and then to make a sudden movement, stopping to hear all the stolen hermit homes tumbling down the coral as the crabs pulled their feet in. They appeared to have reached an evolutionary block. Actually, sitting quietly in the early morning soup was really rather pleasant, doing little but chatting and letting our minds run in neutral for a while. We were to learn that 'Solomon Island time' was a real entity and would often check on a time for an event with: 'Is that half two Solomon time, or half two?'

We were finally picked up and taken off to the rather grand sounding Ministry of Health, over the road and up a bit from Central Hospital ('No. 9' or 'National Referral Hospital' depending on whether you were an elderly local who could remember the Americans building their ninth Military Hospital during the war, or a bureaucrat trying to impress foreign aid workers). The journey time could be extended by traffic jams caused by the rush-hour cars (all two hundred of them) trying to negotiate the huge potholes outside the Ministry of Transport, but we were lucky the first day. At the Ministry of Health we met Jimmy Rodgers, the other Undersecretary of State for Health. He was a very pleasant, slim chap with impeccable manners and beard, who rightly had the reputation of someone who could get things done – a very unusual specimen.

After introductions: 'I'm very glad to see you both. As you know, Temotu has been without any full time doctors for over 18 months, and the Principal Nursing Officer has had to run the whole Provincial Health Service on his own. Luckily, in Wilson Lyno you will have one of the best nurses in the country as your PNO. Right, shall we have a look round the Hospital? Sorry? Oh, don't worry about the children, we will find someone to look after them, or in fact why don't you bring them along as we go round the hospital?'

On enquiries re contract, reimbursement for flights, work permits, visa extensions, etc: 'I'm afraid your contracts aren't ready yet, but the Prime Minister's Office says they should be in two days' time – but they tell me your inducement payment is indeed ready now.' What inducement payment? Why hadn't we been told about it when it would still have been an inducement? Oh well …

Over the next few days we were shown around all the departments in the hospital, met most of the consultants, including a mad Irishman called David Fegan and a rather Germanic Swiss surgeon called Hermann Oberli who both had us over for supper. We also visited just about every ministerial building in town; these were all very similar to one another in that they appeared absolutely deserted. Whenever we actually managed to find someone they had no idea of the whereabouts of the office of the person we had an appointment with. When we managed to find the correct office the person was never in, and his secretary knew neither a) where he was, nor b) when he would be back. The kids enjoyed shouting in the echoing corridors, but in an effort to keep the dust down we didn't let them run round too much. However the chief accountant in the Prime Minister's office was a revelation. Not only did she go to work, but she worked at work, and worked hard. She answered the phone and even occasionally answered letters. Maima was the most wonderful, efficient person working in a morass of mediocrity. A lifesaver thrown into sharp relief by the total lack of competition.

One evening back at the hotel, standing in the relative cool beside the sea outside our rooms, I saw a UFO. A beautiful elongated silvery-white shape moving across the sky and slowly blotting out the stars in front while revealing those behind. I poked my head into our neighbour's room to ask the Solomon Island doctor in there to come out and have a look.

'What do you think it is?'

He craned up. 'I don't know – beautiful though, isn't it?'

The odd thing was, that standing in the luke-warm air coming in off the Coral Sea in a silent dark city on the other side of the world, it didn't seem at all out of place. I felt not a tinge of surprise although it was the second UFO I had seen, and I don't even believe in them.

*

Between plodding the corridors of the ministerial buildings and the hospital and wandering the hot, dusty or muddy streets of Honiara (depending on the weather) we found time to have siestas, swim in the pool at the dishevelled posh Mendana hotel and attend some post-natal sterilisation operations which we would be expected to do in Lata. We also managed to cadge a Suzuki jeep off the WHO via Jimmy Rodgers and had a good look round. There are still lots of reminders of the ferocious battles that took place over Henderson airport during the Second World War: guns in the jungle, small arte-fact museums, Quonsot huts etc. We had brought a Lonely Planet guide with us to the Solomons and from its pages we made up our own battlefield tour, visiting Red beach (site of a wasted Banzai charge by 800 Japanese against entrenched machine-gun wielding Yanks) at the bar across a small river. Basically the Japs were all mown down – obviously hadn't read their First World War history books. We saw *the* original Foxhole (a five foot by three foot concrete-lined hole beside the road that Colonel Fox used during the battles); a Memorial in the hills – up some appalling roads; some underground bat-filled bunkers and a very good military museum at Betikama where incongruously they keep a crocodile behind some wire. It is fed on chickens – the kids loved it. We were also ambushed by a ravening horde of gigantic, vicious, brutal hungry mosquitoes and had to beat our own retreat out of a coconut plantation without getting to see something so interesting I can't remember what it was. All these places are out of town towards the international airport, but we also went out west to Bonegi beach. This is where the Japs ran two ships ashore in a last-ditch attempt to get sufficient men and materials onto the island to see off the round eyes. These round-eyed Americans were still clinging on to the rather good airstrip (now read Henderson International Airport – that good), which the Imperial Japanese forces themselves had built. Enough to have irri-tated them in the extreme. Unfortunately the efficient Yanks noticed, and sank the ships and tanks and jeeps and food and medicines and munitions and of course the men accompanying them. Poor sods. The ship known as Bonegi I is just offshore and as it has superstruc-ture above the waves is easily snorkellable. I was more interested in Bonegi II and made enquiries in town with a view to scuba-diving on it.

'Have you ever scuba-dived before?'

'Yes.'

'Do you have any certificates or logs?'

'None whatsoever.'

'That's fine, when would you like to go?' And so it turned out. I was let loose with Luke, a very black black, hip, cool local from Western Province who was a diving instructor. We snorkelled about twenty yards out and then dived down to what had once been the bow of Bonegi II before it had been blown off. Initially I wondered what all the fuss had been about diving in the Solomons, but then the visibility suddenly cleared and there sat a huge ship, listing over on her port side and disappearing down into the murk – quite a sight. If it hadn't been for the fact that one of my recurring nightmares as a child had been to be trapped under the hull of a huge ship I would probably have enjoyed the first fifteen minutes of the dive a bit more. We swam down the side of the ship – in reality the keel as it was on its side – then we came up and over and down through a shell hole in the deck and into a near-deserted hold filled with shafts of sunlight streaming through other holes and cracks. It was extraordinary to be floating in the middle of the hold in the middle of a ship in the middle of the ocean. Although we didn't see any, the poor old Japs were never far from the forefront of my mind. Amongst the fish and corals and plankton we found plenty of evidence of their intentions: bullets and live shells, and of their everyday lives: bottles and tiny fine ceramic rice bowls. On our return Luke said that although the wrecks were protected Australian divers had nicked most removable artefacts. He wasn't upset, just stating a fact. An amazing place.

The date of departure for Santa Cruz came and went three or four times, but people (the secretary, Ezekial, Jimmy, the hospital superintendent and the parrot belonging to the second relief Monday hospital driver) kept forgetting to book the flight. We had time to take all our heavy non-essentials down to the wharf to be loaded onto the good ship *Mawo III*, having been into QQQ in Chinatown to get food supplies from the ever-smiling fat proprietor Michael. Even the Mawo beat us to Santa Cruz. Most of our questions remained unanswered: What sort of hospital was in Santa Cruz? How many staff? What was our house like? Did it have running water? Electricity? A telephone? How far from the beach was it? No one knew.

But suddenly we were off, sitting in the back of a tiny inter-islander hopper with twenty-three people (all carefully weighed) and piles of luggage (also weighed) crammed into nineteen seats. No live chickens though. We stopped at Makira so that a couple of drums of aviation fuel could be rolled out and hand pumped into the plane, the fuel having first been checked for impurities by splashing the first litre into a 300-ml soft-drink bottle which was held to the light and pronounced clean. We saw little of Makira except a beautiful coral/mud/grass airstrip between swaying coconut palms beside the shore, and a rather nasty little shed. Then it was up and away again into the blue, no sight of land for two hours until the rather oversteep descent to another grass airstrip, this time the International Airport of Santa Cruz.

We were met by dozens of brown and black smiling faces, cheerful and jolly. 'Welcome, welcome'. Tall, squinting Wilson Lyno the PNO was there, immaculately turned out in his nursing uniform of white-collared shirt and creased shorts. His great big callused feet overflowed a pair of long-worn flip-flops. He introduced us to some of his trusty staff including his round, smiling wife Ellen, and then an array of cheerful nurses of various hues. He called forward the lady who was to be our housegirl and Hilda, for that was her name, stretched up and placed sweet-smelling frangipani-flower leis round our necks – wonderful. We realized that their very evident joy at our arrival probably had more to do with the lack of medical top-cover they had had to put up with for nearly two years, rather than anything specifically about us. Still it was rather nice to be wanted. Wilson arranged for us to sit in the back of a pick-up truck to be taken along the dusty coral road through Lata station to what initially seemed our rather imposing house. Here were all the belongings that we had put on an aircraft in England and more recently entrusted to the *Mawo III*. The crew on the ship had forgotten to charge us for the privilege. We were shown round the house by Hilda, a plump, smiling Jehovah's Witness, and found she had cleaned and scrubbed the place for our arrival. We did indeed have electricity, and a telephone and a brand new fridge freezer. A 600-gallon water tank and a great big garden. The station of Lata had a hot-bread shop and lots of small dusty stores selling tinned tuna. Some stores sold the real thing, frozen solid. Everyone spoke Pidgin and some spoke English and some a combination. It was all rather overpowering, but Wilson told us not to come down to the hospital until the next day. What a good chap.

What a great place.

CHOISEUL PROVINCE GOVERNMENT
PROVINCIAL OFFICE
PO BOX 34
CHOISEUL BAY
CHOISEUL PROVINCE
SOLOMON ISLAND.

Permanent Secretary
MHMS
P.O.Box 349
Honiara

Your Ref

Our Ref: CHP:1/19

Date: 16.5.#

Attn: Assistant Director of Nursing Services

Dear Sir,

RE: PAYMENT OF FARE ON POSTING AND DISTURBANCE
ALLOWANCE

Further to reference HMS 5/1/9, dated 3/2/# refers.

1. The respond to your memo by DPHS/Ysable, F08/11/3, dated 14/4/#.
DPHS/WP, FW 7/1/8, dated 7/5/# , my endorsement of the same CPH: 1/19,
dated
20/3/# , need to be considered , especially the comment raised by DPHS/WP ,
para 2 to 6, same to my para 1 to 3.
2. It is now evidence that the Ministry ignores the inputs and directly
Implement the memo HMS 5/1/9, that the Province has to meet recurrent costs.
3. The posting orders, copy received for a Registered Nurse employed from
Central Hospital to Choisel and a SNO/Choiseul posting order from Choiseul
to Malaita confirms the receiving provinces to meet travellings and
disturbance allowances.
4. It would be impossible for the two remote provinces to contact each other
and arrange for travelling of officers rather than the MHMS as the head Ministry
to co-ordinate posting arrangement.
5. I still have strong feeling that the directives on PHS grant be committed
for matter possibly not within the interest of all the Provinces, in terms of
recurrent budget allocation and further request the MHMS to re-consider revoke
the decision and accept responsibilities by making additional recurrent estimate
at its budget to cater for such head/subhead. Malaita PHS would find it difficult
to meet expenses for luaggages and for the staff from Choiseul to Malaita,
especially
Choiseul to Honiara as provinces need a co-ordinating body in Honiara for such
Arrangement and there would be now not possible.
6. Lastly but the least, I wish to thank the MHMS to offer Annual Leave to
the deployed Reg. Nurse (Mr . R. Pulupa) before transferred to Choiseul. This
has been the issue I have concerned about to my para 4 of my letter CPH/1/19
dated 20/3/#

Thank you.

B. Sasa, DPHS (Ag), Choiseul Province.

Cc: DPHS – Provinces

Chapter 2

Welcome to Lata

2nd April 199#
Permanent Secretary
Ministry of Health & Med. Services
PO Box 349
Honiara

Dear Sir,

Re: HOSPITAL SECRETARY, SUPERVISORY POST, LEVEL 5

I believe that Lata Hospital has an establishment for the above post.
As a new Director of Health Services I would find help in the Office extremely
useful and I would appreciate it if you could advertize the post.
Many thanks.
I look forward to hearing from you.

Yours faithfully
Dr D. Arathoon.
Director of Provincial Health services
TEMOTU PROVINCE

                                    CC: PS/Temotu

Having spent a day and a night in Lata, our minds were full and our bodies exhausted. We had been introduced to innumerable very important people (the Provincial Minister of Health didn't bother to introduce himself for eighteen months ... strangely just when his political campaign started ...). We met all the nurses whose names I promptly forgot – Sarah having a memory for these things. Then there were the staff in the malaria lab, the hospital lab, the X-ray room and the pharmacy.

The nurses obviously knew what they were about and looked very smart in their uniforms, in contrast to the average person in town. The sartorial elegance of the average citizen of Temotu has to be marked on the negative side of the scale. Clothes are not chosen in the mornings for much beyond covering the naughty bits – upper thighs in women and the shorts area in men. In addition, due to their rather constricted views on religion the Melanesian women seem to choose rather sack-like clothes in which to dress – usually a long baggy T-shirt with a below-the-knee skirt over a pair of shorts – belt and braces as it were in case the wind got up. This does make them somewhat shapeless to our jaded western eyes. Even if they wore the sexiest clothes possible (a terrible thought if you have lived in Temotu for any length of time) the Melanesian women would still carry themselves in the same rather plodding manner to reduce their profile on any nearby male radar. The Polynesians on the other hand could not hide their shapeliness and sexuality if they had to wear a full chador. They have immense grace and physical style, presence and poise. An amazing contrast. The actual clothes anyone wears may be worn in any state of disrepair, or any state of grubbiness, and whether they are inside out or not depends entirely on how they were taken off the line. Now, I am not one for dress sense (or regular shaving even) but even I was a little taken aback by the fashions on display. But the nurses looked great.

Sarah and I were conducted around all the inpatients in the slowly decaying 48-bed hospital by a bevy of the aforesaid nurses. We were very impressed by their clinical skills and by their management of the problems. Quite often the main problem would be followed by :

'... and she has malaria as well.'

'Ah ... so what should we do about that?'

'Oh, she's already had PT.'

'Oh ... good, good, er ... who's next?'

We found out soon enough that PT is 'presumptive treatment'

but tried not to look too stupid until it was explained to us later on.

Malaria is incredibly common in the Solomons, and looked upon as just one of those things – much like a cold would be regarded in the West. So much for all the horror stories we had heard back in the UK. When it is all round and diagnosed and treated quickly then it is accepted as a minor hazard – like driving on the motorway. Most people on malarial islands have a decent immunity to the disease built up over many infections since childhood. The nurses told us that women in labour who are found to have malaria beg not to have their treatment until they have delivered, as the treatment itself makes them feel so shabby. They also say that occasionally they get a visitor from one of the outlying non-malarious islands who becomes extremely unwell with malaria, which would be what would happen to us whities if we got it. I couldn't decide if getting malaria would be rather romantic, or rather stupid.

In the afternoon of our first full day I was sitting in my new office thinking about having a look at the overladen in-tray, when a nurse from Outpatients popped in to say that there was a girl they wanted me to look at. Outpatients seemed to function as an extended Casualty, a walk-in clinic where most problems got seen and sorted out. Putting the escape from paperwork down to good luck this first time I followed the nurse into the clinical room, to be confronted by a nineteen-year-old girl called Alex who was attempting to vomit up her life's blood all over the floor.

Oh God ...

The chloroquine she had taken for three days for malaria had given her a bit of indigestion and she had started vomiting blood an hour before over at the school on the other side of the bay. Alex had got to the hospital in the leaky school canoe. The girls were putting up an intravenous line and I found her conscious but shocked, with a pulse of 96 and a blood pressure of 80/50, just enough to keep her old kidneys going. At least this was not a tropical medicine type of emergency, and I had some clue as to what to do. We took blood for a blood count (7.4 – should be at least 12) and cross matching and then the lab tech (? Richard) set out to look for wantoks (i.e., family or people that 'tok' the same language – Pidgin is not the most descriptive of languages) who might be prepared to donate blood, and who might have the correct sort of blood group. With some intravenous fluids going, Alex's blood pressure soon picked up and although she remained peaky, her vomiting settled and she was able to report that she had not passed any stinking tar-like stools (or 'sitty' as the locals say).

After a couple of hours someone was found who fulfilled the requisite criteria and we started Alex on her first pint of donated blood. I wandered back to the office to look at the in-tray. Even before I had managed to lift the first important document I was called back to see her (it couldn't have been more than twenty minutes) as she felt worse and had 'come out in a rash'. I felt joy at the interruption to my paperwork with a what-the-hell's-going-on anxiety in my own belly.

To compound her problems Alex now had a good-going transfusion reaction. This was probably her first, and it was undoubtedly the first one her doctor had had to deal with. She was covered from head to foot in an itchy sort of rash (urticaria) which was just starting to make her lips look Monroe-esque, her blood pressure had plummeted and her pulse was up again. I stated my clinical judgement, to looks of relief from the nurses who had no idea what was going on.

'Okey-doke ... let's get that blood down, change the giving-set and give her a bit of saline – yup a litre will do ...' The giving-set is the tube which runs from the plastic bag with the blood in to the small canula in the patient's arm. It filters the blood and controls its rate of flow. It had to be changed as it was contaminated with the donated blood which was causing the reaction. '... What sort of antihistamines have we got?'

'We use promethazine, Doctor – how much should I give her?'

'How much in that vial?'

'Twenty-five milligrams.'

'That sounds fine ... now, what about a bit of IV hydrocortisone – have you any in here? ... yup ... yeah, a couple of vials will do – give her that now and can you make sure we have some adrenaline about in case she doesn't respond? Thanks.'

But she did respond and all her allergic symptoms settled over the next hour or so. Her blood pressure stayed up and we kept the only other unit of blood we had as an emergency. Just as I was heading off home for a cup of tea, the ward sister said, 'We've started her on presumptive, Doctor.'

'Oh really? Wh— I mean good ... good. Er, call me if you need me later.'

Why on earth were they treating a patient for malaria when in fact they had a gastrointestinal bleed? Especially as that had been the cause of the problem in the first place. The chloroquine she had been given at school had irritated her stomach sufficiently to cause it to bleed. And now they were giving her more chloroquine – this was quickly becoming a circular problem. What was going on? A discreet word with Ellen Lyno educated us: a proportion of the population has malaria at any one time, one of those could have been Alex's donor and the rule was to treat all those who received blood with chloroquine. Whatever the cause ...

One of the reasons for coming halfway round the world was to escape the midnight phone call, so you can imagine my horror that night when the phone went. I was mighty bleary.

'Oh Doctor, come to hospital.'

'What ...?'

'Come to hospital, Alex trow up for good.'

'Who ... did what?'

'Doctor, Doctor – Alex hem trow out staka blood dis time.' Mild hysteria.

'Hmm. OK, I'll come.'

It was only when I was reaching the hospital that the nurse's meaning reached my consciousness, and sure enough, there was Alex surrounded by pools of fresh-looking blood. She looked pale and had the whiff of sticky tar about her. Memories of standing by a bedside in England helping my Registrar literally squeeze pints of blood by hand into a forty-year-old as she inexorably died, came right to mind.

'Jesus, get that other pint up straight away – also get me another needle and let's run some fluid into the other arm. What's the chance of getting some more blood tonight?' Hopeful look at frightened nurses.

'Me no savvy Doctor.'

'OK, send someone to find the lab tech – Richard isn't it?'

'No more yet Doctor, nem b'lo hem Michael.'

'Michael, Michael, right get him here quickly and we'll try to find some more blood.'

After half an hour Michael duly arrived from his house 200 yards away, with the good news that he knew of someone with O negative blood – hurrah! The universal donor.

'So where's this chap then?'

'Hem stop lo Bay, Doctor.'

'OK, OK, how do we get him here?' In the truck apparently.

'OK, OK, where's the truck driver?'

'Me no savvy.' Hmm.

'So where's the truck?'

'Lo 'der Doctor,' pointing to a white Toyota pick-up with a

broken front spring, sitting under a small metal canopy at the bottom of a short steep slope outside the malaria lab. There was no way out except up the slope behind the truck – so I jumped in, found the correct key on the bunch Wilson Lyno had given me before and then found that the battery was flat. Small cold sweat. Richard/Michael, both night nurses and a couple of arm-twisted but enthusiastic passers-by pushed the truck as far backwards up the slope as possible. I put on the footbrake, put her in second and gave the word to push, hoping to gain enough speed in the twenty yards of flat ground to start the engine and slam on the brakes before I demolished the pharmacy store. It took us three goes but finally the truck started. The fuel gauge read zero and the head-lights were none too bright, but we set off for the 'Bay'. It was hot, the road was pot-holed, coconut fringed and virtually invisible. I had no idea where we were going, and the headlights were fading. As we turned onto the bay road the moon glinted on the calm sea which we could see through the coconut palms to our left, and gently lit the white coral road ahead. The moonshine was some-what brighter than the Toyota's headlamps.

'Slow now Doctor ... tink tink blo me hem stop close up.' We were getting near.

'You mean you're not sure?'

'Me sure Doctor, hem stop close up.'

We struck lucky at the third house, and I was most surprised to see John, the hospital clerk, emerge from a leaf house – so that was 'the man' with O negative blood. A doubly useful chap.

We got John back and he gave a unit and a half of blood. Alex settled, didn't have any more reactions and I was left wondering if I should try and arrange a charter flight now at 4 am to get her to Honiara, or get a couple of hours' sleep and then try to arrange one at a more godly hour. And then, who to arrange it through ... the physicians or the surgeons? In the end I went to bed.

At 6 am the phone went again. In the time it took me to answer I persuaded myself that they could only ring at that time if something awful had happened. But no, they rang just to let me know that the blood had run through and they had put up some more saline.

'Alex, hem arright Doctor – hem no trow up dis time.'

I still wonder why they phoned. Being awake and it not being too horrendously early, I decided to arrange the charter – I plumped for the physicians and got a rather grumpy David Fegan on the line. He soon cheered up and said he would sort out sending a plane to collect the girl.

'Oh, and I will let the surgeons know she's coming.' So now I knew.

The charter duly arrived in the afternoon, by which time Alex had decided to have another bleed. She was stable-ish so we put her in the back of the sturdy broken-springed Hilux, handed both bags of saline through the window to a stranger who had appeared on the back and took her to the airstrip three minutes away. There we were confronted by two problems: the five-seater plane did not look big enough for a stretcher and nurse, let alone the two sitting cases who needed to be sent to Honiara (a newborn without an anus and an elderly man requiring a prostatectomy). Even worse was Alex's uncle, a bearded ruffian who was insisting on going with his niece. After great arguments I told him he could not possibly go as he could see how little room there was. (Fred, we found out later, was no relation whatsoever but just a schoolteacher hoping for a free ride to Honiara – not that anyone mentioned it at the time, of course.)

The Kiwi pilot and I moved round some of the seats in the aircraft while Alex lay on a stretcher beside the plane in the sun. To shade the poor patient Sarah borrowed an umbrella from one of the many umbrella-toting people present who had come down for all the free entertainment. Alex was much less worried by the sun than by the fear that in her position on the ground someone may be able to get a surreptitious view of her thighs – she was in agonies trying to keep covered.

Finally, the interior of the plane was ready and the Kiwi and I manhandled the ten-stone Alex on her stretcher into the cabin. By now sweat was dripping off the end of my nose onto the poor girl's face – small price to pay I reckoned. The others got in and away they went.

Later that day I was again eyeing up the paperwork when Wilson Lyno, the Principal Nursing Officer, popped his head in.

'Welcome to Lata, Doctor.'

'Thanks, Wilson.'

Lata Hospital
Santa Cruz
Temotu Province
9th May 199#

Dr. David Fegan
Central Hospital.

Dear David,

Before she left Elizabeth Rodgers asked us if we would send you a list of adult
cardiac patients who could do with seeing the visiting cardiac team in
September. So here it is ...
1.   Lora Yamgala, Age 29 yrs, Otabwe (Reefs), mixed mitral disease
2.   Mary Wia Age 18 yrs, Meneu, MS and pulm HT.

That's it. Had a good search round, but not surprisingly most of our cardiac
patients are Paediatric or dead.
Regards to Jackie and hope to see you sometime.

Yours sincerely
Dr David Arathoon
Director Provincial Health Services
TEMOTU PROVINCE

Chapter 3

Coconuts and Clams

Lata Hospital
Santa Cruz
Temotu Province.

17 June 1996

Albert Noel Punufimana
Director Nursing Services
Ministry of Health Medical Services
Honiara.

DPHS file.

Dear Mr. Punufimana

Many thanks for your fax and subsequent letter regarding the behavior of RN T. Teika.

To reiterate:
This man had complaints made against him while working at Nuoba. He received a written warning from his immediate Supervisor (Selwyn Hou) at Manuopo. He then absconded from his post without permission, and came to Lata where he received a second written warning from myself. He then flew to Honiara against very specific verbal and written instructions from PNO Wilson Lyno. His conduct is unprofessional.

He **is** wanted at Manuopo. They have had to put themselves to great inconvenience to cover his unauthorized absence and are therefore short staffed. He would be under the direct day to day supervision of Selwyn Hou. His attitude while at Lata has nothing whatsoever to do with his attitude when he is again placed out in a peripheral clinic.

He is currently working in the Out Patient Department of Lata Hospital under the supervision of ANO Yvonne Sisiolo. I am not sure what sort of message you wish to send to my nurses working at distant Health clinics. They probably assume that if they want to change their working environment all they have to do is leave their post without permission, and then they will be employed at Lata hospital. This is an unbelievable situation and I will have no more to do with it. I have asked ANO Sisiolo to report to me on the behavior of Teika, but I doubt anything he does now will bring upon him the disciplinary action he deserves.

I hope you understand this situation has placed me, and all my senior nurses in an extremely difficult position.

Yours sincerely

Dr. David Arathoon.
Director Provincial Health Services
TEMOTU PROVINCE.

I was somewhat overdressed for the occasion in that I had on a pair of shorts and a T-shirt over my underpants, unlike Meg and Barney. We were standing around a fallen coconut just outside the verandah, each with our hands on our hips and each frowning. This was an important decision and we wanted to get it right.

'What about over there?' from Meg, first pointing at the sprouting coconut at our feet, and then at the base of the nearest coconut tree ten yards away.

'Dad, Dad, look ...' Barney bent down and turned the coconut over to reveal a white squiggly worm of a root poking out from the opposite end to the tiny green shoot.

'Isn't that amazing Barnes? No Meg it will have to be away from all the other trees; at least we know which way up it goes,' looking around and eyeing up all the spaces in our garden.

A few years previously in a fit of efficiency (and to overcome the niggling problem of all the doctors in the country being on strike) central government had employed twenty Philipino doctors. They were obviously a bad job lot and were sent home in disgrace after a year or so. Anyway the hapless chap who had been sent to Lata seemed to have let the place get to him, and had gone a bit potty, according to Hilda. Still, thousands of miles away from home, in a foreign culture, and most importantly on his own, I can understand his reaction. He had become paranoid, but while working his way there had started peeing against the wall of the hospital mid ward round; then he took to peeing on the floor of his (now our) house at night. Towards flipping time he slept with a bush knife under his pillow and instructed his gardener to chop down all the shrubs and bushes around the house that had, until then, proved a haven for all the whispering, sniggering, tiptoeing, bush knife-wielding, red-eyed, wild-haired locals of his imagination.

Poor old Dr Philipino was finally pushed right over the edge and back to his mother's bosom by a young man who came into the hospital with a hernia. Through some administrative cock-up he failed to get the patient onto a scheduled flight out of Lata, and had then had to watch him slowly die of a strangulated hernia. It must have been awful for all involved. We found the records of the horrendous event mouldering away at the back of a drawer in the house. A measure of the state of the doctor was his handwriting, which deteriorated along with the hernia, and came to an abrupt end just before the patient. The whole episode was relayed to us by Wilson when we showed him the hospital notes we had discovered.

So that was why our garden was a bit barren, according to Hilda anyway. And that in turn was why we wanted to plant a coconut. That and the fact I thought it may be the only lasting achievement of our stay. I think I was right.

'Now, we have got to find the spot furthest from all the other coconut and ... er, what did Hilda call those other trees Meg?'

'Alitays.'

'Yup, from them as well. OK Barnaboy, you go off and count how many steps between that one and that one, and Meg you do the same between those two,' pointing out three hugely tall coconut trees and one Alitay.

Using this accurate scientific method we plumped for a spot down towards the most massive Alitay tree which was at the edge of the garden and near the clump of finger banana trees. Meg reckoned this Alitay looked a very likely place for a tree house and I could but agree.

Barney carried the coconut against his chest down to the selected spot and Meg followed with the bush knife while I coordinated the event. The bush knife we had brought all the way from QQQ in Honiara, but we may as well have bought it in Birmingham, as that was where it had been made.

I used the knife to dig a hole to put the coconut in but soon came up against rather unforgiving coral – so that's why the coconut trees in our garden had most of their roots above ground. We plonked the chosen nut in the scrape and all carefully heaped what soil we could around it to keep it upright. Meg was dispatched to get some water and she returned with a bucketful and Sarah. We emptied the gallon or so round the potential tree and stepped back to admire it – it looked grand. We needn't have bothered with the water though as several hundred tons of it fell on our garden that night.

'Shall we have a look round the rest of the garden?' from Sarah.

'Yup, let's get Hilda to tell us what everything is.'

So we wandered round in a little group being told what each thing was. We recognized some: pawpaws, bananas, pineapples (none in fruit) but the majority were new to us. By the time we were standing on the cover of the septic tank at the back of the house – the best place from which to see the distant twinkling blue blue waters of Graciosa Bay – we had had pointed out to us cutnuts, soursops, oranges incongruously high up thin spindly trees, gnali nuts and all sorts of other wonders. According to

Hilda the local kids would nick our produce if we didn't keep a close eye on it all.

When we first arrived in Lata we had been presented with Eric-the-gardener. He was to be paid the princely sum of SI$13 (£2) a day to work three days a week. Hilda was a little unsure of him and told us that the older John-the-gardener used to work for the doctors. Eric seemed to be doing an adequate job and he certainly mowed the extensive bushless, shrubless grass with an efficient constant forehand/backhand swish of his long stemmed brush knife.

We could see him now behind us beside the water tank stand grubbing weeds out of the coral soil to try to make the bare patch behind the kitchen look more lawn-like.

Hilda showed us the bright red fibreglass water tank with some pride. Not many Jehovah's Witnesses worked for someone so important that they had a large red water tank, and, wonder of wonders, a small electric pump to get the water into the house. Pretty hot stuff. She pointed out the blue snake of a pipe on the ground which would top up the tank for half an hour very early each morning and evening to augment the water off the roof which was channelled into the hole in the top of the tank via a rickety piece of 'roofing iron' (corrugated iron or 'Copper' in Pidgin – God knows why) held up with two pieces of rusty wire and one piece of string.

I wondered why the blue pipe was on the ground and archly thought I would save myself two years of 5.30 a.m. starts to the day by picking it up, climbing onto the tank stand and pushing it through the hole in the top of the tank. To prevent it falling out I had to push it virtually to the bottom of the tank.

'That look all right, Hilda?'

'Er ... me no savvy.' Daft woman.

Not so daft the next morning when I went to check the level in the tank to find only two inches in the bottom as the rest had siphoned out through the blue pipe.

'We'd better get going if we're to be ready to go down to the beach with Helen.' We had rushed through our ward round by 9.30 on this Friday in readiness to be taken to her favourite beach by Helen the VSO legal advisor. Of course we remained on call; well, there were no other doctors to cover the hospital for each and every 24 hours. We followed Sarah into the kitchen and gathered swimming togs and flippers and snorkels as Helen had promised to pick us up at 9.30. It was now 10.30 and we were beginning to realize that Helen had indeed taken to Solomon Island time. Sarah even had time to nip off with Hilda to have a look at some of the local stores to get a few essentials. I hid my poor Pidgin by staying behind to await the legal advisor.

Time is the one thing that Solomon islanders have in abundance. There is never any temptation to rush, which could be construed as laziness. Actually I looked upon it as filling the day. There are plenty of fish in the sea, there is lots of land to garden, lots of rain-fall and sunshine to make things grow, and so not much to do. Shopping in the stores was one of the few things that wives of provincial government employees could do to fill the day. Each store was much the same as all the rest. Each had the same single room with a wooden floor, a wooden counter and dusty wooden shelves for the same produce as the other stores. Prices were all much of a muchness and all stores ran out of the same things at the same time when the ship was due in. Owners of stores tended to come and go a bit as they found it difficult to compete, not with other stores but with their Wantoks who helped themselves to items for free. However there was great kudos attached to being a store-owner.

The whole time we were in Lata, whenever we entered a store the place would go quiet and everyone would step away from the counter to let us go first so they could see what the white man was going to buy. Occasionally we did manage to watch others doing their shopping. It was fascinating: first an item would be selected – viz a bag of rice; an enquiry would be made as to its cost, say $20.50; the customer would hand over $25 and the boy behind the counter would reach for his calculator and start to stab it: 2 5.0 0 C C C 2 5 . 0 0 - 2 0 . 5 0 = C C C, 2 5 . 0 0 - 2 0 . 5 0 = He would then hand over $4.50 change. The customer would then select the next item and so on ad infinitum, or so it seemed.

Around 11 a.m., just as the sun was approaching its zenith, a sweaty flushed Helen appeared up the garden path. She was of middle height, plump (well ... fat), had curly light-coloured hair and a large smile. She was always kind to us. However because of the late start and the midday heat this first trip of ours to the beach nearly blighted our relationship from the start.

We set off walking from our house, past the library, the police station, adult education, the agricultural offices, post office and finally the hospital – waving to the girls in the nursing station and making swimming motions with our hands while shouting 'Luova' as that was where we were going. They looked a bit anxious. We carried on along the impressive cambered crushed-coral road (thank you the UK) down to the airstrip. Here three things happened. Firstly our two children ran out of steam and had to be carried, secondly the coral road took a swerve right and headed towards the bay (I was alarmed to realize that I recognized none of it although I had only recently driven along it at breakneck speed) and we headed off across the airstrip towards the fabled 'Luova'.

Forty-five hot-sweaty-dripping-panting-child-carrying minutes later we arrived at what was to become *our* favourite beach. There was a gently sloping white coral sand beach, at the top of which were some shady trees and at the bottom of which was a beautiful mile of sheltered sea. That mile away lay Malo Island, and between our beach and Malo was coral reef and a deep channel for inward and outward ships. We collapsed in a humid heap under the trees and some local kids came to watch us from the safety of two feet away. Helen shooed them off. After a while we managed to rouse ourselves to a snorkel, carefully obeying Helen and keeping our T- shirts and shorts on (i.e. all our clothes) so as not to upset the morals of the Christianized locals. If we thought the view across to Malo was stunning we were in for a real treat once we had on our snorkels and masks. The sea life was incredible. Magnificent. We were stunned. The variety of corals, the colours of the fish and the clarity of the sea were quite outside our experience. That and the rather gentle temperature of the water very nearly made up for Helen's lateness and our impending and presumably hotter return to Lata. With hotter and miserable children.

We probably went down to Luova beach at least once a week for the whole of our stay in Lata. Each time we found something new: a different fish, a stranger shell or just someone new to talk to. A rather special place. Well, once we had had the 'toilet beach' pointed out to us, anyway.

In a land of very few flushing loos, where everyone eats reef fish, the toilet beach is ubiquitous. Each village has two areas of beach set aside for human stool production. One for males and one for females. Most venture down to the specified beach around dawn to perform and then don't go again till the next day. They don't seem to drink or pass urine in daylight hours either. We were never sure of the correct procedure at a toilet beach. Does one nonchalantly squat looking out to sea to admire the view, or face inland to keep an eye out for peeping Toms? I think each unto his own. As Helen said, 'One should always ask the position of the toilet beach before swimming at a new beach for the first time.'

The strangest thing was that it seemed to do no one any harm. Certainly the reef fish prospered and, apart from times of drought, we hardly ever saw cases of diarrhoea and vomiting in the hospital. In fact a laudable practice made possible by the lack of population pressure.

That very first time at Luova I found a grove of giant clams only fifteen yards offshore. There were forty-eight of these huge creatures, all arranged in neat concentric circles. Each was open and showed off his iridescent insides to me floating a few feet above. The largest was about three feet across and the smallest one foot. I was quite lost for an explanation as all the clams we had seen previously had been in ones and twos and often entirely embedded in the coral, whereas this grove were all quietly sitting in a small sandy spot. Very odd. I got Helen over and then Sarah, and they were both as mystified as I was. So as not to give their position away I told the kids that they mustn't mention them to the locals and to look nonchalant when we went to view them. I thought they were some natural gathering of blue and green and turquoise lipped giant clams and I didn't want to let on to the locals where they were in case they got eaten. We realized after a couple of weeks as their numbers and positions varied that they were in fact someone's larder.

After an hour or so of swimming, beachcombing, shell collecting and lazing around we set off back towards Lata. Our way lay along the coast on a tree-shaded path through a minor village and some small gardens. Most of the homes we passed were custom built, made of wood and roofed and walled with woven banana leaf sections. Lovely and cool. One large house stood out on its own. It was raised up about ten feet on timber pilings and had a couple of large water tanks. All the visible wood had been sawn to shape and the roof was iron. Rather hot looking. Helen told us it had been built by Habitat under the chairmanship of the ex-United States president Jimmy Carter. It was now lived in by Sam, the secretary of the Temotu church of Melanesia. We got to know him later, a tall black-haired betel-chewing, unshaven light-skinned man from the island of Tikopia who was the right-hand man of the Bishop, a sturdy close-cropped grey-haired darker-skinned ex-rugby playing Tikopian. Both good chaps.

A little further along the path we noticed that someone had put a monstrous pineapple in the small leaf lean-to which, in my ignorance, I had taken for a shrine on our outbound journey. It seemed that if it was an offering it was to Mammon, as there was a price tag on it and a small jar for dollars next to it. Why were all our own prickly pineapple plants empty we wondered? We couldn't collect more than a few cents between us and had to forgo the monster pineapple this time. But from then on we always took some dollars in our pockets on our trips to Luova and took home some amazing fruit and vegetables. Mammon ended up with damp currency more often than not.

We stumbled back up the hill from the airstrip into Lata station and staggered up our path onto the veranda, where we offloaded children and had a sit down before running a cold bath to get the salt off. Hilda was in the kitchen.

'Hi Hilda, how are you? Er, where's Eric? Gone off already?'

Silence.

'Hilda?'

'Me no savvy.'

'Come on Hilda, you must know if he's gone home.'

'Hem say head blo' hem, hem sore for good.' A headache. Actually he had looked a little peaky when we had seen him earlier. Perhaps he had malaria? But Hilda wasn't happy about something. She wasn't going to let on too easily what it was, but she made sure we knew that she knew ... something. My Pidgin was not up to an investigation anyway. We would have to wait and see.

'Oh doctor, Bakila hem tellem come, "So how, doctors like lookim TB pasent?".' Oh my God, we had forgotten the TB patients. In our haste to get away by 9.30 we had overlooked walking down to the TB block at the end of the ward round. The head ward nurse, John Bakila, and his entourage did not think it their place to remind us at the time. Hence the anxiety on the faces of the nurses when we had done our swimming mime. John had obviously struggled with the problem of trying not to tell the doctors what to do, *and* at the same time get his patients seen. In the end he had walked up to our house and left a message with Hilda.

Sarah asked Hilda to bath the children, and she and I dashed off to the hospital to damply review the TB patients. They were all their normal cheerful selves and said not a word about the water dripping off their doctors.

Lata Hospital
Santa Cruz
Temotu Province.

21 May 1996.

Thompson Teika
RN Nuoba Clinic.

Dear Thompson

I was most surprised to see you at Lata today. You have not had permission to leave your post in Nuoba and by traveling here you have neglected your duty. You have also left a Nurse Aide on her own in a clinic which requires a Registered Nurse. I am very upset by your conduct and I am writing this letter as your **second written warning**. I see from recent correspondence that you have already received your first written warning from Selwyn Hou, your immediate supervisor.

We are trying to arrange for you to work at Manuopo under direct supervision for a few months. This of course entails many other people to be inconvenienced.

I hope you appreciate this. Until you leave to return to the Reefs you are not allowed on Hospital grounds.

I hope you understand this.

Yours sincerely

David Arathoon

Dr. David Arathoon.
Director Provincial Health Services
TEMOTU PROVINCE.

cc: PS/Temotu
cc: PS/Public Service
cc: DNS/MHMS
cc: PS/MHMS

Chapter 4

Spirits

Lata Hospital
Santa Cruz
Temotu Province

16th July 199#

Permanent Secretary
Ministry of Health & Med. Services
PO Box 349
Honiara

<u>Attention:</u> Dr Lester Ross

Dear Madam

I would like to bring to your notice the fact that Dr. Henry Kako (who did a locum in Lata before our arrival) ran up substantial telephone bills while in Lata. He still owes the Provincial Health Services $1,398.92 from unpaid telephone bills. He is now working in Kilu'ufi Hospital as you know, and has not even bothered to answer our written requests for the money. I have spoken to Dr Carroll and he has done all he can to help. I wonder if it would be possible for you to deduct the unpaid sum from his pay and forward it to us ?

I would be grateful for any help you can provide.

Many thanks.

Yours faithfully

Dr. David Arathoon
Director Provincial Health Services
<u>TEMOTU PROVINCE</u>

Quite soon after our arrival, Meg and Barney both started at the local 'Kindy' and brought home the obligatory cold. However it stimulated no asthma in either of them, which was good as they both had dreadful asthma back in the UK.

Around the same time I managed to cut off a fingernail while slicing up the latest bit of Bullumacow. The animal was so fresh when I went to collect our 5 kg that it was still twitching. It was always a bit hit and miss getting Bullumacow meat. The animals were either walked down from the farm inland, past our house (eagle eyes swaying in the hammock) and on down past the hospital (ditto in the office) to the wharf where it had its throat slit, or it came already slit-throated in bloody pieces in a grubby glass fibre ex-fish container canoed over from Malo island: the word gets out that something is up and Sarah and I spend a few fruitless hours wandering down to the wharf and back to see if the meat or animal has arrived. The nurses of course rely solely on telepathy, and suddenly without a word they're off, clutching their valuable plastic carrier bags, and the hospital is left empty. But how do they know the meat is ready? I've no idea. I was somewhat reminded of the meat collection when I sawed off three-quarters of a different fingernail while I was cutting up a bit of bamboo with which to make a hanging chair, also for the verandah. It bled like a stuck Bullumacow gazing its last across the bay.

Why 'Bullumacow'? I'm sure you wonder. Well, Pidgin is a descriptive language (not a language at all really, merely a pre-Creole, but one mustn't quibble) and I suppose not everyone can tell the difference between a cow's dangly bits and a bull's dangly bits, hence Bull-um-a-cow. Anyway, it was so tough, due to lack of hanging, due to the flies, due to the heat, etc. that we always had to mince it all in my mother's old mincer and then freeze it.

Now, the cattle themselves were magnificent beasts. We often saw them in their coconut paddocks, and they always looked sleek and cheerful. They didn't seem to get any noxious tropical diseases and had a happy and fulfilling life until they were chopped up, weighed out and placed in little plastic carrier bags.

I found another use for the mincer, which was the manufacture of cocoa paste. The beans are grown on Santa Cruz and then get fermented in large wooden boxes for a week before being dried for two days in a converted copra dryer. This consists of a twelve foot by twelve foot tray suspended over the heat emanating from a near-horizontal chimney made of empty 44-gallon fuel drums heated by an open fire at the bottom end. This is lovingly attended by a chap whose job description includes virtually continuous drinking of SolBrew and hourly raucous laughter with his mates. I bought the beans and roasted them in a pan and minced them into a bitty paste. We made a form of hot chocolate drink by merely adding hot water, milk and sugar. Bit chewy towards the bottom, but fine for us.

We heard on the grapevine that Dr Szetu, the (only) eye surgeon, was soon to come on tour. Eric, our particularly fine eye nurse, set about gathering patients, which left me free to try to find someone to make us a canoe. Having already spent what seemed like months trying to get someone to cut us a dugout canoe (one of the most ubiquitous of objects) we found one Ben-the-boat-builder down at the bay. He seemed to be some distant wantok of John-the-clerk who made our negotiations on cost very convoluted:

'So John, when are you going to find me someone to make me a canoe? What about you doing it for me?'

'Oh Doctor,' ostentatiously scratching his chin with an inch-long non-labourer's thumbnail, 'me worka long hospital.'

'Hmm ...'

'One fella man lo' bay, nem blo' hem "Ben", hem savvy good how now for workem canoe.'

'Yeees ... but have you asked him if he *will* make me a canoe, John?'

'Me askem finis.'

'Well, what did he say?'

'Hem say by hem workem.'

'Great. When will he start? How long will it take? Oh, it won't cost too much will it?'

'Ya.'

'Er ... Ya it will, or Ya it won't?'

'Ya, by you payem lelebit no more, no staka selleni tumas.'

'Ah, so "yes it won't cost too much" then?'

'Yeah man.'

'Hmm ... er, how do you know this Ben-chap, John?'

''Hem brudda blo' me.'

'Ah ha, not cost too much eh? Now let me see, you two fella garem same Mammi?"

'Er ...' Complete bafflement at my brilliant pre-Creole attempt.

'OK ... how about: Mammi blo' hem same same allsame Mammi blo' you?'

'No more yet,' laughing. 'Hem no really brudda blo' me.' It

seemed that in fact John's father was just a good friend of his 'brudda's' father.

'OK, OK. Now how much is this "no staka selleni tumas?"'

'Me no savvy.'

'Oh God ... would you ask him for me, John?'

It turned out that 'no stakka selleni tumas' came to SI$350 (about £50) or at the going rate of $14 a day, 25 eight-hour days' worth.

John took us off en masse as a family up the head road for a mile and then across the gardens to a patch of forest which was the boat-building site. It was wonderful to see a canoe literally being shaped out of a forest giant (stump at one end, spray of branches at the other end and in between, disconnected but still in line, the proto-canoe) by Ben, his wife and kids. I had to have a go with the axe and then to pose à la gondolier at the back of the boat sitting in its sea of chips. A few days later we helped Ben carry the boat to the head road so it could be trucked to his home to be finished off with his fine adzes.

Soon we got word that our dugout canoe was finally finished – hooray! I went down the bay with John-the-hospital-clerk to collect it from Ben-the-boat-builder's house. The canoe sat right outside Ben's front door, nestling in a heap of paper-thin adze shavings. The Beauty. We heaved the canoe down to the sea. There was a great gathering of locals, mostly kids, who had come to see the white man make a fool of himself. I duly obliged. I jumped in and John-the-clerk pushed off from the shore and joined me, first in the canoe and immediately afterwards in the lukewarm waters of Graciosa Bay – much hilarity from the shore, and steam coming out of the doctor's ears.

'I thought you said you knew how to handle a canoe, John,' and *sotto voce*, 'Jesus Christ ...'

However we only turned turtle once more on the one-mile paddle back to the wharf. Once there we got a few able-bodied chaps to carry the canoe up the hill to the hospital so that Peter-the-Tikopian could add an outrigger. He was the husband of one of our patients who was to deliver in Lata so that we could sterilize her afterwards – Tikopians are renowned for their outriggers and fertility. Anyway, over the next few days I found every excuse to nip out and have a look at him putting on the outrigger. The boat looked beautiful when finished. Not a nail in sight, all tied together, (not with 'custom rope' this time but with 80 lb breaking strain fishing line), and totally solid. Then Peter made us a longer mast (gulp) and finally a sail out of flour sacks, which are apparently superior to rice sacks, but being white, not so colourful as the bright yellow Solris bags. We went for a trial run down at the wharf – with the outrigger on the boat was so stable that two people could stand up in her at the same time. We took it to a quiet little bay round the corner where a family said they would keep an eye on it for us.

Sarah and I took the kids out for an experimental sail one weekend – rather a disaster actually. The tide was out but there was a goodly wind blowing. If we stayed inshore we kept out of the big waves, but bottomed out on the coral. Twice we ventured further out and the waves came over the side and swamped the boat. It didn't actually sink (they can't ...) but it's difficult to make headway when the hull is under water. Meg was completely calm but three-year-old Barney went off his head while sitting safely in the underwater canoe with his lifejacket on – he never forgave us. We only seemed to have two inches of freeboard, and I contemplated tacking on another six inches or so with some thin boards and caulking. Or should I have a larger one made?

We did sail her successfully, which was enormous fun as long as there weren't too many people on board (i.e. only one ...). In any sort of wind it was difficult to tack, but gybing seemed a bit easier (got all the jargon, you know). I thought that once it was a bit more seaworthy, and our Environmental Health team had made us an anchor out of a piece of three-inch pipe and concrete (to replace our dubious chunk of coral), we would venture out to different parts of the reef that we hadn't yet explored. Or should I have a larger one made?

Dr Szetu, the eye surgeon, finally came on tour. He comes to Temotu every two years or so to cut out people's cataracts and insert IOLs (intra-ocular lenses, to those in the know – the ultra-violet light wreaks havoc with human eyeballs in the tropics). Because no ships had gone round the outer islands since we had got word of Dr Szetu's visit we only managed to gather together twelve patients. All the others would have to wait another two years ... or more. He didn't mind as he had done sixty-eight operations in the province of Malaita the week before. He warned us that if we wanted Hermann, the very pleasant, brilliant but rather pernickety Swiss surgeon to come on tour (which we did), we would have to tighten up on our instrument sterilizing, etc. We learnt a lot.

Just after Szetu's visit and while our canoe was having its outrigger fixed on we had an unusually busy time in the hospital, probably made worse by my frequent absences down by the TB block watching the canoe being outriggered.

So Sarah was particularly busy. She did two Ventouse extractions (the Ventouse apparatus looks like a sink plunger connected to a bicycle pump and is used to help in the delivery during difficult births. It looks archaic but works well and is safe), delivered a breech (her first), and eviscerated her first eyeball. Dr Szetu said we were the only provincial doctors he had known to do eviscerations – the others always put their patients on a plane and sent them to him. That's probably because all the other provinces are nearer Honiara than to Vanuatu (unlike us) and have at least one flight a day against our two a week (when we were lucky). Now, an eyeball may look soft and fragile but once someone has shot it with a wooden arrow and the eye has got infected in the two days it takes to get to hospital, it is found to be *very* tough. It requires very sharp scissors to puncture the white in order to cut off the whole of the front of the eye so that you can remove the jelly, lens and retina with a bit of gauze and a bone scraper hijacked for the purpose. All under local anaesthetic of course, and a touch of Valium to help them forget the experience. But we learned something new every day, and anyway Dr Szetu gave very good instructions over the phone ... which by chance was working.

Sarah also made a couple of spectacular diagnoses, considering how few investigations were available. The first was a baby of six weeks with a bleeding diathesis (bleeding disorder) of unknown cause. The child stood little chance; three out of four of its siblings had died from a mysterious illness. We now knew what that had been and could make this little mite's few years of life more comfortable. The other was a newborn who had difficulty breathing. Sarah reckoned it had a tracheomalacia (an unusually narrow breathing tube). This was rather 'poo-pooed' by the paediatricians in Honiara when we finally managed to get through to them on the phone. After a couple of weeks, when they eventually consented to see the child, they agreed – and then immediately put it on a plane for further treatment in Australia. Easy for them to do.

There seemed to be a lot of domestic violence around, Sarah (again) had to tie off one poor lady's radial artery after her pleasant Christian husband had severed it for her in a drunken rage. Actually she was lucky, as she had parried his knife-thrust to her stomach. Then we saw a five-year-old girl who had both the bones in her forearm broken by a kick from her father (she went swimming in the sea after a couple of weeks – the plaster fell off and we never managed to trace her again although one of the nurses said she saw her in the distance and she looked all right); and another father who managed to fracture his own arm by smashing it on a bookshelf in frustration at his son. Considering that everyone wandered around with great big bush knives all day long it's amazing that many more people weren't stabbed or cut. Actually even toddlers can be seen staggering round clutching kitchen knives close to their vitals before they are strong enough to lift a bush knife. But I suppose, as they say, it's not the knives that are dangerous but the people that wield them.

Then the worst thing to happen to us since we arrived occurred – enough to banish canoes from my thoughts and bring me into the hospital full time again: the death of a sixteen-year-old girl from meningitis. She breached our clinical defences and before we knew it, was at death's door. She started hallucinating and was convinced that her grandfather had come over from Tinakula (the local volcano island) to collect her – he had been dead for some time and the volcano had been deserted for twenty years. In the end she had a convulsion one night and stopped breathing. By the time I had been called and got to her she was lifeless but still had a pulse. After an hour and a half of effort she was still lifeless, still had a pulse but I was assisting her breathing with an endotracheal tube and a bag.

It was hopeless.

We were in the small, ten foot by eight foot hot, humid, dripping isolation room with about twenty relatives and assorted onlookers crowded round the bed. I was sweating like a worried white doctor a long way from home – the sweat dripping off my nose and chin onto the poor girl. A decision had to be made. I handed the bag over to the nearest relative and gave simple instructions on its use. I asked her parents to come with me to the quiet of the nursing station. Her mother was a well-educated retired teacher. I explained the desperateness of the situation. Mum was calm and said the girl's grandfather was still here from Tinakula.

'Has he come to take her back with him?'

'He's not really here ...'

'I know ... it's his spirit ...'

Short pause. 'Yes, he's here to take her away with him – please take out the pipe and stop breathing for her.'

This was followed by a great sense of release on my side. She and

I went back to the girl, shooed away everyone mum did not want in the room, and stopped all medical activity. Not very pleasant.

In fact pretty dreadful.

After that we were left pretty washed out and began to wonder if we were doing anyone any good by being in Lata. We felt very low and so jumped at the chance of some rest and rehabilitation suggested by Helen, the VSO legal adviser. She took us off to the village of Nea for a weekend with the family of Mathias. The village is on the south side of Santa Cruz and is reached by driving for half an hour along the crushed coral road (heaving sighs of relief at being away from all but the worst emergencies in the hospital) and then striking off on foot over gardens, coconut plantations and the bush on a very muddy path, carrying various children in our particular case. Nea is right on the sea at the base of a very steep coral cliff, halfway down which is a beautiful spring that provides the village with water, water which has been filtered and purified by a couple of hundred feet of solid coral. At the point where the water springs cool-ly from the rock face, someone had thoughtfully jammed in two pieces of split bamboo over which the water flowed, so that by merely our bending at the waist the water ran into our mouths and then over our heads – bliss.

Mathias is a big man in the village and a quieter, more pleasant, smiling, cheerful, helpful man you could not wish to find. We were put up in a hut that he borrowed from one of his wantoks (a cousin's stepsister's husband ... or some such) which was 15 yards from the sea, beside a tiny beach which looked over a channel 200 yards across to an uninhabited emerald islet – all rather amazing. Mathias and his extended family were trying to encourage eco-tourism and we were some of their first guests. So for a small fee they put us up, cooked for us and showed us round the village and later showed us how to make Tapa cloth. Because the house was raised up five feet on poles and because it benefited from all the sea breezes, the mosquitoes were kept away, but we slept under our nets anyway and sprayed the floor with repellent to stop the tiny little red fire ants from interrupting our sleep. On very firm leaf mats on the even firmer floor. We had a great time with the village kids leaping into a brackish pool near the sea, and later snorkelled off the island. We were paddled over there in pairs in a rather leaky dugout by a boy who must have been at least eight years old. The snorkelling was breathtaking: the coral completely virgin, quantities of new fish species; and deeper down, patrolling the channel, some languid white-tipped reef sharks.

The highlight of this pleasantly lazy weekend was being taken into the 'booss'('bush' to you and me) to be shown the Tapa cloth manufacturing process. Tapa is a material made from the bark of a specific tree, which was worn by the locals before the arrival of the whities with their cotton goods. Anyway, we wandered off into the booss, stopping only at some giant Taro plants whose leaves were cut for us to use as custom umbrellas against the drizzle, and found the correct type of Tapa tree of the correct age and girth. This was speedily hacked down with a booss-knife (only to sprout again in time to be harvested in another three years), and the bark removed with a sharpened stick. On the way back to the village to wash the bark in the sea, one stops off at a different tree species, scrapes the lichen off its exposed roots and then collects a little of the bark. This is used as a fixer for the black dye used to put patterns on the cloth. The bark, having been washed in the sea (whether the sea has to be full of sweet potato peelings was never made clear), is then pummelled on a flat piece of wood with a grooved mallet, which seems to be passed down from one generation to the next. This causes the bark to become thinner, wider, more pliable and in effect more cloth-like. It is then washed again and left to dry. Remember the other small pieces of bark? Well, they are mixed with water and then all the juices are squeezed out to make the fixer. To make the black dye the villagers collect soot from a piece of resin left burning under an upturned battered aluminium pan (the resin collected from yet another type of tree) – it smells rather like frankincense when it is alight. The soot and fixer are then carefully mixed together to the right consistency with a forefinger in an old coconut shell. The dye is applied to the Tapa with a variety of shaped bamboo sticks to make patterns representing all manner of things including sharks' teeth, frigate birds and root vegetables. Now, how on earth did they find out about all those tree species and their potential uses? We were amazed.

On our rested and somewhat recuperated return from Nea, Wilson told us that the breadfruit picking season had passed for another year, thank goodness and luckily for the local women. I don't know if you remember, but breadfruit was one of the causes of the mutiny on the *Bounty*. Captain Bligh had a shipful of young breadfruit trees which he was taking out, I think to the West Indies, to see if the slaves would deign to eat them (I suppose Europeans in the nineteenth century considered all black people would eat the same food wherever they came from). To keep the trees alive he had to cut the water

Mathias making Tapa cloth.

rations to the crew – not a terribly sound idea when they had been away from home so long *and* had just spent time among the topless beauties on Tahiti. The rest is history – and quite a good story at the time. In fact very interesting until something more interesting occurred, e.g., Captain Bligh precipitating another mutiny, this time on land at Botany Bay. God, he must have been a twit.

Anyway, breadfruit is one of the staples out in the Solomons and grows on trees up to one hundred and thirty feet high. The men of the society have unanimously decreed that it shall be women who venture up these trees at this particular time of year with ten-foot-long poles to knock the breadfruit down to the earthbound (and jolly sensible) males. Thus all the injuries, caused by the action of gravity on the human body when it lets go of a branch to enable it to poke that very last breadfruit that is *just* out of reach, happen to women. I suppose it's possible for a man to get hit by a well-aimed breadfruit, or indeed a poorly aimed female – but they usually have time to step neatly aside. We had no deaths our first year, but amongst the lesser injuries were a fractured lumbar vertebrae ('broken back'), a rather nice star-shaped fracture of an acetabulum (the socket part of the ball and socket hip joint) and a compression fracture of the hip – the woman, when she had come round, thought she had been attacked by the 'Wildman'; she brushed herself off and calmly walked back to her village. All the treatments were the same, and luckily low tech: bed rest for three weeks.

Our good Christian nurses told us a little about the 'Wildman':

'Ooh Doctor, no good you lookim dis fella "Wildman".'

'Why not? What's wrong with the poor chap?' My Pidgin was still not ready for general conversation.

'Ooh, Wildman, hem brava no-good man.' Brava meaning very or extremely.

'So, how do we get to meet him? Where does he live? What does he do?'

'Ooh Doctor, hem stop long booss. S'pose you lookim dis fella Wildman by you die quicktime.'

'Er ... so if I see the Wildman, then I die?' Sounded a little unusual.

'Yes Doctor. Tink tink blo me, dis fella Wildman hem brava no-good. S'pose hem lookim olketa, by olketa die finis.' This all sounded complicated and I had to have a guess at the nurses' meaning.

'Soo ... you can't see him without dying?'

'Yeah man.'

'Hang on – do you mean "yes you can't see him without dying" or "yes you *can* see him without dying"?' Apparently it was 'yes you can't ...' Pidgin suddenly seemed a rather semantic form of communication.

'So what sort of people see him?' I was really struggling with the whole concept. A tribe from the mountainous interior of Santa Cruz who preyed on the villagers and killed them to conceal their identity ? Who could tell?

'No more yet Doctor, you no savvy good.' Sniggers amongst themselves. It seemed that the Wildman was some sort of spirit who could be called up by a villager to help settle a dispute by looking at another villager and hence doing away with him.

Ahh ... dawning of understanding ... an Evil Spirit lurking in the bosoms of these Christianity-crazy locals. It slowly added up. After all they had only been introduced to the 'light' over the last couple of generations, and lots of their previous pagan beliefs still hold sway.

As for Tinakula, the active volcano twenty-seven miles to the north ... well the very Devil himself lived there. You can see evidence of it two or three times a day when smoke pours from the top. At least they haven't had to change any fundamental beliefs regarding the Devil ...

Works Officer   Health Education Unit
Lata   Lata
Temotu Province.   Temotu Province.
                     10th June 199#

Dear Sir

RE: HEALTH EDUCATION DOOR

The above underlined has been damaged following its key lost.
The door was left open every time which has resulted in things
gone missing in the office. Therefore I'm asking for your immediate
help to repair the door before the office gets empty.

Your help will be very much appreciated and I leave things into
your good hands.

Regards
John Peter Metoula.

Health Education Officer
Lata Hospital
For: Director Health Services
TEMOTU PROVINCE.

cc: Treasurer (TP)

cc: DPHS (TP)

Chapter 5

Bowels, Boats and Books

Faxed 11/6/96.

Lata Hosp, Santa Cruz, Temotu Province, Solomon Islands.
Tel: 53042 (home), Fax :53044   11/6/96

Attention : Students John Pratt & Leon Clark

Dear John & Leon ,

Thanks for your fax concerning a possible Elective out here with us on Santa Cruz . I spoke to the Undersecretary of State for Health yesterday & he also seemed to think it would be all right if you came out. He would like you to fax your Cvs to him (with a covering letter of introduction etc) & I think it wouldn't go amiss if you could also get a letter from a tutor or even the Subdean saying what wonderful chaps you are -- and fax that at the same time. The fax should be headed : "For the attention of :Drs Ezekial Nakuru (Undersecretary of state for Health) & Lester Ross (Medical Superintendant of Central Hospital)".I will give you all the phone & fax Nos at the end. Lester would be better to deal with as you may get a reply from him.....

Your fax was a little bit broken up, but I think you want to come in Jan & Feb of 1997...is that right ? There shouldn't be any problems on our side--although we hope to go to New Zealnd for 3/52 over Christmas. Your main expenses are going to be the airfares out here --we flew United to the States & then New Zealand air & finally Solomon Airlines to Honiara. From Honiara you then need to take a small interisland plane--either Solomon airlines on a Wed or Sat, or Western Pacific on Tues & Fri. It is probably cheaper to book all the flights from UK. I don't know how long you have got , but it may be worth spending some time in NZ for instance, on your way out--you would be more acclimatized to the heat & anyway its rather a beautiful place. Its not desperately hot here (us 30°C) but the humidity is high so its a bit enervating. Theres not much to spend your money on when you get to Santa Cruz, but if you spend a few days in Honiara you could get some diving in (2 good Japanese transport wrecks & a B17 close offshore) That would cost a bit (presently $150 per dive or $250 for 2 dives).Probably best to bring your own snorkelling gear.

The work here varies a lot depending whats on the ward (presently 7 cases of 'Santa Cruz fever'). The nurses are mostly pretty good & really act as (rather good) Housemen, alot of new cases appearing on the wards between rounds with their Rx started. We also have a Community Health team which visits villages 2-3 times a week to innoculate kids & treat any thing that comes up.If you have any ideas for projects while here let us know & we will try to help. Don't however feel you have to.

If none of the above puts you off then perhaps the fact that we have 2 kids (aged 3 & 4) will.... actually they are pretty house trained.

If theres anything else you need to know then let us know.We need to know the dates you would like to be here as soon as possible.
Here are the Nos :Drs Nakuru & Ross at the Ministry of Health & Medical Services :

Fax	20085
General Office	20830
Undersecretary	23404.

Dr Ross at Central Hospital 23600, ext 219

Hope to hear soon,
Yours sincerely,

David Arthwan

DPHS

'I can't believe it ... what utter, utter rubbish ... to think we paid good money for this ... this crap.' Before coming out to Lata, Sarah and I had reckoned that we probably had two good years of reading ahead of us and had decided to take advantage. We had gone out and bought masses of books. All those classics we had never had a chance to read, all those tomes which would take a little concentration. Anything really.

'God, it makes me mad, absolutely hopping mad.' And I really was hopping around our living room getting hotter and hotter by the minute, aching to lash out at someone.

'I have got to *do* something or I will explode.' We had filled one of the two heated cupboards in the house with our small library. These cupboards were ingeniously simple. They were plain wooden built-in cupboards with a large door and a concrete floor. Just above the concrete was a light bulb socket. When the door was shut, the 60-watt bulb slowly raised the temperature of the cupboard and kept the air dry and hence kept the mildew at bay. This particular cupboard in the spare room had slatted shelves on both sides; ideal for books, cameras, films and any odds and ends we didn't want fungus to grow in.

'That's it, I'm bloody well going to complain to someone.' In choosing which books to include in our library we often checked the backs of unknown ones to see which 'experts' had said what about them. Occasionally, as in this particular case, it was a mistake to believe the recommendation on the back, and an even worse mistake to spend good money buying the book and carrying it halfway round the world. We had bought so many books that our finances got stretched to breaking point and we even had to borrow money off an unsuspecting relative on our way through New Zealand.

'Right, let's have a look ... which bastards said this was a decent read? Hmm ... talking through their rear ends the lot of them.' I decided to get something on paper there and then before going down to our Wednesday morning ward round. I was planning on going over to the Reef islands the next day for my first visit to the largest of the outer clinics and wanted to get everything as ship-shape as possible before I left Sarah.

Among other subjects, Sarah and I had decided to read books on the First World War. We started with Siegfried Sassoon and Robert Graves, and then went on to Erich Maria Remarque (although I had read *All Quiet on the Western Front* and *Three Comrades* before; *Three Comrades* made me pretty sniffy the second time round as well.) Then Denys Reitz and finally onto Solzhenitzyn and *August 1914.* All amazing, gripping, chilling and excellent. We also looked to see if anything more contemporary had been written on the Great War. Completely by chance we discovered Pat Barker and her brilliant trilogy (eventually a trilogy anyway). Unfortunately I also picked up a book called *Birdsong* back in England, and noting it was:

a. Large,
b. Set in the First World War, and
c. Had been reviewed favourably by some people we had heard of, I bunged it in my WHS basket and brought it all the way to Lata.

In the greater scheme of things I would not usually worry about reading a mediocre book, but we were in a strange situation in Lata where we couldn't just pop out to a shop and buy another book if the one we were reading was poor. Now I really resented wasting time on a book that I had only continued with because I kept expecting it to improve. We each read for at least four hours every day and each minute of that time was precious. And now I had just wasted this unrecoverable time completing *Birdsong.* I don't think I would have been so incensed if I had read it before the other First World War books, but unfortunately it had been the very last.

'Hang on a sec Sarey, let me just jot down a few notes to remind myself how utterly pissed off I am, then I shall be with you.' I wrote a few red-hot phrases on a piece of paper and then followed Sarah out to the hospital. 'I want you to have a look at that young chap I admitted yesterday.' I had seen a man of about twenty-eight years the afternoon before with some very unwestern complaints centred around his chest. I had no clue what was wrong with him but he hadn't looked quite right. Halfway through the ward round we came to him, sitting on his bed with his young bashful wife. He looked OK but the nurses reported that he had needed oxygen during the night. Oxygen? Virtually unheard of in Lata hospital. We had another look at him and found nothing. Moving to the next patient we waved a cheery goodbye to Stephen and his wife, but told the nurses to keep him in a bit longer. At the end of the ward round I went to find Wilson Lyno in his office to make final arrangements for our trip to the Reefs the next day. He had gathered sufficient fuel for the trip and had arranged for one of the provincial drivers to take us.

'Wilson, how long is it going to take to get to Manuopo?'

'Maybe four hours.' I wondered what "maybe" meant.

'In that case we should leave at 6.30 – is that OK? I mean 6.30 really, not Solomon time. Will that be OK with the driver?'

'Yes, by me tellem Simon too.' Simon being one of the senior nurses involved in community health; he and Wilson were off to inspect the clinic at Manuopo while I had a look at some patients they had gathered for me. I had doubts about Wilson's ability to get everyone ready by 6.30, even when 'English' time had been specified.

Strangely enough I was correct. I had a peaceful half an hour to myself in the gentle breeze down at the wharf in the morning before our team arrived in dribs and drabs. We pushed the very fine strong aluminium canoe down to the water, attached a 25 hp outboard engine and put in a couple of extra plastic drums of fuel, some drugs for Manuopo and some mail for the Reefs. Setting off, the bay was a peaceful calm, and I settled down to the trip. Soon Tinakula the volcano came in sight, and then Luesalemba, the secondary school on the north of the island, followed by Nolua and then Taepe villages, each with their own lone dog on the beach, before we headed towards the empty horizon to the north. On coming out of the bay the calmness of the sea changed, and as we left the shelter of Santa Cruz island for the great empty horizon the canoe started groaning up the backs of the increasingly large waves before scooting down their fronts. The wind got up, the horizon remained very horizontal and I wondered if I should ask how the driver knew where we were going, compass-less as he was. However our 25 hp outboard drowned out all but the most important conversation, such as: 'We should bail now,' from Wilson to me. I began to get a little anxious, having heard horror stories emanating from the Western Province where doctors had been known to drift for days when an engine failed on tour. I had not heeded one of the only pieces of advice I had been given in England which was always to make sure there was a spare engine and a couple of split pins in the boat on all sea-going outboard canoe trips. I felt foolish. In the Western Province there are loads of islands scattered on all horizons, but here, with the low lying Reef islands invisible, the only obvious land was behind us and receding fast. The wind continued to build and I started to get wet and chilled and sunburnt all at the same time. I got some moral support from the thought that by now Sarah had probably posted my blistering remarks to Quentin Crewe and his band of fellow novel reviewers re the crappy *Birdsong*.

I started humming repeating phrases to myself to make the time pass and to keep my mind off the depth of the sea and the flotation characteristics of a swamped all-aluminium canoe. Suddenly I saw a silver winged shape shoot out of the water in front of the boat and speed off down a wave gully – wow, my first flying fish. A new mind filler: timing the flights of flying fish. What an amazing adaptation. I could just imagine a barracuda down below in the depths tearing in for the kill only for his silvery angelic victim to go into warp drive and disappear from barracuda-consciousness. Barracudadom's loss and my gain. I timed one twisting, turning wave skimming flight at sixteen seconds, which remained my record for two years.

Sitting on my life jacket for comfort, I changed buttock position for the ninetieth time to ease the numb sensation of three brocking hours when Wilson leaned over and pointed at a large blob which had appeared off to the left. 'Matema,' he yelled in my ear, thinking I had some clue what he was on about. I grinned and nodded vigorously hoping that that would speed our voyage. Above the engine he then explained that Matema was one of the outer Reef islands. Phew. Just then the engine took the chance to up and die with a final flourish of revs. Silence apart from ringing ears. It looked an awfully long way to paddle a large, heavy aluminium canoe with one old dilapidated paddle through bungalow-sized waves. Having scanned the horizon to look for help I turned round to ask Wilson what we should do now, only to find the driver and Simon wrestling with an open plastic drum of petrol, which they were trying to slop into the outboard motor's fuel tank. More than half made it into the tank and with a few sharp pulls on the starter rope we were off again. I feigned indifference, but silently thanked God that, with the ringing in their ears, the other three didn't seem to have heard my whimper at the sudden onset of the silence. Soon all the other islands came into view. I asked to have Pigeon Island pointed out to me in Mohawk Bay as I had been invited to sleep there during our stay in the Reefs. The island belonged to a very elderly white lady and I looked forward to meeting her.

The wind and waves dropped in Mohawk Bay and suddenly we were scooting a few feet above the coral. The tide was receding fast and it became obvious that we would soon have to stop the engine and paddle, then punt, and finally get out and push our boat. We got in and out of the boat for the next hour or so and slowly edged deeper into the mangroves of Lom Lom Island.

We finally arrived at Manuopo and were met by the smelly

Walking on water, Reef islands.

water's edge by the immaculately turned out head nurse. In contrast I felt grubby and dishevelled after our canoe trip. He took us the fifty yards to the clinic, which was large and grand by Solomon standards. Outside the clinic there seemed to be a jumble of wires lying on the ground. Wilson said it was the clinic's radio aerial that had been blown out of a tree a couple of weeks ago, which was why Lata hospital had had such poor communications with Manuopo recently. 'Have we?' Apparently we had. I asked what was required to get the aerial back up and working. A rope and someone able to shin up two trees. Hmm. Inside the clinic I was plonked behind a desk and the first of my outpatients was shown in from the inquisitive queue outside. I hadn't the nerve to ask after drinks or food. Most of the patients' problems were not life threatening but were sufficient to get to meet the new doctor. Wilson, who was a Reef islander, knew most of them and translated and provided background information when I could drag him away from his official inspection. After a surprisingly short time we were offered some rice-y sustenance and some precious instant coffee for lunch, the yet-to-be-seen outpatients being shooed away and told to come back at the next visit from the doctor.

Then I was taken on a tour of the clinic by the head nurse, his nurses, Wilson, Simon, the canoe driver and some wives and children. We started at the well-equipped malaria lab (there is no malaria on the Reefs ...), then went onto the poorly equipped but beautifully organized pharmacy store and ended up on the wards. Manuopo is the only clinic in Temotu large enough to cater for inpatients. There were three inpatients. One elderly prostatic man who had been catheterized was easy. He had to go to Honiara 'slow time' to be reamed out. A very elderly lady (elderly or chronically overworked in the gardens, either or) who was terminally ill wanted to go back to her village to die. Fair enough, another easy decision. Last of all was an extremely poorly looking young man of three years with a distended belly, a fever and a pained face. He was reported to have come in with 'belly pain' two days before and had been kept in as he hadn't improved. Not only was he unhappy but also he couldn't keep anything down and so they had quite rightly put up a drip. Then he had stopped opening his bowels except for a little ... well ... sort of pasty red material. Good God, perhaps my consultants back in Barts had been right and the patient would tell you the diagnosis if you only gave them the chance. Or in my case if my questions went in English to Wilson, in an unspecified village language from Wilson to the boy's mum, from mum to boy and all the way back, thereby giving me time to cogitate the problem as we went along. Not that this needed much thinking about as it was clinically a case of intussusception (where the bowel gets blocked when it invaginates upon itself) and the boy, Jimmy, was obviously in great danger. It was the sort of thing one reads in all the textbooks but never gets to see as a general practitioner. I was so chuffed at making the diagnosis that I very nearly forgot to place a hand on Jimmy's tummy. However this boy needed to get to Honiara if he was to survive. The next scheduled flight out of Lata would be Saturday, which he wouldn't make, so I would have to arrange a charter – hopefully for tomorrow, Friday. He should live that long. But how to get him to Lata? More to the point, as Wilson reminded me, how to contact Lata, there being no aerial on the radio here in Manuopo and all ... Oh God, how things gang up on you when you have a problem. If we couldn't contact Lata soonish Sarah wouldn't have time to arrange a charter for the next day. There again it would all be a bit futile if we couldn't get Jimmy to Lata – neither Wilson nor I thought he would survive the trip we had just made in the canoe. But miracle of miracles, a message came through on the grapevine, even as we stood a little despondently in the ward, that HMV *Butai* was in Mohawk Bay and would be going to Lata tomorrow. Messengers were sent off immediately begging passage for Jimmy and a nurse, and requesting the ship set off at dawn. What a stroke of luck. That still left the niggly problem of contacting Lata before it was too late to arrange the charter.

Wilson had a plan, which did not include my suggestion of shooting one of the staff at the clinic and using their guts as a rope to haul the aerial into place. He knew of a village that had a chief who had a radio whose aerial was up and working. The radio had been bought for the village by the local politician just before the last election (funny old thing) and the chief had decided he should be the one with the key to the radio hut, which was of course fair enough.

We ambled away from the clinic following Wilson and headed westwards through gardens and land lying fallow and some huge old trees. Wilson was having a wonderful time, a big man amongst his own, on a mission to save a life. I just wished he would inject a bit of urgency into his passage, and more to the point, explain what use a radio was to us. No one would be listening in at the hospital as they only manned it twice a day at 8 am and 3 pm. It was now half past four and I was seething with frustration. We wandered along intersecting footpaths for twenty-five minutes or so and finally arrived at the village. While we were still on the edge of the village Wilson did his distant communication trick with his eyebrows and a few apparently whispered words to his friends at least fifty yards away. I had come to suspect that Solomon islanders communicated by telepathy, so good was their hearing and understanding of body language.

He was obviously asking if anyone knew where the chief with the key to the radio hut had got to. There still seemed little urgency, and the kick-about football match with a rag ball continued apace in the mud in the centre of the village. Wilson beamed at his wantoks and let me know what was going on: 'By you-me wait lelebit,' his English slipping into Pidgin. We perched on the verandah of the padlocked radio hut while a succession of passers-by stopped and passed the time with Wilson. After an unspecified time a middle-aged man arrived with a large key and let us into the hut. He got the radio going by attaching a tractor battery (recharged from a solar panel on the roof) and seemed to be trying to contact the fisheries department in Honiara. He was successful and handed over to Wilson, who had a chat and a bit of a laugh with the lads in the fisheries department in Honiara. I was completely baffled but luckily Wilson signed off and told me what was going on: 'By-you-me-everyone wait first time.' Aaah ...?

We waited and waited for what seemed an hour (but in fact was twenty minutes). In that time, the chap at one of the only radios in Honiara which is manned twenty-four hours a day (i.e. the fisheries one) spoke to his boss who then telephoned the fisheries in Lata. They in turn wandered up to the hospital and spoke to John Bakila, who wandered up to our house and asked Sarah if she could come down with him to the radio room in the hospital in order to speak to me. I couldn't believe it. One minute I was wondering what on earth Wilson was doing, chatting to his friends in the fisheries in Honiara when what was obviously required was *action*, the next minute the radio crackled into life with Sarah's voice. Fantastic. I quickly explained to Sarah the problem with Jimmy and asked her to organize a charter flight for the next afternoon. We signed off, the chief unplugged the tractor battery, locked up the radio hut and wandered back to wherever he had emerged from, and Wilson looked chuffed with life. An amazing chap.

Back to Jimmy to check on him, and to explain to his anxious parents that we hoped he would be under the surgeon's knife in Honiara by this time tomorrow. I was exhausted. The driver drove and pushed me back through the mangroves to Pigeon Island. I had arranged with Wilson to head back to Lata from Pigeon the next day at 8 a.m., hopefully with HMV *Butai* in hot pursuit.

Pigeon Island is a tiny (? five-acre) raised coral islet, which belonged to Diana Hepworth. She and her two sons Ross and Ben were rarities in Temotu in that they were white, and they were successful traders. I had met the just-becoming-plump 35ish-year-old Ross a couple of times on Santa Cruz and he seemed a decent sort of chap. I had not yet had the pleasure of Ben, and he was away from Pigeon, Ross informed me when he greeted me at the beach below the steps leading to the family-run store. He was accompanied by a large young boisterous Rottweiller who looked pleased to see me. Ross explained that it was only because I wasn't black that he was friendly, as they seemed to have raised a racist dog. I was now even more knackered and still in my salt-encrusted and damp sea-crossing outfit, topped with a rather spectacular coiffure of sea-salt matted hair. Not that the delightfully eccentric Diana minded a jot when we were introduced. She turned out to be a tall, slim, grey-haired elegant lady who had spent her married life with her husband Tom sailing the seven seas on a Brixham trawler, trading and seeing the world between modelling assignments. She sat me down for supper and Ross produced an achingly welcome can of cold beer and we chatted. By the end of supper I was seeing the world through the wrong end of a telescope in my weariness and mild inebriation of a second beer; nevertheless it was fascinating hearing all Diana's stories and seeing her old photos. It seemed that many years ago they had set up a small store on 'our' emerald green islet off Nea ... I had to get to bed.

Ross took me back to 'his' side of the island to what seemed to be a wide covered walkway with a huge television blaring and lots of young locals slouching around watching some weird programme in American, a generator distantly pounding. There seemed to be a couple of white children asleep on mats in a room off the walkway. Ross said they were his children, and this walkway was his home. It was all so strange and incongruous, and all viewed at such a distance of tiredness that I was unsure if I was already asleep and dreaming or not. But I wasn't, because as soon as I got to the guesthouse overlooking the bay the mosquitoes started on me. I had been promised a complete absence of mosquitoes by Diana not ten minutes before. Bloody things.

The next day dawned fine and clear. I had breakfast with Ross and his two boys and a large, shy, smiling local girl called Peggi who was his wife. Wilson et al. arrived from Manuopo with the good news that Jimmy and a nurse had been delivered to the *Butai* by 7 a.m., the sun was shining, the wind had settled and the waves were smaller, so we set off towards the large blob of Santa Cruz just to the left of the cone-shaped billowing, mini-erupting island of Tinakula. Everything was going our way at last.

We blazed back to Lata with the little 25 hp outboard happily raucous. Hardly a couple of gallons had to be bailed out and we arrived back wet and cheerful with HMV *Butai* entering the bay behind us. I left Wilson and the boys to sort out the canoe while I tripped up the exposed coral to the hospital in town. The nurses informed me that Sarah had nipped home for lunch. Cheerful still I went the last few hundred yards to the house, admiring the enormous yellow carapaced spiders in their webs on the telephone wires. Bloody great monsters, they. My tired cheerfulness only lasted a few seconds more, when, after a welcoming kiss, Sarah informed me that the bureaucrats in the Ministry of Health wouldn't sanction a charter from Sarah as she hadn't seen the patient. Aaagh ...

The time was ... 1.30 pm;

It usually took about four hours to arrange a charter;

It took three and a half hours to fly to Lata;

It was not possible to land at Lata after dark, as there were no lights;

The sun goes down at 6.30 ... Oh God.

I had to sit dripping on the verandah to think while we had a cup of coffee. I couldn't even raise the energy to climb into my beloved hammock. Well, Jimmy was probably nearer death than twenty-four hours, so we had better have a go. Instead of phoning the Ministry of Health (who would all be at lunch or otherwise engaged) we decided to telephone Solomon Airlines direct, to check if they had a plane to charter.

It was an inspiration, and we got through to an immensely helpful young man who said 'Leave it to me, I'll get back to you.' *And* he did, which shocked us to the core. At 2.30 he phoned back to say they should have a charter ready by 3 pm when the flight from Gizo came in. And, by the way, he had OK'd it with the Ministry of Health. Fantastic. I phoned the surgeons to tell them the story so far.

At 3.15 we got another call from Honiara airport to say there had been a small hold-up as the incoming flight from Gizo had been delayed. Could we arrange a full load of fuel our end, as they would not now have time to top up in Makira on the way out? Wilson sorted it. A little mental arithmetic and a glance at my watch showed they were pushing it a rather fine. Another call at 3.30 – they were airborne. Hooray.

Sarah and I went back to make Jimmy as comfortable as possible and to instil in the nurses that once the plane was spotted speed was of the essence as it would be getting jolly gloomy. The local grapevine was in full swing and already quite a few people had made their way up from the bay for the free entertainment.

A few anxious hours lay ahead of us so we decided to while away the time by doing a ward round. Our minds weren't really on the job in hand so it was a shock to get to Stephen, the chap with the undiagnosed chest problem, to find him that awful grey colour which only particularly unwell dark-skinned people are capable of. He was lying in the arms of his smiling wife who was sitting on his bed cradling him while twisting her head round to chat to her friends through the louvre windows. Right in front of our aston-ished eyes Stephen died. One second an unwell looking young, newly married man with no diagnosis, the next dead. I spent a few very miserable minutes rushing to theatres and back to get the intu-bation set and put a tube into his lungs in the full view of uncomprehending and still cheerful wife, friends and wantoks. They were mighty surprised when I announced his demise. Incredulity followed by terrible keening, shrieking and wailing. We escaped into the paediatric ward.

At 6.30 the plane was heard. The sun being below the swaying palm trees and night approaching fast, the pilot had no time for a check circuit and had to bring the plane straight in. It was dark within a few minutes. Of course the 'speed' we had instilled into the nurses was of no avail and it was some time before Jimmy's mum could be traced (visiting wantoks in town) and we could chivvy all interested parties down to the dark airstrip. As we were setting off Wilson ran out of his office and stopped the truck to tell me the Ministry were on the phone and did we want to order a charter? Down at the airstrip the refuelling was in hand so the pilot and I rearranged the seats inside – it was getting to be a habit. Jimmy and various wantoks were put aboard and while we strapped them in, the one last and vital question came to me. How on earth were they going to take off in the pitch-black moonless night? I need not have worried. The Chief of police was there. He beckoned me over to his truck and drove down to the far end of the airstrip while the aeroplane taxied to the other end. He turned the truck round to face towards the plane, hidden from us by the gentle hillock over which the airstrip ran. At least the pilot would have a light to aim at. The policeman and I bravely left the truck and edged towards some handy coconut trees. We could hear the noise of the engines begin to wind up, at which lines of bright flaming kerosene-soaked rag torches lit each side of the airstrip. These were being waved enthusiastically by young men who had been organized by the police – wonderful.

The sound of the engines grew and grew and then the lights of the plane bounced over the hillock towards us in the silky-warm darkness. Like some mad animal the aeroplane roared up and away over our heads, but the roar didn't die away and I realized that it was me and all the other onlookers yelling and shouting with relief and hairtingling unbridled joy. WOW.

Jimmy survived.

Lata Hospital
Santa Cruz
Temotu Province

5th July 1996.

DPHS

Chief Adminstration Officer
Ministry of Health & Med. Services
P O Box 349
Honiara.

Dear Sir

Please find enclosed the list of Medical employees requested by your good self.
Unfortunately we were unable to provide you with it by your deadline as your request only
arrived here 2 days after the deadline.

Yours faithfully

Dr. David Arathoon.
Director Provincial Health Services
TEMOTU PROVINCE.

Chapter 6

Dozy Dogs and the Midday Sun

TEMOTU PROVINCE

LATA
SANTA CRUZ
SOLOMON ISLANDS

The islands of:
Ndeni (Santa Cruz)
Tinakula
Reef Islands
Fianu
Materna
Nupani
Nukapu
Nifiloli
Duff Islands
Utupua
Vanikoro
Tikopia
Anuta
Fataka

In reply please quote reference No.

Chief of Police
Lata

DATE: 1/5/96·

Dear Sir,

I would just like to express my appreciation for your invaluable help with the Charter flight on Monday 29th of April. You and your boys did a sterling job with no fuss or bother. Fantastic. I am sorry we had to rely on you for the use of your truck, but as you know the medical truck is in a very poor state of repair & is currently off the road.

The sick child made it to Central hospital and is recovering from an emergency operation.

Please pass on the thanks from everyone in the Medical Division to your men

Yours sincerely,

DPHS, TEMOTU PROVINCE.

cc Premier, Temotu Province
   P/S, MHMS, Honiara.

'The kids seemed to have named that disgusting foul filthy cat "Nessie".'

'Hmm.'

'You know, that skinny black and white stinking feline which has been meowing round the back door.'

'Hmm.'

'Well, what do you think?' I was holding up an X-ray of a rotting big toe so that Sarah could see it against the light.

'What I think is that *I* am trying to concentrate on this amputation – bit higher – and you wittering about that stupid cat is not helping.' She was bent to 90° at the waist, over the suppurating foot of a fisherman who had trodden on a fish bone three months previously, and was squinting up at the X-ray. 'Anyway, Hilda says it belonged to our predecessors.' So that was it.

'But what about those pigging feral dogs? They will get Nessie as soon as we have wiped the pus and mud off the damned thing.' We had become worried by the stray dog population which was increasing and becoming ever more brazen – even sleeping in half dozens on my vegetable patch. I had thrown trainers at them and even had a shot with a bow and arrow, which we had been sold by a diminutive grizzled local who had pitched up at the door out of the blue. The aforesaid Wilfred had promised that the six-foot polished bow was designed to kill ... 'Pigeons?' – 'No, for shootem man.' So much for 'man'. In my rage at the sight of the dogs one day I had reached for the bow, strung it expertly and blindly as I kept one eye on the snoozing dogs and then run out onto the verandah. I pulled the custom string to its fullest extent, sighted along the trembling arrow at the nearest dog, and had then been given the fright of my life when the bow burst in two with such a loud bang that the dogs all woke up, haring off into the coconuts on my exasperated:

'*Jesus*, Wilfred.'

'The cat has survived this long, so I should think it will be OK ... now let me see – where do you think I should put the suture line?' She had removed the distal phalanx, gnawed at the end of the proximal phalanx with bone nibblers (as instructed by Hermann) and had left sufficient skin to put the sutures wherever she wanted. 'This way?' flap down, 'Or that way?' flap up.

'Er ...'

'Along the top seems most sensible,' saith the surgeon, and that's what she did.

*

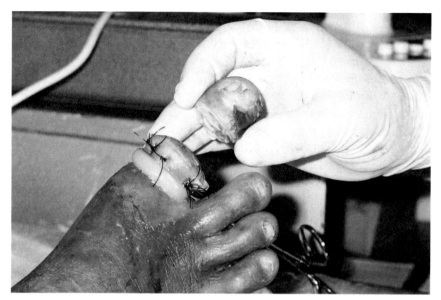

Amputation.

After washing up and sorting the rest of the hospital for the morning we wandered back towards our house looking forward to the single cup of coffee we allowed ourselves each day from our declining stock. I was to spend a couple of hours in the afternoon discussing the forthcoming celebrations for the Second Appointed Day with Barry, one of the Kiwi VSAs. Like each of the other provinces in the Solomons, Temotu had its own special day during which it celebrated its formation. For some obscure reason this was known as 'The Second Appointed Day' – not only in Temotu, but in all the other provinces as well.

'That was quite some racket eh?' We grinned at each other as we trudged the few hundred yards up the glaring white coral road to our home, remembering the impressive noise the congregation had made over at the Bishop's church celebrating Easter a couple of days before. We were unsure why the Tikopian bishop had invited us, but it had been amazing. During the hymns the sheer volume of noise in the open-sided, tin-roofed, coral-floored church had taken us by surprise. After being overwhelmed for a few minutes by the physical enormity of the sound, our ears became acclimatised sufficiently to distinguish the harmonies; they were beautiful. The children had stopped trembling by the third hymn. We turned off the road onto the path leading to the house still shaking our heads and giggling.

'Look – look there, and in broad daylight as well.' I picked up a handy lump of coral and flung it at the retreating pack of dogs who had been lounging right beside the verandah and who now laughed at us over their shoulders. 'Bloody things. You know, after I have had a chat with Barry I am going to do in that scabby Labrador look-a-like that's always hanging round the hospital. Guess how?' The remedy having come to me in a flash.

'How?' Raised eyebrows.

'A massive overdose of ketamine, followed by a trip in the hospital truck to the cliff at the end of the airstrip and then a quiet drowning – God I can't wait'.

Barry was a large balding overweight moustachioed New Zealander of about sixty years with amazing drive and determination. He was a little non-PC in that he thought that the First World could teach and help the Third World. Goodness knows how he got through the Stalinist VSA PC radar when he had been chosen to come to the Solomons. Put it this way, he and Helen did not get on. Hardly on speaking terms in fact, which made it difficult and sometimes rather amusing for Sarah and I.

Barry ran the Temotu Development Agency (TDA), which tried to support small commercial ventures in the community. This usually took the form of loans to buy outboard motors, chainsaws, canoes, seeds or just about anything if you could persuade Barry it was a good idea. Initially the locals thought this was great, but they became very puzzled when asked for their repayments. They were aghast when Barry took back the precious chainsaw after six months of lack of repayments. I don't think Barry was on to a winner but he was nothing if not persistent, and he had some rather far-fetched plans: an oil press to extract coconut oil from copra; a ship for the province; he even contemplated assisting the provincial government towards beaurocratic efficiency ... His house was across the netball pitch, past the motor workshops and down the hill towards the town generator.

On the way over I passed 'the' mango tree opposite Wilson Lyno's store. Surrounding this was the market which was usually a sea of mud, mango skins, banana skins, betel-red spittle and coconut husks. Unfortunately no canine corpses. One of Barry's ideas was to build a foot-high platform for all the women stall-holders to sit on to keep them out of the gloopy mud. The idea had not come to fruition. It seemed to be blocked at every turn – town council, provincial government – as usual it was difficult to know what the problem was and where it lay.

From Barry's bungalow I was aware of the deep 'thrub' of the diesel generator, but he insisted he no longer noticed it. As was his wont at home, Barry was only dressed in a pair of shorts and sandals ... apart from a haze of sweat. We got down to business.

'So Dave, waddya think?' he asked after an hour or so. I thought his ideas were tremendous: canoe races and 'Iron Warrior' and 'Iron Mary' races. To my mind his plans for prize money were a trifle excessive. (Helen agreed with me).

After a series of canoe races in the bay, he planned the 'Iron' races. These consisted of a canoe race to the bottom of the bay, followed by a run back into the station, stopping only to shoot arrows at a target for the men, and to carry logs on heads for the women. This was to be in addition to the usual custom dancing competitions and vegetable and livestock competition. Fantastic.

'Hey Dave, this year the New Zealand High Commissioner and his wife and son will be coming – do you reckon we should have a barbie? What about taking them out for a trip to Tinakula – there's an idea. Could we borrow a medical canoe and outboard? I am sure TDA could find some fuel – do you know of a driver who would take us?' Phew, that was Barry all right. I promised to make enquiries; anyway I had never been out to the volcano island. That would be a good way to celebrate the province's special day.

I didn't tell Barry about my plans for the scabrous dog which haunted the hospital.

However, I thought I should inform Wilson Lyno. He looked extremely sceptical, with his eyebrows rising so far as to nearly meet his mini afro. Of course he could not say that he thought the idea was that of an idiot, but it was apparent he thought so. Over his afro in fact I could see the morning volcanic haze slowly rising from the hidden Tinakula to remind me, so I made enquiries about a driver for the trip to the volcano. Wilson Yamalo the hospital handyman was the man.

I had seen the filthy leering yellow cur snoozing under the hospital truck on my way through the hospital ... little did he know that the truck would soon be part of the end of him, ha ha ha. I sauntered past the wards to the operating theatre to get a vial of ketamine. The theatre was at the end of one arm of the hospital, opposite was the malaria lab and making a third side to a natural rectangle, about forty yards by twenty yards, was the covered walkway. This was to be the site of the ketamine overdose ... ha ha ha.

Now ketamine is used a lot in the Third World because it is an amazing drug for anaesthesia. It can be used either intramuscularly in a highish dose where the onset of action is some minutes, or intravenously in a lower dose with a rapid onset, and shorter action. (The dog would get it intramuscularly.) The patient loses consciousness and major operations can be carried out as long as the airway is maintained. It is brilliant where there are no anaesthetists or blood oxygen monitors. There are a few strange potential side effects: often generalised muscle contractions (making pushing guts and wombs back into abdominal cavities rather trying) and bad dreams. The bad dreams are countered with Valium which does nothing whatsoever for the dreams, but makes the patient forget them. Sometimes the dreams are all too real and the patient moans a bit, and writhes. Not that I cared about dreams, moaning and writhing with the dog.

I pushed open the door of the operating theatre reading the vial, and as I came into the sunlight I looked up – straight into the brown eyes of the yellow dog that had moved and was now lounging in the shade of the large concrete water tank. He grinned at me and wagged his tail. I grinned at him. He got up stiffly and made towards me, head down and panting in the heat.

'Not yet, crazy dog, not yet.' I turned into the clinical room to check the dose.'Now I wonder how heavy that bloody thing is ...' I was gazing up at a chart stuck to the wall (protected with an old XR film) that indicated the dosage of ketamine for any given weight – of humans. Once my eyes had become accustomed to the relative murk of the clinical room I ran my finger over the XR wondering what weight I should use. I glanced back out into the white hot blazing sunshine to gauge the weight of the yellow one who had staggered back to the shade of the water tank. He was watching me.

'Hmm ... let's say he is about 50 lbs ... that must be 25 or 30 kilos ... double the dose to make sure – right ho.' I had made my decision, drew up the clear ketamine liquid and went to see if I could find a piece of string to tie up the dog with while I injected him. He followed me with his eyes, wagging his dusty tail when I inadvertently caught his eye. Wilson Yamalo had an old piece of string and I persuaded John-the-clerk to come and help.

It was much easier than I had supposed. Not only was the dog fetid and filthy, but he was also curious and trusting. We got the string round his neck and attached him to one of the rusty bedsteads which seemed to be stored in the open behind the water tank. He grinned inanely and wagged his tail. Quite a few faces had appeared at the windows of the wards and the nursing station. Was there to be entertainment?

'OK John, you holdem tight.' John held the dog's head and neck, trying to keep his fingers out of the worst of the suppurating sores. I carefully injected the ketamine into his neck and stood back. The dog had hardly winced and continued to grin and leer and wag. What a lot of attention – when normally all he got was abuse and a flip-flop up the bum. What nicesh people these Uprightsh are ... Hmm dozy dozy, jusht have a bit of a lie down ... the shade looksh rather far awa ... rather far aw ...

The dog went down slowly. John and I stood back. This was going to be easy. We noticed a few twitches, and then a couple of muffled 'Humphs' through blowing lips. Soon this built up and within two minutes the dog was on the move, scrabbling round and round on his side attached to his bedstead by the string, making more and more noise. Boy, it looked like an interesting dream. I hoped he would gradually settle down so we could lift him onto the truck. But he didn't. More and more people appeared to watch. The noise grew and grew. Suddenly there was an ear-piercing, shrieking 'Ho ... how ... **hoowwl**' from the dog. I anxiously glanced up at John – he looked very pleased with the proceedings. The noise built and built and the movements became wilder and wilder until it looked as though a banshee was having an epileptic fit. I was flabbergasted. All around me were cheerful amused faces. 'What fun,' they said. Not 'What an idiot the doctor is,' but more 'Wow, a shrieking helpless dog thrashing around in the dust – great.' The epileptiform movements of the dog made me realize something heroic was called for.

So I retreated to my office forty yards away, behind another building and the other side of two closed doors. The noise remained terrible. I retired home.

The dog lived. Our children christened him 'Scabby' and he adopted me. From then on whenever he saw me he would hasten over in his grinning leering cheerful way and try to rub his facial scabs off onto my legs. He had to be physically restrained if we wanted to go anywhere without him.

How strange life can be. I had, with all intent, tried to murder the mutt, and he thought I was the biz ... I didn't know what to think.

Sarah did though: 'You're a twit.'

Dr. David Arathoon   12 September 1996
Director of Health & Medical Services
LATA

Dear Mr Director,

I am now in possession of your letter. Surprisingly, it was very fast
coming in. I did not expect you to write, because I do not want to waste
my time with stubborn characters.

You did this to the most senior officer of the Medical Division in Temotu
this year. You refused to pay their airfares during leave resulting in
the family having to meet their own expenses. You have no value for the
welfare of your staff. What is your money compared to the lives of the
people in Temotu. Your policy is man made and can be adjusted to suit
prevailing situations in Temotu Province. We who served here for life
have experienced those difficulties than you do. I am concerned about
the welfare of my wife. It was you, because of your incapabilities, who
decided to send her to Honiara. And it is you who should understand simple
concepts. You have no experience in Temotu.

I am a member of the Provincial Government and I know what I did. If
you have no concern for other peoples welfare, say so. Travelling in
Temotu is difficult and this fact you must learn to humbly accept.

I am surprised that you value your wife so much. Why can't you do this
to others. If you continue to be stubborn, as you did so this far, I
will continue to shout at you.

Gone were the days when whiteman would sit in their glass house, looking
over their shoulders to see what is next.

You have lighted a fire, but at the wrong end, and is now burning out
of control. I will expect you to travel by sea during your mid term tour
since ANNUAL LEAVE is not EMERGENCY.

I shall wait for more.

MUSU L. KEVU
Deputy Provincial Secretary
Temotu Province

cc: US/MHMS - Health Care
cc: PS/MHMS
cc: PS/Temotu Province
cc: Provincial Premier
cc: Provincial Police Commander
cc: PNO/Lata

Chapter 7

Fun, Fire and Water

Lata Hospital
Santa Cruz
Temotu Province.

12th September 1996

Musu Kevu
Deputy Provincial Secretary
Lata Provincial Office
Temotu Province.

Dear Mr. Kevu

Herewith the letter explaining our conversation this morning. We send patients to Honiara 2 ways. If it is an emergency they go by air, if not an emergency then they go by ship. I hope you can understand this as it is not a complex idea. If a patient wishes to fly to Honiara, but we do not consider it an emergency, then we will put the seafare and they can make the airfare from their own pockets. This also should be understandable.

On another point, I WILL NOT have you shouting at my wife, or indeed myself. If you are unable to understand simple concepts then it is yourself you should get angry with not others. Should behave in such an aggressive, immature manner again in my office then I shall forced to ask the police to forcibly remove you from the Hospital grounds. As a member of the Provincial Government I think you will agree that it is unseemly to behave in such a manner.

Yours sincerely

Dr. David Arathoon.
Director Provincial Health Services
TEMOTU PROVINCE
cc: Underline by Healthcare
cc: PS/MHMS
cc: PS/Temotu
cc: Provincial Premier
cc: Provincial Police Commander

We were in the back of the hospital pick-up, heading along the bay road towards 'the water source'. So many things had happened in such a short space of time that Helen had decided she should show us as much as she could before she left to return to the UK. That was one of the things that had happened: Helen had received her leaving date. As there had been hiccoughs in both the weather – not enough rain for the time of year – and in the water pump – not working often enough to supply Lata town with water – we were off to see the water source five miles away at the bottom of the bay. This was the water that was pumped up to Lata and ended up coming through our blue pipe (now left entirely alone on the ground, except when it flowed . . .). It also flowed into a large water tank further up the hill from the station. Or should have, but it hadn't. Helen suggested we all troop to the source with our soap and shampoo to have a rather long-needed wash. I was very excited by the trip, as I had gleaned from the Lonely Planet guide that Mendana himself had set up camp down near the water source on his troubled stay on Santa Cruz. There was supposed to be some evidence of his stay in the form of ditches and ramparts – perhaps the local crabs had dug up some coins or ceramics – I could hardly wait.

Don Alvaro de Mendana y Neyra had come out from Peru to the Solomons in the late 1560s but it had taken him until 1595 to raise the finance to return (even having named the islands after the fabulous wealth of Solomon). He discovered Santa Cruz in September 1595 and set up camp 'down the bay' at Pala. A jolly sensible decision as he had access to a permanent supply of water, unlike modern day Lata-ites. There was pretty much immediate strife with the locals and by the end of November the so-called settlers returned to Peru leaving fifty of their number behind, dead . . . not only from malaria. Poor old Mendana was one of those left behind, presumably rotting in a grave somewhere even now. I don't think the Spaniards and the locals understood each other:

'And why shouldn't we eat each other?'

'And why shouldn't *we* eat those free roaming pigs?' etc, etc.

Quite a few of the fifty were killed by the locals; no one knows how many locals were killed by the Spanish – but they were so used to death and cannibalism that they probably forgot all about it come the next intervillage dispute, war and then feasting.

What else had happened? Well, Hilda had finally come clean about Eric-the-gardener and his recurrent headaches and deteriorating work: alcohol – gasp. Poor old Jehovah's Witness Hilda could hardly bring herself to say the word, but she had got rid of Eric and had installed in his place John-the-gardener who had served our predecessors loyally. John was superb. Three times a week he would appear from who knows where and set about the garden, planting up vegetables and keeping an eye and a brush knife on the grass. (My goodness grass likes lots of rain and warmth and light – if only it could find a tiny bit of soil on the coral.) He was about fifty years old (give or take a couple of decades), slim, smiling, quiet, humble and completely content with life. Luckily he also didn't mind the children jumping on his back as he squatted to weed. He chewed betel constantly, and usually had a garish red dribble from the angle of his mouth. He was utterly trustworthy and worked hard. Rather a gem. He also had a secret source of coconut crabs which he would occasionally bring us to eat. What a chap.

Doctor/gardener, gardener/doctor.

Sarah had been invited by the Bishop to go on his next tour of the outer islands – and I was not jealous at all. At all . . .

The Second Appointed Day had been and gone. As I had been assigned one of the judges of the custom dancing competition I had shaved, put on a pair of clean shorts and a clean T-shirt and had been in position in the grandly named football stadium at the appointed hour of 9.30 am ready for the action. I was, of course, alone. i.e. no one else, dancers, villagers, supporters, fellow judges etc, turned up until 11.30. I was somewhat put out. The dancing was very unusual. Each participating village had a different get up: different pattern of white lime paste on different parts of their anatomies, different types of different vegetable matter draped over different limbs and differing amounts of breasts on display. The dances ranged from fast and furious to slow and literally stomping. And I was supposed to know which was best. I made my votes and left while the other judges totted up the scores. Sarah helped judge the vegetables and livestock. There was one cacao pod in the cacao pod section, so that wasn't difficult and all the judges could agree. The main judicial dispute arose at the goat section. One of the judges seemed to favour a certain goat amongst its colleagues. Sarah had to admit it did look fatter than average, but that was only because it had been killed by the feral dogs the evening before and had become bloated overnight. After seeking advice it was agreed that a smaller but live goat should

Custom dancing competition, Santa Cruz.

win. Full marks to the owner for entering the deceased anyway. The other competitions were just as fierce. The canoe races and Iron races had been a great success. Huge crowds on the wharf, cheering each race, collision, capsize and crafty corner cutting. Later I was mocked as I set up the archery targets for the Iron Warrior race. It was obvious to everyone except myself that the targets were too big and much too close, 'cos of course they are all such spanking good shots. In the event, one of the four targets was hit once in the outer circle by one competitor and all the others were ... misses. I wasn't quite sure what to make of that.

Sarah was off to the fabled island of Tikopia with the Bishop – and I hardly cared. She would be going via Vanikoro.

Two days before the Second Appointed Day, Christophe had arrived from New Caledonia. One minute he wasn't there, the next he was – Third World style. No advance warning. Helen had immediately fallen in love with the dashing Frenchman. He had come to examine the 'treasures', which had been recovered some years before from the wrecks of the ships *Astrolabe* and *Boussole*. All the artefacts that had been brought to the surface had been put in a very insecure room in the government building if they were robust enough, or in the case of the delicate wooden pieces into a freezer

Relics from La Perouse (and Sarah . . .)

in the fisheries building. This was because the fisheries had a back-up generator if the town genny broke down, and the cold of the freezers would preserve the wood where the heat and humidity outside would destroy it. Actually when Christophe opened the freezer he was met by a pile of sawdust, as some years before the freezer had been switched off, and then unplugged for good measure. He was a bit upset. Christophe had come to log what was left of the artefacts, and to see if the locals would mind if they were taken away to New Caledonia to be preserved before being brought back to Lata as soon as a purpose-built, air-conditioned, museum was built, i.e. never ...

The story of these two ships is fascinating. A French chap called Le Compte de la Perouse led an expedition in 1788 and was unfortunately caught on a lee shore in a terrific cyclone off the island of Vanikoro. His ship the *Boussole* was driven onto the outer reef and sank quickly; the few survivors swam ashore to be eaten by the locals. The *Astrolabe* heroically made for a gap in the reef to rescue their colleagues (and presumably to get into the quieter water inside the reef) but unfortunately the gap was a false passage and the ship became impaled on a coral spike. Most got ashore, fended off the replete locals, recovered wood and tools from the ship, built a fort and sat down to think. What they thought they should do was to build a two-masted boat from the retrievable parts of the ships – so they did, and sailed away, never to be heard of again. They left two of their members behind who were reported to be alive in 1820 but had disappeared by 1827 when an Irish trader called Dillon popped by. There are two further interesting points. After he was cast adrift with eighteen members of his crew in an open boat, Bligh actually rowed past Vanikoro while the French were still on the island. Bligh refused to land as he had been attacked by locals at a previous island. He did however, in a typically British way, make it back to civilization instead of romantically sailing off into the wide blue yonder, à la France.

One of the chief officers of the ship *Astrolabe* was a Monsieur Ducorps. He has the distinction of having the Solomon Island White Cockatoo named after him, unfortunately with a spelling mistake due to a transposition of letters, which has persisted: 'Kakatoe ducrops'. Poor old Froggies, even the name of a cockatoo which 'only screeches when startled' is a cock up.

As Barry had suggested we had made a trip to the volcano island of Tinakula. It turned out to be quite an expedition with Christophe, the New Zealand High Commissioner's son and a couple of Peace Corps teachers from the only secondary school in Temotu swelling our ranks. We had set off mid morning the day before the Second Appointed Day in two canoes because of the numbers who wanted to go. It was a lovely day with little wind and a beautiful blue sky reflected in the huge calm ocean. The volcano is twenty-six miles from Santa Cruz and was gently smoking as we approached from the south. On closer inspection it looked to be a perfect cone rising straight out of the sea with what looked like runnels down the side. It was an aching emerald green of the purest hue, stunningly lovely. At the base of the island we could see waves breaking on black volcanic rocks and the black of the rocks and the foamy white of the waves contrasted sharply with the green of the rest of the island. The wonder of it stopped the excited holiday chatter on both canoes and we gazed rather calf like at the slopes and steaming top. The canoes slowed as we came closer and our necks craned further back.

'Wow,' was the most appropriate comment.

Sarah and I were in the second canoe and as we gently motored round the west side of the island we heard gasps and shouts from the canoe ahead:

'Jesus.'

'Oh my god.'

'Look at that ...'

'Flipping heck.'

We thought something catastrophic had happened, and in a way we were correct, only we were forty years late. We went further towards the north of the island and suddenly saw what had caused the outburst from the leading canoe. From the 2700-foot summit to the base in the sea a huge part of the north side of the island was missing, replaced by an ugly black, brown and ochre moonscape of boulders and rocks. God it was ugly. Wilson Yamalo told us that there had been a massive landslide in the 1950s and the north side had been desolate ever since. The island perfection was ruined. Or perhaps it was enhanced by the contrast with the hellish north face. I felt I could reach up and peer into the top of the caldera, the side of which had fallen into the sea. However, when we landed on the black sand beach at the base of the slip it was obvious that one couldn't reach the top of the mountain via the unstable north side. In fact, when the excited conversation died down again we could hear stones continuously dribbling down the scarred cheek of the volcano. We wouldn't be staying long. The top was completely protected either by the still mobile moonscape, or the impenetrable jungle elsewhere.

There was only one chance of reaching the summit and that relied on finding what was in the runnels we had seen on the way in.

We learnt a valuable lesson on the way back to Lata. Our canoe with all its fifteen horses galloping behind could not get round the eastern edge of the island due to invisible but powerful currents. It took us ten minutes to realize that we had been motoring flat out past the same water-splashed rock without getting anywhere. On that shore-side rock stood a scrawny dishevelled flea-bitten lone dog watching our lack of progress. What was he doing on an uninhabited island? Tinakula had been abandoned in the 1970s because of regular very powerful earthquakes. He couldn't be twenty years old. What was he doing, how had he got there, what did he eat? Not a lot by the look at him. The other canoe with twenty-five less-gasping horses outboard turned back to see what we were up to.

'Oh ... nothing, let's go back the way we came shall we?'

The Bishop and Sarah would soon be off on his ship the *Southern Cross*, and *I* would be left in charge of the children. And the hospital.

'That's Dan's and Brenda's house.'
    'What?'
    'What?'
    'Over there, no on the left, no ... well we're past now but I will show you on the way back.' Helen had been pointing out the sights to us from the back of the noisy truck to the water source. These consisted mainly of tiny villages which merged into one another, the odd dancing circle paved with coral (and surrounded with coral), and the ubiquitous standpipes ... most unattended and gushing onto the ground. How come they had running water down here, and we didn't have up on the plateau?
    'Who are Dan and Brenda?' We had been in Lata months now and had never heard their names before.
    'Oh, they have been here for ages, seven or eight years I should think.'
    'What on earth for?'
    'They're Bible translators ...'
    'Ah.' Difficult to know what to say about that, 'Right ... er, how far now to the source?' at which we slowed and turned right, off the road onto a winding track between the coastal coconuts. Two hundred yards on we came to 'the water source'. All along the track I had gazed excitedly from side to side.

Water source: Sarah, Barney, Meg, and John Melalao.

'Helen, have you ever seen any ditches or ramparts down this track?'

'What and what?'

'Ditches and ... oh never mind.'

The water source was a calm, beautiful oasis. Or would have been without the noisy concrete pump house. The water rose crystal clear into a rectangular pond three feet deep and about thirty yards across right at the base of the coralline cliff, which led vertically a couple of hundred feet to the plateau above. The water was so clear as to be nigh on invisible, the playful fish filling it looked as if they were swimming in air. All around was verdant growth. The water spilled over a small weir into a second and much smaller pool, just right for bathing in. (The pump extracted the water from the top pool.) Goodness it was cold. The children screeched and wailed but we pretended not to hear above the thumping from the pump house. For us adults it was ecstatic. Cold cold water on hot sweaty greasy grimy ingrained pale skin. Fully clothed of course. Wonderful. The bottom pond emptied in its turn over a weir and became a river which ran straight to the sea. The flow was pretty impressive and I contemplated making a guestimate of it, but decided my brain had been fried and then frozen too quickly to make a decent answer likely. So I decided to walk round the periphery of the source. At the very base of the cliff there were a couple of small ponds-cum-caves where the water could be seen to well up. As I stepped over one of them I noticed something long thin and banded. I gulped. It looked not unlike a water snake. It *was* a water snake. I hurried back.

'Come and look at this ...' Sarah duly did, and gratifyingly recoiled as I had.

'Thanks ...' Well she had better get used to it, off as she was to the wilds of the outer islands with the Bishop.

I did have a look amongst the bowls of the coconut trees between the pools and the sea searching in vain for shards of pottery, gold coins or anything really. The local crabs were not up to much and had brought precisely zero to the surface. Copra hadn't been collected for some time and the undergrowth was too dense for more than a random look round. Nothing. I slowly retraced my steps – and nearly fell into a ditch. Wow! Hooray. Old Mendana had stood on this very spot, probably gazing worriedly across the ditch at the gathering locals. I could hardly believe it.

In fact no one else did believe it. 'Probably just a drainage ditch.' Ha, I say. There are no drainage ditches on Santa Cruz. And anyway my ditch is in exactly the position marked in the Lonely Planet guide – so there. I remained chuffed.

We set off back to Lata. Helen forgot to show us Dan and Brenda's house again. We drew up into the hospital and one of the nurses came out of the nursing station. It was Ellen.

'Cindrella, hem start for bornim pikinini. Stakka blood ...'

Sarah and I looked at each other. Someone with a weird name was well into labour but bleeding profusely. I took the children home to Hilda while Sarah went to examine the poor potential mother.

Benjaim Builua   20th September 1996
Health Education Unit
Lata
Temotu Province.

Dear Ben

I was surprised to see you at the hospital today at 7:30. Most
of the time no one seems to know where you are or what you
are doing. I have heard that you spend a lot of time at
Minevi with wantoks - how can you possibly do your job in
Lata efficiently if you sleep at Minevi?

Any way, I am thinking of doing a survery on how much time is
actually spent at work by employees of MHMS. Firstly I want
to do a pilot survey and I have chosen you to study.
I would like you to come to John Melelao's office each morning
between 7:30 and 8 am. He will keep a record of when you came
to work and when you don't. If you know that you will be
working at night, I will still expect you in the mornings, but
obviously you can take time off in the afternoons in lieu of
your night work. In addition I want you to liase with Edwin -
Daulu so that you can go out twice a week with the CHT and
start doing regular Health Education in the villages. In
addition I would like you to drop off in my office each Friday
a note of what you propose to do with your time during the
coming week. Please start on Wednesday 25th September.

Many thank for your help.

Your sincerely

David Arathoon

Dr. David Arathoon.
Director Provincial Health Services
TEMOTU PROVINCE.

Chapter 8

Seized by Events

(*Et tu* Cindrella)

Lata Hospital
Santa Cruz
Temotu Province.

23rd July 1996

New Zealand High Commissioner
Honiara.

Dear Rhys

Many thanks for the cheque for $5,000, it will be put to good use. I am sorry it has taken me so long to get round to acknowledging it, and I don't even have the excuse of pressure of work. I also enclose the acquittal form because although the money has not all been 'spent' you might have to wait over a year or more for the community Rehabilitation team to use up their $1,000 share.

Thanks also for the round robin letter and photo of Sarah at work under the tree. We have also had a look at Barrys Photos which are amazing.

I'm afraid that if you keep extending invitations to us to come and stay then you might very well be taken up by us and both children. However, we don't plan go to Honiara before December on our way out to New Zealand for a holiday, so you are safe for a while.

Regards to Margaret.

Yours sincerely

David Arathoon

Dr. David Arathoon.
Director Provincial Health Services
TEMOTU PROVINCE.

I got back to the hospital to hear Sarah's verdict:

'Well, she's in early labour, quite regular contractions every ten minutes or so, but the most obvious thing is that she is bleeding heavily . . .'

'You don't think . . .'

'I have to say I'm not sure, she's stable at the moment but of course I can't examine her PV. The foetal heart is OK.'

'I had better go back to the house and get that surgical textbook then.' Our greatest worry was that Cindrella might have a placenta praevia, where the placenta, which provides the unborn babe with its nutrition, covers the entrance to the cervix and therefore the real world. Now the placenta is a very bloody organ and if nothing is done in placenta praevia, as the cervix dilates in labour, it starts to pump blood, not to the excited babe which thinks it is about to start life, but to the outside world through the mother's vagina until first one and then the other dies. A lingering death, which can become precipitate if a larger blood vessel ruptures. This unspoken diagnosis we did not want. We didn't have the facilities to stop the labour, the next plane wasn't due for two days, and if we did manage to arrange a charter all the action would probably be over by the time the plane landed. All this was going through my mind as I returned for the surgical textbook. We had to find out if the placenta was lying over the cervix. The only way to do this would be to examine the labouring Cindrella vaginally. Such an examination would have to be done on the operating table because the examination itself can cause catastrophic bleeding and an emergency Caesarean section has to be carried out. My mind whirred. I returned with the book.

'We will have to examine her on the operating table,' said Sarah. 'I will let the nurses know that we need to operate immediately if we confirm a placenta praevia.' There, she had said the dreaded words without causing any deterioration in Cindrella's condition.

'Hang on a sec, I had better have a look at this book first.' I had decided that if a Caesarean was to be carried out then I should do it. Sarah was aware that I had in fact done two Caesareans many years before as a junior hospital doctor. The difference was that they had been 'cold' (or planned) and I had had a very competent experienced senior registrar across the table from me 'assisting', and an anaesthetist, theatre sisters, midwives, porters and of course modern equipment. This on the other hand was looking potentially very hot.

Sarah and I had a good look at the instructions in the surgical manual. I had only seen what are called 'lower segment' Caesareans where the womb is opened across-wise (horizontally), low down. This gives best results and allows the womb to heal up well with minimal scar tissue, so that further pregnancies are put at least risk. However, in this case I was scared that if I opened the uterus low down I might go straight into the placenta, as it would have to be low lying if it was covering the cervix. If it was . . . It all depended on the initial examination followed either by a huge sigh or frantic surgical manoeuvres to get the babe out before any excess bleeding we had caused by the examination caused exsanguinations. If we did go in I thought we should do a 'classical' section where the uterus is opened vertically and well away from the lower part where the placenta would be lurking. It was a risk as neither of us had seen it done and it would leave Cindrella with a more fragile uterus in subsequent pregnancies should she, of course, survive our imminent ministrations.

Then what about the anaesthetic? Often these days Caesareans are done under a spinal anaesthetic where a tiny tube is introduced into a woman's back through a needle and local anaesthetic is inserted with ensuing numbness. This allows the surgeon to operate while cracking dirty jokes with the patient. There are lots of advantages, not least avoiding a general anaesthetic and all the risks that entails. The mum is awake throughout and can be given the babe straight away, suckling if she so wishes while she is stitched back up. Then of course pain relief is not a problem afterwards as more local can be pushed through the tube as and when. Neither of us had ever attempted a spinal anaesthetic and actually they had the reputation of dropping the blood pressure which may not be a good idea if our poor patient was bleeding all over the place already. We decided we didn't want to be scrabbling around with a needle in the spinal cord of a very pregnant lady, in labour with a potentially life-threatening condition, where time would be of the essence.

That left only two alternatives:

1. A full general anaesthetic; however we did not have any of the necessary drugs or equipment, let alone any form of anaesthetist.
2. Ketamine . . . oh dear, with all its possible drawbacks including uterine contraction at perhaps an inopportune moment. Oh well, needs must when the devil drives.

'So, Wilson,' to Wilson Lyno, 'who can give the IV ketamine, pethidine and Valium while Sarah and I operate?'

'Melau, by me tellim come,' – the laid-back Simon Melau of

community health team fame. I wondered if anyone knew where he was, or how long it would take him to get to the hospital.

We gathered all the relevant staff (including a fast appearing Simon) and explained what we needed to do:

a. We needed to examine Cindrella to ascertain if she had a placenta praevia.

b. We would need to operate immediately if 'a' was positive, as carrying out 'a' could cause heavy (for heavy read very heavy) bleeding.

'OK?'

'OK,' 'OK,' 'OK,' 'OK,' 'OK,' etc.

About twenty minutes later we all seemed ready, Yvonne was scrubbed to assist, Ellen was ready to receive, Simon was at the top end all ready.

'Everyone ready?'

'Yes,' 'Yes,' 'Yes,' 'Yes,' 'Yes,' etc.

'OK then,' from Sarah, 'I will have a look-see and tell you what I think,' at which she carefully and gently pushed a speculum in to enable her to visualize the cervix. 'There's quite a lot of blood in here ... I'll just remove some of it ... oh gosh ... you know, I think it is a praevia ... do you want a look?' I jolly well did.

As I changed places at the bottom end of the theatre couch to examine Cindrella's innermost parts I asked Sarah: 'Have you ever seen a praevia before?'

'No, have you?'

'Er, no ... never, let's have a look ... Dear God I think it is as well. What did you see – a sort of livery cotyledony-looking bleeding thingy poking out ... and lots of blood?'

'Yeah.'

'Right that's it, let's go. Simon, put her to sleep and we will scrub.'

Due to all the unforeseen circumstances which forseeably pertain in the Third World it took another twenty minutes to put Cindrella under. Simon wasn't entirely sure how much ketamine to give and had to slowly wander off to find some more, not all the necessary instruments had quite been sterilized and there was only one pair of sterile gloves for Sarah and I to share. However Cindrella stayed calm, her blood pressure stayed up and slowly slowly everything came about so I could make the first incision.

I cut Cindrella open from umbilicus to pubis and gently dissected my way through the midline (having taken a bit of time to find the midline) to avoid cutting through muscle. I didn't know whether to extend the incision above her umbilicus and nor did Sarah. We decided to leave it below for the time being and extend if necessary.

'Has John given any blood yet?' Our universal blood donor hospital-clerk had been persuaded, with another tin of tuna, to forsake some more of his valuable blood in case we needed it. In case? It was a certainty.

'By me chekim,' from Wilson Lyno, who soon reported back that John had given a pint and a half.

We were now faced with an enormous looking uterus, which had come through my initial incision and was proudly standing looking at us through the parchment of the peritoneum. This I nicked and pulled apart to reveal the engorged muscle of the uterus. More for a breather and a chance to get my nerve up I asked Wilson to bring over the surgical textbook and hold it under the two working bulbs of the four-bulb operating lamp so I could see what to do next. It all sounded a bit bloody. I glanced at Yvonne's tray of sterile instruments and swabs and realized with a start that there didn't seem to be any swabs larger than four square inches ... where were the huge great ginockerous blanket-sized swabs we would need for the impending outpour? Yvonne assured me that these were the biggest she had. I had often seen the nurses in their nursing station quietly chopping up strips of gauze to put into packs for operations but had never realized they only made one size. Actually only half of them would be making the swabs because the other half sensibly would be taking advantage of the quiet time to stand behind the gauze-choppers using their finger nails to CRACK headlice. Not that that thought helped me now. I looked down at the pathetic sucker machine, which should have been the answer to my prayers. Sucker machines do just that, and provide suction down an easily manipulated tube so that blood and assorted debris can be quickly cleared from the field of vision of the surgeon. Our only sucker had seen better days and hadn't been serviced for at least ten years. His partner in crime had been sent off to Honiara to be serviced three years beforehand, but had disappeared into the maw that is medicine in the Third World, and had never been heard of again. Wilson had refused to let the other one go because then we would have been left with none. Now we did have one that was as good as useless in this sort of case. We would have to cope without ...

'Can we get that blood up now Wilson? I think we'll need it pretty soon,' I was right there, 'and just check her BP and pulse

before I incise this ... thanks ... OK at your end Simon?' A nod.
OK Yvonne?' Another nod. I pointed down: 'About here?' to Sarah,
and yet another nod.

I put the scalpel in and then everything became a bit of a blur ...
I opened the uterus without cutting the babe (hooray) and the
blood started flowing ... then I put in my fingers and pulled up and
down in the incision to enlarge it, and the blood flowed ... I
grabbed the babe and yanked her out (for it was a 'she' I did notice)
and gave her to Ellen, then because pressure had been released the
blood really started coming ... I scraped out the offending placenta
... there was so much blood filling the recently emptied uterus that
I couldn't have sworn that it was low lying ... the blood flowed and
flowed ... the babe was alive and our feet were getting wet. Actually I was soaked through, but blood was only responsible for my
feet.

We had to slow the flow enough to get a few stitches in ... to
slow the flow. I had to be able to have some idea where to put the
sutures in to slow the flow and to do that I had to be able to get a
glimpse of what was going on ... oh God.

'Yvonne, givvus a wadge of swabs ... what? No a great fistful.'
She did and I put them into the wound and pressed hard. In a few
seconds they were soaked, but on lifting them out I got a sight of
where the bleeding was coming from.

'OK, let's do that again, but this time when I pull them out hand
me a three-oh catgut suture and I will try and get some stitches in
before she pegs it ...' So I alternated handfuls of four-inch gauze
with two or three sutures, and slowly the storm settled to a gentle
downpour and my mind came back from autopilot to the very near
present, having absconded for a while. I was amazed to find that in
the middle of the worst of it I had extended the original skin incision to above the umbilicus so I could get a better view ... couldn't
remember doing that.

'Anyone been counting swabs?' I asked in a conversational way.
No answer. One of the most important routines in an operating
theatre, back all those thousands of miles away in the UK, was the
nurse's mantra of counting the swabs. All the swabs that went onto
the operating table were counted, and all the used swabs were hung
up and counted again by two nurses in unison, in a bid to make
sure none were left inside the patient. All the First World's swabs
are also marked with a radio-opaque strip in case they *are* left in,
to make it easier for the patient to sue the surgeon. To make him
feel even better about leaving a swab inside a patient. I looked up

from Cindrella's insides to see everyone (bar Sarah) looking at me quizzically ... then I shot a look in the general direction of where I had been chucking the bloodied four-inch swabs in my haste. There in the corner of the operating theatre against the wall was a decent-sized pile of uncounted very bloody gauze swabs ... none of which, I knew for a certainty, contained a radio-opaque strip.

'Er ... I wonder if anyone knows how many swabs we have used?' Lots of blank faces.

'Er ...'

'Don't let's worry,' said Sarah, 'I'm sure you haven't left any inside ...' I looked again at the now closed (and miraculously blood-tight) uterus and wondered what to do. We had no idea how many swabs we had used and so would have no idea if we had left any inside even if we counted those lying curdling on the floor. In the haste and flux of our combat with the uterus it had occurred to neither of us to count swabs on and off the table. Now, did I risk opening the bloody uterus again with all the risks associated or just carry on and trust to luck? Odd as it may seem it is extremely easy to inadvertently leave all sorts of flotsam and jetsam in an abdominal wound, even if you are a real surgeon. What to do, what to do?

'Oh bloody hell, I think we have to risk it. I reckon her chances of making it are better if we *have* left one inside and she gets septic but makes it to a proper surgeon in Honiara rather than if I open up the uterus again and can't for instance stop the bleeding a second time. bloodybloodybloody HELL ... sorry Wilson.' I apologized to Wilson for my unchristian vocabulary and closed Cindrella up, layer by layer. She was still alive, the babe was definitely still alive from the terrific racket going on at the far end of the hospital, and Sarah and I had survived, so all was well so far. The staff behaved as if we had done what was expected. We thought we were pretty damn heroic, and they thought we had just done our job. They were right, but we were pretty buoyed up.

As Cindrella was wheeled out of the operating theatre beginning to grumble and mumble the girls started to clear up the mess I had left behind. They picked up all the soiled swabs and instruments I had dropped and then started to swab up the pools of blood and slightly smaller pools of sweat we had left behind. In a bit of a daze Sarah and I got out of our operating gowns and greens and quietly got dressed, quietly went over to see if Cindrella was OK and then quietly sauntered up the road to our house. The sun was still shining which came as rather a surprise ... one instinctively feels that the sun should set after an epic. It was late afternoon and we

found the children in the special care of Hilda. We sat on the verandah and had a quiet cup of tea. Well Sarah sat while I lay back in
my hammock slung across the corner of the verandah. The blue
waters of Graciosa Bay winked at us through the coconut trees and
we slowly started to un-numb. It had been a mite hectic from start
to finish and we finally had a chance to unwind.

'God, I hope she makes it ...'

'Yup ... same here. We better think about going inside soon, out
of the mossies ... hey, and guess what?'

'Huh?'

'I had better think about packing ...'

'Huh?'

'You know ... I'm off on tour tomorrow with the Bishop ... hey
hey.' She was right. I just hoped Wilson had got everything ready
from the hospital point of view as neither of us was up to much
now.

'You lucky bugger.'

8th September 1997

Mr. Justin Mutukera
X-Ray Technician
Lata Hospital
Temotu Province.

Dear Justin

I see that you have gone against my explicit written instructions
and left your post here in Lata to attend a religious conference
without leaving your position covered by a locum. You will re-
call that both my letters to you of: 1st September 1997 and
1st July 1997 state unequivocably that you could only go to the
first General Assembly of the United Church in Honiara if you
had locum coverage.

By your action you have disobeyed a direct instruction from
your Director of Health, but what is worse, you have let down
the people of Temotu and yourself as a professional person.
I do not understand your actions. I am writing to the PS, MHMS
for advice on what to do with you.

Yours sincerely

Dr. David Arathoon.
Director Provincial Health Services
TEMOTU PROVINCE.

Chapter 9

Gatherings, Greetings and Goodbyes

TEMOTU PROVINCE

LATA
SANTA CRUZ
SOLOMON ISLANDS

The Islands of:

Ndeni (Santa Cruz)
Tinakula
Reef Islands
Pileni
Matema
Nupani
Nukapu
Nifiloli
Duff Islands
Utupua
Vanikoro
Tikopia
Anuta
Fataka

In reply please quote reference No. F: 04/1/4   DATE: 29th August 1997

The Director
Provincial Health Services
LATA
Temotu Province

Dear Dr. David,

RE: ERADICATION OF FERAL DOGS IN LATA

Your letter of 25/8/97 in respect of the above is well received and
here being acknowledged.

While your idea is in line with that of the T & CPB, the Board is yet
at this stage to meet and deliberate on resolutions on the same. There
are resolutions awaiting the Board's deliberations, which if resolved
become Regulations that can be further adhered to.

With the above mentioned, your office is hereby duly informed that
permission in respect of the above is granted on the following conditions:

* that the general public is well informed by any means of publi-
  cation, notices or media for awareness.

* Materials (items) for use in the exercise are available and
  inspected before use.

and remember to be friendly with the environment.

Yours Sincerely,

SIMON UESIKOKE
Secretary/T & CP Board/Temotu
Temotu Province

The hammock, the good old hammock. What a wonderful invention. Small, simple, cool, cheap and just wonderful. I was lying in my very own string number on the verandah, as was my wont, gazing into the middle distance and letting life and the tiny gentle breeze waft over me. Would Sarah notice that I had indulged in more than our allotted allowance of one cup of coffee a day whilst she had been cruising with the Bishop in far-off archipelagos? Was the drop in the quantity of instant coffee in the tin steep enough to warrant questions? I hoped not, and decided to keep my indulgent excesses to myself. I reached over to my daily allowance balanced on the tiny mug-sized platform I had nailed to the edge of the verandah within easy reach. Ah life ... I glanced over to the magnificent Polynesian paddle Sarah had brought me back from her voyages – it was a beauty – hand carved out of one piece of wood, carefully finished and then priced with a large red marker pen on the blade. I couldn't wait to try it in the canoe after the plane had come in with the mail and gone out with Helen. The coming and going of the twice-weekly plane was always quite an event, usually due to the anticipation of getting mail followed by the frustration of not getting any because someone had forgotten to deliver it to the International Airport in Honiara from the central post office ... or more commonly because the chap employed to pick up the mailbag and place it upon the plane hadn't got out of bed to do so. However it all caused some enjoyment, and the frustration of lack of mailbags was often cancelled out by meeting for a chat with Brian the middle-aged Kiwi pilot we had become friendly with. This time the plane's movements would be watched even more closely by all as Helen was due to leave.

I was also musing about cogs in my half-aroused state on the verandah. Cogs and Cindrella and how one's survival (so far) seemed to bring the grinding cogs of our First World into play with the jolly, laid-back cogs of our current Third World. I could see the rotating and counter-rotating interdigitating raucous cogs of the First World, through my half-closed eyelids, slowly drifting from stage right to intermesh successfully with the Third World cogs of Santa Cruz. I was pretty pleased with my visual metaphor and my thought that Cindrella's survival and that of her newborn may have had something to do with the meshing of both worlds. Not that Cindrella hadn't given us pause for thought on and off since her operation. Initially she seemed OK and came round from Simon's coolly executed ketamine anaesthetic with barely a grunt or a shout. She had suckled early and well and thus reduced the noise in the hospital to its more recognizable level of the background creaking of insects. The babe had done brilliantly in the unselfconscious manner that babes, with no idea of the greater world and its worries, manage. Then after about thirty-six hours Cindrella started getting occasional elevated temperatures. She remained well. Was it malaria? Or was it the start of a huge internal abscess forming in her recently chopped-about womb – forming around a neglected swab that had been neatly stitched into the wall of the uterus in my hurry? God only knew. Then having had her chloroquine for a presumed bout of malaria (from John-the-clerk?), she worsened. Should we treat her for scrub typhus? I asked Sarah on one of our infrequent radio calls while she was cruising the South Seas.

'Have you had a look at her wound yet?'

'Ah ... yes ... hadn't thought of that.' So I did, and there lay our problem – a wound infection. A large red tender indurated lump at the lower end of what now looked a rather enthusiastic incision. Was it merely due to a small collection of pus in the suture line, or was it due to a small collection of pus in the suture line surrounding a piece of gauze carefully stitched into said suture line? I nicked out four or five of the skin sutures and a disgusting blob of greeny pus plopped out – not followed by pieces of half-digested gauze – hooray. The pus now liberated, Cindrella went from strength to strength and our cogs came closer together.

Sarah and Helen's trip with the Bishop had been a resounding success and great fun was had by all ... all who were on the trip, that is. Sarah was in a very privileged position being the doctor on one of the infrequent tours of our outer islands. The Bishop's ship, the MV *Southern Cross*, not only had a beautiful and apposite name but also provided decent accommodation. Sarah and Helen had a cabin to themselves, access to a shower and more often than not ate with the Bishop and his large jolly wife, Mamma Christina. When she went ashore Sarah nearly always went ashore with the first group and came back last, spending as much time ashore as possible. Being a somewhat religious cruise there were feasts at each stop. Apart from the doctor, for anyone to earn the right to attend the feast, church and a sermon by the Bishop had to be enjoyed first. The doctor usually had a clinic to sort out and while everyone else literally sang for their supper (or lunch) she could whip through the waiting patients (patients who by this time had been waiting the better part of two years ... 'So doctor, if you want to attend church, we are quite happy to wait a couple of hours longer ...') and then go and explore the islands. Her favourite islands were Tikopia and Anuta, being respectively a tiny dot in the ocean and an even tinier dot in the ocean. Put it this way: Anuta had a population of 200 and was 400 metres long by 400 metres wide and was hundreds of miles from Tikopia, which was substantially larger in both respects and just as far from the next piece of inhabited earth. Tikopia had a clinic, which was much too large for its population and was hence dilapidated and under used. The Anutans had decided to reject every offer of a clinic, which pleasingly had not harmed their populace, and meant that Sarah performed her ministrations under a tree in the public gaze. Anuta did not have any communication with the outside world except for the occasional passing ships (having rejected innumerable offers of radios ...) and Tikopia's clinic had a huge set that didn't work at any time that we were in the country.

One of the most famous anthropological books written is called *We, the Tikopia* by a chap called Raymond Firth. It was published in 1936 after Firth had spent a year on Tikopia in the 1920s. It is staggeringly meaningful, boring and vengeful particularly against a certain medical doctor: W.H.R. Rivers. Virtually every mention of Rivers concerns where he went wrong and misinterpreted the society on Tikopia. Rivers did visit Tikopia, (aboard the *Southern Cross* ...) and subsequently published a book called *History of Melanesian Society* where he frequently refers to his studies on Tikopia. What Firth can't bear is that Rivers spent such a short time on Tikopia (some say twenty-four hours – ouch) and yet was able to glean so much, whereas one can't help thinking that Firth spent a year there, and was subsequently led further up the garden path than his predecessor. I thought Rivers was a complete hero. After studying the Pacific peoples he returned to Europe in time to psychologically treat the injured of the Great War, particularly one George Sherston aka Siegfried Sassoon, whom Sarah and I had spent so much time enjoying through the eyes of Pat Barker in her trilogy and indeed through his own eyes in *his* trilogy ... what a tiny place the world seems to be sometimes. Rivers reported that the size of families on Tikopia was restricted to four children, any subsequent sprogs being buried alive at birth. John Dillon, the Irish trader who had popped into Vanikoro to look for Froggy survivors from the La Perouse expedition, had previously reported that for every man on the island there were three women. He put this down to the fact that after the birth of the first two males into a family the rest of the male progeny were put down by being strangled at birth ... all pretty gruesome. Firth, in his rather nerdy manner, plodded around the small island for a year and counted all and sundry ... managing in his pedantic fashion to miss out an entire family. This was a significant chunk of the total population. What a der brain.

Rivers comes across as a quiet, calm, forgiving, peaceful chap. I don't know if this was innate or only occurred after his stay on Eddystone island (the position of which is a complete mystery to me), which came to fill his hallucinogenic dreams later whenever his bouts of malaria troubled him.

'Hiya ...' A distant shout wakened me from my half sleeping state. I turned my head to see a white pair passing the library and heading our way. The male was tall and well built with long very black hair around his shoulders framing his large happy bearded face. He was pretty well turned out. His companion was small and petite with a very pretty head atop a charming physique concealed in an overly voluminous dress. They were both sweating profusely and moving quite slowly as if they had just walked six miles in the morning heat. A pair of yachties come to ask inane questions? No, it was Jake and Amy, a very young pair of newly married Peace Corps teachers who had indeed walked from work at the Bishop's school six miles away. They had come over to see Helen off and to check the mail. They were definitely the exception to the rule of the Peace Corps. I found the whole idea of a bunch of under-educated, young, and most alarmingly, overtly religious Americans (of all things) 'doing good' to the poor old Third World very frightening. Perhaps the locals would think we were all like that? Luckily the locals had too much sense. This pair were abnormally normal. Well mannered, quietly spoken, educated beyond their years and best of all had common sense. They also didn't flinch at a hike in the heat to see friends. I could now make out the sweat running down their faces. Meg and Barney were leaning over the verandah waving furiously across the gap of all of twenty yards.

'The others said they would be coming over later.' I groaned inwardly, 'The others' being a group of female teachers who fulfilled all my prejudges of the aforesaid American organisation. The only sane member of their coven (a tough gay lady who brooked no nonsense) had left to return to the States, after her allotted two years, leaving the rest mimicking a flock of brainless chickens.

'Would you like to stay over?' I hastily enquired, hoping therefore to preclude any of the chickens from inviting themselves. Jake and Amy collapsed on the verandah and accepted a drink before accepting my offer and then wondering aloud if there were any children in the vicinity who may be interested in ice cream after the plane had gone? I am a complete ice cream addict, but even I had to grit my teeth at the local ice cream. Meg and Barney knew no better and were soon bouncing on the Americans.

Sarah came out onto the verandah and we had an excellent chat for some time before Sarah looked up and said, 'Ah, here come the others now . . .'

I was up and away like a scalded cat.

'Where are you off to?'

'Er . . . I had better make sure the hospital truck's got enough fuel in it . . . then I'll go over to Helen's to pick up all her stuff and take it to the airstrip. Anyone else want to come?' Jake and the children decided a trip in the back of the truck was just the thing and we sauntered to the hospital, remaining thus at waving distance to the chooks. The truck and new driver collected, we drove to Helen's, all clinging on in the back and making out that the journey was much more scary then it really was. All Helen's gear was loaded on and a rather teary Helen joined us on the back for a regal journey through the station to the airstrip, the children waving at all their friends, and Helen waving to all hers. Approaching the airstrip down the hill, we heard the aircraft in the distance, which was a good omen as it wasn't renowned for being on time. There was a great gathering at the airstrip, all come to say goodbye to Helen who was greatly loved by everyone . . . except Barry of course.

The aeroplane hummed over the coconuts at the far side of the airstrip and did a tight turn at the eastern end before executing a perfect landing. We all agreed that it must be Brian at the controls. He got out and organised the refuelling before heading over to chew the fat with us and donate some Australian newspapers to the Arathoons. Meanwhile the great gathering had formed itself into a long line of people all waiting patiently to say farewell to Helen as she moved tearfully along. Friends and housegirls, shopkeepers and local politicians all intermingled and happy and sad. Brian got a little tetchy as he had been forewarned of some impending bad weather, but he managed to control his urges and we finally walked Helen up to the door of the plane, gave her a final hug and bid her goodbye. The plane droned down to the eastern end of the runway and disappeared out of sight over the hill before we heard the engines roar and it reappeared bumping lazily along to take off, swing round and make a fly-over with all of us waving madly. Good old Brian ...

'Hey Jake, what about a barbie down at Luova? I'll see if Barry wants to come.'

'Great idea. Where was he by the way?'

'I think he must have had something to do in the office ... er did you see if any mail sacks came off the plane?' In the excitement I had forgotten the most important thing.

'Yup, looked like four to me.'

'Blimey, four, we had better get over there.' He and I rushed back up to the post office were we could see Henry the postmaster sorting through a pile of mail.

'Henry ... how long will you be?' We interpreted his muffled answer as twenty minutes, but were back within ten in case we had heard wrong or in case he had underestimated his abilities ... but he hadn't. We finally got our mail and leafing through it slowly meandered back to the verandah. Most of it was as expected or at least recognisable ... weekly newspapers a couple of months out of date, a few postcards and letters from those in the family who understood the importance of the mail. One letter, however, stood out. A large plain envelope addressed in an unknown hand to me personally. Most strange.

'What do you think?' I enquired of my spouse.

'Better open it and see I suppose,' saith she, pretending she didn't understand that this could be *anything*.

I quickly tore open the envelope to find a letter beginning with 'Dear Dr Arathoon' and a hasty glance showed it ended with 'Yours sincerely, Quentin Crewe.'

'Oh my God ... he's replied to that ranting raving lunatic letter I wrote.'

'Who?'

'Jesus ... what's he said?'

'Who?'

'Do you think I dare read what he says?'

'Who?'

'OhGodOhGod ... I was so rude about what he said about that stupid book.'

'Who? What book?' Sarah finally lost patience and took the letter from me. 'Ah Quentin Crewe, ya, have a look, see what he says about your "blistering" letter,' and she handed it back to me, handling it like any normal letter while I took it like a hot coal.

It was a fantastic letter, even going so far as to agree that *Bird-song* wasn't all it was cracked up to be and that he had been quoted out of context for the blurb on the back. Apparently the next book was even worse and he suggested I avoid it. Wow. He didn't mention my comments on his inability to spot a decent read and was generally very kind. He went on to tell me about an author he had recently been introduced to called Patrick O'Brian who wrote maritime novels set in the Napoleonic times. Would I like him to send me a couple of O'Brian's books ? Would I?? Wow. I showed Sarah the letter. I felt buoyed up at having someone famous taking the trouble to write to me and at the same time very embarrassed to have my rantings answered with such a kind offer. I dithered about writing back to accept his offer – for all of five seconds.

My reverie of communing with the rich and famous was broken by the raucous sound of Barry's tractor heading across the station and up towards our house. He stopped below the verandah, switched off and popped in to see if we were all ready. We were and loaded our gear onto the trailer next to Barry's barbecue and bits of wood and pots of food to be cooked. Then the children were loaded while the rest of us gathered at the back of the trailer ready to push. A few unsuspecting but game passing pikininis were hauled over to lend weight to the task.

Barry stood up from the hard metal seat of the tractor, looked over his shoulder at all of us and shouted: 'Ready?' We all yelled back. He leant back and reached far far back behind himself with his right arm, left hand on the steering wheel. He gradually brought his right arm forward and let rip with: 'Wagons roll!' and pointed straight ahead. We pushed like mad, the children and pikininis screamed with excitement and the tractor slowly began to pick up speed until Barry let his foot off the clutch when the engine coughed and then roared into life. We all leapt aboard (including the pikininis) and set off at pace (a gentle pace that is) to Luova. The racket from the engine prevented all but important conversation. I was still buzzing from my letter and decided on the spur of the moment to do something exciting.

'Hey ... you know that canoe we saw last time the ship was in?' I shouted in Sarah's ear.

'Which one?' she yelled back.

'The durn great big one ... the one we watched them loading *eight* barrels of fuel into.' She nodded, not wanting to battle the noise unnecessarily. 'Well, I'm going to get a decent-sized canoe made ... and I am going to call it *Bucephalus*.'

'What?'

'*Bucephalus.*'

'Why?'

''Cos I feel so damned chuffed, that's why.'

'No I mean the name ...'

'He was a sturdy steed ...'

'Ah.' She gave me one of her looks, but I was still grinning inanely.

We had a tranquil quiet restful relaxing time at the beach, slowly getting the barbie ready while eating some of Barry's raw fish slices he had 'cooked' overnight in lime juice. The food was cooked and shared. Swims were swum, chats were had, drowsiness and contentedness ensued. I dreamed of *Bucephalus* ... down here at the beach, big enough to get everyone into with a sail large enough to take us over to Malo island. God it looked good.

Unfinished ocean-going Tepuke canoe and doctor.

1st July 1997

Justin Mutukera
X-Ray Department
Lata Hospital
Temotu Province.

Dear Sir Juh

FIRST GENERAL ASSEMBLY OF THE UNITED CHURCH IN HONIARA -
SEPTEMBER 6 - 21 1997

You may attend this meeting on the following conditions:

(1).   The time you spend away will came out of your annual-
       leave.

(2).   You don't expect me to pay any of your expenses.

(3).   You arrange a locum to cover your abscence.

Yours faithfully

Dr. Arathoon.
Director Provincial Health Services
TEMOTU PROVINCE.

Chapter 10

Thrown:
Up, Over, Along

LATA HOSPITAL

15th April 1997

Director of Health Education
Ministry of Health & Med. Services
P O Box 349
Honiara.

Dear Sir

On the 10th of April 1997 I accompanied two (2) of my CHT Nurses
to the island of Nupani, where they were to do a leprosy survey.
Whom should we find skulking upon the island but one Ben Suilua,..
He was by then over 5 weeks late from his annual leave. At least
one boat a week makes the return journey from Lata to Nupani.

Very nearly every day radio contact is made between Lata and Nupani,
however, Mr. Suilua made no effort to use these ways to return to
work. He could have made arrangements before he left on leave to
be picked up at the end. Our nurses were told that the elders on
the island repeatedly tried to encourage Mr. Suilua to return to
work but his answer was along the lines that he was the boss and
would return when it suited him.

In my last letter I mentioned that Mr. Suilua was worse than useless as a Provincial Health Educator. Let me expand on this:
He is useless because he does not work, (in the last 13 months he
has put on one 40 minute play about malaria and given a one hour
lecture to a single village on Vanikoro - thats all) but he is
worse than useless because his very presence here leads everyone
to believe that we have an efficient Health Educator in the Province,
which we patently do not.

I am sending Mr. Suilua back to Honiara on the next ship and I hope
you can do something with him.

Yours faithfully

Dr. David Arathoon.
Director Provincial Health Services
TEMOTU PROVINCE.

It had been Wilson Lyno who had persuaded me that we should tour around Santa Cruz by outboard canoe. He said we could visit all the clinics and at the same time quieten down a local politician who was seeking re-election by pushing for a clinic on the offshore island known as Lord Howe island. That's not exactly what he said of course, but reading between his words, that's what he meant. I could have got him to write my post-tour assessment report on the desirability of said clinic before we set off, but these political actions have to be plodded through. The whole day was a bit of a trial, made worse by the lower colon of a pig; we sweated across crocodile-infested Lord Howe Island to the beautiful western shore of sand and wind to chat with the locals and wait until our politician had done his best. Wilson wisely used his time by purchasing a large happy pink and white boar which was herded back a different way through the infested muddy interior of the island. On reaching the canoe the boar's back legs were bound together, then his front legs were bound together ... he continued peaceful and contented. He was loaded into the canoe and we set off. Unfortunately we could find no way of cobbling his backside together and he proceeded to pass wind and copious amounts of stool for the rest of the day.

We visited clinics and were treated royally at each with rice dishes and perfectly turned-out nurses. Not one patient was examined by the doctor although they had all had radio warning of our tour. Lovely. By the time we reached the south-eastern corner of Santa Cruz the wind had decided to get up and we found ourselves gazing at the oncoming waves with cricks in our necks, all the while blindly bailing with whatever came to hand. This helped remove some of the porcine effluent, but it was as quickly replaced. The movement of the canoe in the waves caused piggy to be thrown up, only to come crashing down onto the bottom of the canoe through the colonic sediment. By now his cheerful grin had been replaced by a worried frown ... was it the attitude of the boat? Or had he finally realized what Wilson intended doing with a hammer and bush knife on piggy's first (and only) visit to Lata? The boar tried manfully to peer over the side of the canoe into the green and white depths, but got a whack on his snout and a: 'Sit *down* bloody pig ... sorry Wilson,' from me as I could feel the canoe lurch under his weight. He settled back with the look of a Catholic monk heading towards a Protestant pyre.

Meanwhile I had a tremor of déjà vu when the nearby shore stopped rushing past, and began to creep past, and then seemed to stop going past (à la Tinakula) ... oh God ... but a final twist on the handle of the outboard and we were round out of the worst of the wind.

We carried on round getting more and more exhausted and smelly until a final stop at Taepe village where Wilson wanted to check on something unspecifiable, or at any rate unspecified – there was certainly no clinic there. The invariable lone dog caught sight, or perhaps smell, of us at some distance and had gathered his mangy mates around by the time we landed. So it wasn't just Lata with a cur problem. I felt left out of the loop, ignorant and super-fluous, as I could not fathom what Wilson was up to; perhaps this was the reason for the tour? What a tiring day all round, and now we were in sight of Lata we were held up ... but I was proud of our little clinics. We finally got back after dark, meandering the last three or four hundred yards by torchlight ... phew.

That very night Sarah and I were awoken by the strangely unfa-miliar sound of the phone going. How it happened I am not sure, but Sarah ended up answering it (I played the 'so-tired-by-my-day-that-I-am-still-asleep, card) and announced that they wanted her to check on the old chap with TB that she had recently picked up from Tikopia on her tour. She slowly got dressed and I watched rather satisfied through one half-open eye. Yippee – not me staggering through the murky warm soup to the hospital to sort things out. I dozed off to be woken by a distant creepy wailing noise that somehow seemed familiar ... weird. Just then Sarah returned looking pale and interesting. Pale she was.

'They said he had coughed up a bit of blood ...'

'Ya?'

'Well it wasn't a bit ...' She sat rather forlornly on the edge of the bed with a distant look straight through the wall to the glisten-ing waters of Graciosa bay beyond. I roused myself.

'Er ... what happened? And what's that God-awful frightening racket coming from the hospital? Sounds like the ghouls have been let out ...' But as I said it I recognised it.

'They have ... he's dead ...'

'Er ...'

'It wasn't a bit ... more like six or seven pints ... he was as dead as a door nail when I arrived. Can you imagine what seven pints of blood looks like when it has been coughed up all over the walls and floor ... .and ceiling?'

'God almighty ... blimey ...'

'They were all waiting for me – between the phone call and me arriving he went from a small haemoptysis to a bloody great torrent. A Niagara. He was dead when I got there.'

'God.'

'The relatives obviously wondered what I was going to do to help – but he had been bled dry. I gave them the bad news, and that's when the wailing started ... creepy.'

'God ... er, did you take Jason?' (our resident Kiwi medical student).

'Heavens – forgot all about him.'

'Ah well.'

So we went back to sleep.

I could see Jason now, trying to catch a few minutes' rest, on the back deck of MV *Korpuria*, right outside my cabin. He was a gangly long blond chap, lying on his back with his head up on the step into my cabin (neck bent uncomfortably at 90°), eyes shut, mouth agape, feet infringing not only the personal space of the elderly couple who had boarded at Lata, but their real physical space. They had moved away, either through politeness or because of some olfactory reflex precipitated by his great big feet. It was not a large back deck. I smiled to myself as I remembered his arrival at Santa Cruz sporting the ubiquitous goatee beard. Within a few days he had shaved it off and then announced he never thought facial hair was a good idea. Did we care ...? No. A couple of days later I asked him to see a chap who had arrived in outpatients with a hand injury. Jason and his translator disappeared off for about thirty minutes and then came to collect me to 'present' the patient. I sat opposite the patient and smiled at him. He smiled back. Jason entered into a very long complicated story of how Isaiah had encountered a certain piece of wood from a certain kind of tree of a certain length and weight in such a way as to injure his right dominant hand. I smiled at Isaiah. He smiled at me. Jason ploughed on. And on and on. After a while I could feel my concentration waning. I butted in:

Me to Isaiah: 'So Isaiah, who now you killim?' (Who did you hit?)

Isaiah to me (laughing): 'Oh doctor, me killim one fellow man long Luelta.' (Someone at Luelta bar.)

Jason (looking most upset): 'I like to trust my patients,' and he stormed off.

The nurses and I sorted out Isaiah's classical boxer's injury of a fractured fifth metacarpal. But it about summed up Jason and his Jason-centric view of the world. As did his disregard of the poor elderly couple on the back deck.

So this was touring the outer islands. We had set off one late evening from the coast beside the Bishop's school, to awake the next morning without the Bishop and not in the Reef islands as promised, but at Nolua on the opposite side of Santa Cruz. There was no clinic there so I had a wander round and then watched the loading of some copra. That evening we set off for the Reef islands only to awake the next morning at Utupua. What a beautiful beautiful island. No wonder the Bishop had bought some land there on which to retire. Where was the Bishop? Why wasn't he aboard? No one knew, so I stopped worrying. We approached Utupua in the early morning haze, gently passed through the fringing reef and then motored slowly round to the west. I kept watch on the port (or island) side and watched the greenery and sand go by. Peaceful, quiet, restful. After a languid ten minutes my eyes caught sight of another pair of eyes watching me from ten yards away. What sort of creature was that? I wondered. I was about to ask Wilson, who was further up the deck, when I refocused and then the cuddly little sea creature wasn't ten yards away ... he was thirty yards away, and he was an enormous glinting-eyed grinning crocodile. He was

Good ship *Kopuria*.

a whopper, and that was only the bit of him that I could see, i.e. his head. He kept his eyes on me and easily kept up with the ship as it motored along. He was such a shock that I gulped and took a step back from the rail. God he was big. He realized I wasn't about to be stupid enough to suddenly fall overboard so gave me a final leer over his shoulder and disappeared with a swish of his tail. Was he real? When I came out of my catony and asked Wilson, he thought that it probably was, as Utupua was renowned for its crocs.

We anchored off shore, near the village of Nembao and some way from the mangroves further up the inlet. Soon an outboard was seen to approach and aboard was Alfred, one of our very best clinic medics. He took us to the generic British-built clinic, offered us tea and when we were refreshed brought us patients that he had foregathered; what a good, quiet, efficient bloke. The problems weren't too bad and didn't tax my soporific brain too much, although we decided to take a couple of cases back to Lata to investigate them a bit further. Everything seemed peaceful and gentle. I had a quick wash up at the clinic water butt, and then wandered back to the foreshore, straw hat on against the sun, not moving faster than a crawl to conserve the recently showered coolness, to watch the loading of copra. The young lads of the village were in high spirits, flinging each 70 kg bag of copra nonchalantly into a wide-bodied aluminium canoe, filling it to within inches of its freeboard and then with yells and shouts roaring out to the ship to pass the sacks up the side to be put in the hold. Each sack represented a substantial amount of work done by a large amount of people who hoped to make a few dollars on its sale to the buyers in Lata. This didn't depress the high spirits of the youngsters taking the sacks out to the ship. On the second such trip that I witnessed the inevitable happened: the canoe was travelling so fast on its approach and the lad in charge was so intent on proving his manhood by leaving the girly slowing down to the last moment, that the acute deceleration caused the bow of the overladen boat to dip under the waves, literally at the side of the ship. The sacks had certainly not been tied on, they all shifted and three disappeared overboard before (I have to acknowledge) the lightning quick reflexes of all the young males righted the canoe, now half-and-half full of heavy sacks of copra and water ... At least we now knew that copra, when crushed into 70 kg sacks, does not float.

Things quietened down somewhat after that. The copra loading was completed in near silence and when all the other things that needed doing (me looking at the completely decrepit but obviously much used school room for one) had been done, we set off back on the tour. Jason and I had each bought a large live turtle, as had most of the others of the medical establishment. They were rather pleased with us in a surreptitious way as they all knew, as did we, that it was totally illegal to do so. They each came and observed what handsome, large and healthy looking creatures the doctors had bought themselves, loud enough for us to hear. I could see their salivary glands purring away at the thought of these delicious creatures ... Their smugness was short lived however, as upon getting up to cruising speed having left the confines of the fringing reef, Jason and I each lifted our bargains onto the rail ... and heaved them overboard. You would have thought we had torn the last scrap of bread from within the mouth of a starving two-year old from the chorus of disbelief which met this action. If anyone on board had realized what we were up to they would have clapped us in irons to protect us from such a wasteful crime. There were dark looks for days.

We headed for Vanikoro.

A blink of time, a warp.
   A day?
   A year?
The 30-foot yacht slowly manoeuvred through the reef and motored to the mouth of the inlet before turning to starboard up the creek and past Nembao. The middle-aged American couple on board kept their eyes down to avoid any glances from the shore. They shouldn't have been there and they knew it. They had spent eight months sailing the Pacific and knew well enough that they shouldn't make landfall anywhere in the Solomons until they had been through Customs, but to get to the nearest Customs post would mean going right past this beautiful place to get to Lata, and then the prevailing winds would not be helpful for getting back. Anyhow, they knew most people just ignored the rules, but to be on the safe side they cruised slowly past the village and very nearly out of sight to the far end of the inlet, right up in the mangroves. Mr middle-aged American was a consciencscious sort of chap and having let the anchor go he put on his flippers and mask in order to snorkel down the anchor chain to make sure the anchor was secure, in this case in the murky muddy mangrovy waters. After a few seconds his head re-emerged and he took off his mask to say: 'Pretty dark down there,' to his attentive wife

leaning over the rail. 'Do be careful darling' she replied. He smiled, and went back down. Another twenty seconds later he reappeared: 'I think there's a crocodile down there ...' 'Well let's leave it this once ...' 'Er ... let me have just one last quick check,' and before she could say anything he disappeared back into the murk. She watched and waited, twenty seconds, thirty seconds, her anxiety rising with her pulse. What was that swishing?? A few bubbles, no other movement. She was aghast, numbed into immobility. An hour passed. A canoe from the village with fresh vegetables aboard approached. She came out of her terror ... what to do? She wasn't meant to be there, but her husband ... was gone. She pretended he was below decks having a doze and to please come back later. The villagers gave her a strange look and departed. Another hour passed and the sun gathered momentum towards the horizon. She made a decision, got out the dinghy and went back to the village. When they found out what had happened they were horrified and insisted on finding him immediately. They set off in their canoes with paraffin lamps and searched & searched but it was well after sunrise when all bar his right leg was found jammed under a mangrove root.

Vanikoro was immense, dark, brooding and I found it a little frightening. I felt like a child again when you know something awful has or is about to happen but the grown-ups won't tell you what it is. A background worry, an uneasiness, something going on that is not expressed verbally. It seemed to have overtures of the darkness following the Mau Mau in Kenya in my youth. All the short time we were there I felt a little uneasy; I wouldn't have been surprised if Wilson had mentioned in passing the recent massacre at the village up the way where there was no evidence because all the evidence had been eaten ... but he didn't because there hadn't been. I considered that the feeling I was getting may have had something to do with the wrecking of Le Compte de la Perouse's ships all that time ago, but it wasn't that: it was the mass of the island itself, the sheer bulk, the continuous background presence lowering over your shoulder at all times. Relief slowly returned when we sailed away and the island had become a dark shadow on the western horizon and I felt strong enough to give it a metaphorical 'V' sign. Actually, I think it was the weather, as I returned a few times to the place and more than once found it delightful. Strange, eh?

The next morning found us on the approaches to the fabled island of Tikopia, with all the associations it had in my mind: Raymond

Polynesian couple, Tikopia.

Firth, Rivers, Sassoon (why?) and all the rest. I therefore was not prepared for the beauty of the place and of its people. The inhabitants didn't so much have a physical beauty (too much interbreeding I think) as a beautiful outlook on life. For the most they were peaceable and happy with their lot, they all knew where they fitted in the hierarchy which still existed, thank goodness, on this tropical isle. Everyone knew everyone else, and all understood where they stood with regard to the chiefs ... which is something I was unable to work out in two years, let alone twenty-four hours as my hero Rivers had done. The island was an old extinct volcano with a large lake in the old crater. The sides of the old volcano were very steep both on the lakeside and the seaside. On the south-eastern aspect was the little flattish land where most people lived and most gardens were grown. The crater lake very nearly communicated with the sea on the south side and was only prevented from doing so by a sandy bar at the beach. Once a year the bar was breached by the Tikopians, nets having been laid across the canal to catch the fish swept out by the outflow.

We were taken to the dilapidated clinic by Nancy, our nurse, saw some patients – at least two of which had good going pulmonary TB (doctor keeping his oropharynx well averted during examination) and would need to return with us for six months' treatment – examined the total lack of water at the clinic (it would need a

large water tank and a bit of guttering to sort it out ... this was
promised by myself but I caught the flicker of 'In a month of
Sundays ...' go through the eyes of everyone present), and then we
were finally led to Nancy's mother's house for a meal. By the time
I had squatted down onto my knees and squeezed under the door-
frame into the darkness of the hut, I found I was alone with Jason
and Nancy's parents; Wilson et al. were off seeing friends, or
perhaps enjoying the weather. This made initial conversation and
etiquette difficult, but we managed and enjoyed a simple meal of
rice and vegetables eaten off banana leaves, and water drunk from
old tin mugs. The highlight of our visit was due to start soon: the
Tika dart throwing competition.

I know of only 2 places on the earth that have Tika dart throwing pitches: we were on one and were due to visit the other one on
Anuta the next day. We were taken out to examine the pitch before
the event started and while the great and the good congregated. The
pitch is about 170 yards long and consists of a concave sandy track
which has been brushed of all obstructions (leaves, branches,
stones etc). The locals are obsessed with the game and all males
from the time they can stand and hold a wand of wood, practise at
all times and places. Number 2 chief (on whose land the pitch was
situated) was seated at one end of the pitch on the seat of honour;
in fact the only seat. The participating men and boys took turns to
fling their darts down the track. They were magnificent, their
power and control superb. The Tika dart consists of a yard-long
piece of very light wood, on the front end of which is a much
thicker heavier piece ... can you imagine the control needed to
throw such a thing without it tumbling and cartwheeling? Well I
can because I had a go after the event and I managed to throw it all
of 28 yards (schoolboy county javelin champion not withstanding),
and the longest throw in our competition was 140 yards as paced
by an unbelieving doctor. The chap that won was left-handed and
was in fact the reigning world champion and record holder. We
know this because of the 'memory stones' each thrower has, which
marks his best ever throw. These, usually insignificant, stones could
easily be mistaken for one of the pieces of detritus which need to be
moved off the pitch before the start, but hold huge importance to
all. The champ's 'stone' is in fact one of the uprights of a hut, a
special place indeed. I felt very privileged to meet him.

Wilson brought word from the captain of the *Korpuria* that we
needed to be off as he was expecting bad weather before we reached
Anuta. And he was right. The steady MV *Korpuria* did her best, but

World Tika dart throwing champion, Tikopia.

the waves got bigger and bigger, the rocking got worse and worse and the passengers more and more fretful. In fact it was one such passenger who finally got the ship turned away from Anuta and back towards the safety of Santa Cruz. The waterproof fabric sides around the deck had been let down to protect the passengers from the weather, but unfortunately a huge wave hit the back of the ship just as it was at its most vulnerable, swept across the back deck outside my cabin (I had magnanimously allowed Jason in out of the spray) and lifted the poor little old lady who had had so much trouble with Jason's feet right up and away over the side ... in mid plunge her husband grabbed her from the edge of the scuppers and hauled her back aboard. All her baskets of kumera and coconuts and all her mats were lost for ever. Her husband immediately went to remonstrate with the captain who very reasonably decided on altering course. There was some debate about reimbursement for a baby hog which was supposed to have gone by the board ...

As I said to Sarah on our return: 'Bloody hell.'

And a bit later after a restoring cup of coffee: 'Blimey ... hey, do you want to have a look at the new TB patients before we go to bed? ... ha ha ha.'

She said: 'No, let's send Jason ...'

HOSPITAL

5th December 1997

Chairman
Posting Committee
Nursing Division
M H M S
P O Box 349
HONIARA.

Dear Sir

Re: Application for Posting to Makira/Ulawa Province 1998
     By Mr. Selwyn Hou

Currently serving as Nursing Officer at Manuopo AHC, Temotu.

I would endorse Mr. Hou in his request for a transfer. He has
served 2 years in this Province with diligence. He is a most
able nurse, and I would be sorry to see him leave the Province,
but I believe he should be allowed to be nearer to his family.

He has worked hard and achieved much at Manuopo under often
difficult circumstances. Should he be posted out our best
wishes go with him.

Yours faithfully

Dr. David Arathoon.
Director Provincial Health Services
TEMOTU PROVINCE.

Red feather money, Lata. Chief of police, Chief, Father Ini Lapli.

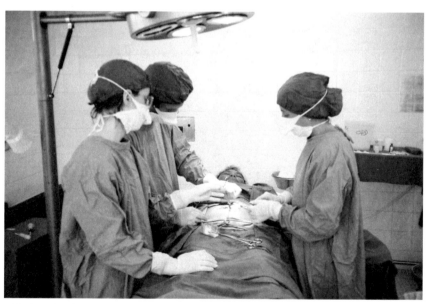

Patient having sterilization under local anaesthetic, L to R: medical student, doctor, fallopian tube/patient, medical student.

Punting out to supply ship, Duff Islands.

Returning from Luova beach.

L to R: Anuta, Kopuria, Moffat, doctor, butterfly net.

Tepukes, crab-claw sails, Lynne.

Polynesian child.

Polynesian child decorated with turmeric.

Polynesian lady, Tikopia.

Punting to man-made island, Duffs.

Chapter 11

Working, Waiting and Wondering

BRIEF FOR INCOMING MINISTER OF STATE OF HEALTH

TEMOTU PROVINCE

GOOD NEWS

1. Rate of malaria has fallen steeply in 1997.
2. As a consequence of this all other diseases in the Province are reduced.
3. June was the quietest month on record in Lata hospital.

BAD NEWS

1. **Communications:**

   a). Shipping service to Temotu very poor

   eg: In December 1996 ordered sufficient fuel for medical use to last a year. To this date only ½ received and we are again without fuel for OBMs.

   Other problems are: Patients Rations, Spares, maintance materials.

   b). Telephone system: i). Extremely difficult to contact Honiara as so few lines out of Province.

   ii). Once through to Central-Hospital virtually impssible to contact consultants as personell on switchboard are under trained and clueless.

   c). Very infrequently get letters from Central Hospital regarding patients of ours that they discharge. This is not only rude but unprofessional.

2. **Budget**

   a). This is paid to us retrospectively so we are always short of money. This year we have been up to seven (7) months overdue. This makes planning impossible.

   b). Amount: Each year we submit a budget for the coming year, but we are never informed if it has been accepted or even how much we will receive if it is not accepted. This makes planning impossible.

3. **Water**

   We have a continuing problem getting sufficient water for the Hospital. At times this year we have had not a drop of water - i.e. insufficient to give to patient to help swallow their medications, insufficient to use the steriliser without carting water in buckets from private houses. The NZ High Commission and RWSS are attempting to help.

(Dr. David Arathoon)
DPHS/TEMOTU

Early morning.

Doctor struggling.

'Come on, come on ...' (groans of concentration and digital exertion) '... bloody thing ...' A sudden 'THWAP' and the working parts sprang back together again leaving the doctor sweating and mumbling, squatting on the verandah with his eldest child looking at the small rat trap that was enjoying the battle.

'Megs, I don't know how I am going to get this bloody thing to work. Nip inside and get me the longest screwdriver you can find and we'll try that.'

She and I had spent most of the weekend constructing a fly-screen door to keep the mossies out when the front door was left open, as it would have to be to get some through-draught into the house. The provincial government had finally replaced all the screens on the windows, which of course prevented the ingress of mosquitoes, but unfortunately there was much less breeze as there were no longer geko-poo rotted holes to let the wind in. Hence the construction of the screen door. We had managed to make the outer wooden frame 'glued and screwed', and filled the central chasm with the ubiquitous couple of dollars-worth of mosquito netting bought from the malaria division. Wilson Lyno had recently become an even bigger man in the community and invested in a store – he had sold us a set of hinges – now all we had to do was think of a way of keeping the screen door shut. I had thought of weights attached to pieces of string which would drop under gravity and pull the door shut, but that idea foundered as soon as I had drilled the first hole in the door frame when the friction/weight/strength coefficient of the string was found to be incompatible with the job in hand. Hence we had ended up with the working parts of a rather snappy rat trap – also from store-Lyno – to push the screen closed instead of pulling it closed with string. I hoped to have the main part of the trap workings attached to the door frame and the thwacking wire rat-neck-splatting arm pushing against the screen door bit to keep it shut. Brilliant idea, but I hadn't got enough leverage to attach the spring to the frame with the spring loaded – hence the bigger, brighter, but most importantly longer, screwdriver. Meg came back with it.

'Daddy, Yin's coming – ooh she's got her puppy. Goody' and she abandoned the life-saving door to trot down to the strange pair approaching. Since her arrival Lynne had made a good impression. For a divorced Kiwi she was fine. She and Barry got on well (which was quite a decent change from Helen) and she had done good

things with the finances of TDA. All a bit beyond me. However –
and I fought to forgive her – in her loneliness she had acquired a
cur puppy. There was me trying to keep the population down (not
very successfully it had to be admitted, with chloroquine-laced
tuna) and there was this newcomer giving all the wrong signals by
upping the flaming canine population. Oh well.

'Waddya up to?' ... puppy sniffing my squatting crutch ...

'I'm trying to get this door finished before our ward round – been
at it all weekend.'

'Oh ... you know you mentioned getting a larger canoe made?'

'Ya.'

'Would you sell me the other one if you do?'

'Well, you know it's not brilliant ... but yup, I would love to sell
it – OK.'

'Great,' and with that she turned to wander down to the TDA
offices. When she was twenty yards away she turned: 'Er ... when
he's a little older,' bending down to coo over her sullen cur, 'what
would you think of castrating little Adam for me?' What an opportunity ...

'Yeah ... I'd love to ... but you may have to get me some instructions. Do you want to come for supper tonight?'

'I'm going to go to Honiara in a few months, I'll ask there at the
vet's to see if they can give you any help, yeah, I'd love to come, see
you later then,' and this time she continued with the soon to be rearranged canine suddenly close to her side. Was it me or did it look
anxiously backwards? I wondered what Barry thought of having
the proto-hound under his feet all day in the office – not that Barry
spent much time in the office.

Sarah came out onto the verandah: 'Come on, time to go.' Time
for the Monday ward round. I donned my smart hospital-working
clothes (i.e. my T-shirt) and we sauntered off – leaving the screen
door and my tools littered about the verandah, the front door shut
against the mossies and Hilda sweltering inside about to take Meg
and Barney to kindy.

'What did Lynne want?'

'Came to make me an offer,' quick look at Sarah's expression,
'well two offers actually. She wants to buy our canoe if we get
another one made, and she wants me to castrate her dog ... nothing
I'd like better except killing the bloody thing. I said "yes" of course,
and invited her for supper.'

'Good.'

We came into the hospital grounds and said hello to our new

truck driver who already seemed much better than the last lazy drunken oaf, and stepped up to the nurses' station, everyone chatty and ready for the off; what a great lot. We strode down the covered walkway to start at one end in the ante/post-natal ward. I noticed a middle-aged man hovering, he didn't look ill but he seemed to be trying to catch my eye. I decided to see him after the pregnant and recently pregnant ones had been sorted. The ward was absolutely teeming with flies; it was always the worst in the hospital.

'Hey Wilson, could we get a couple of cans of fly spray up here? And when we have finished could you see if the cleaners could give it a really good go in here?' It never seemed to make much difference but was worth a try. There were no problems, the nurses had sorted everything that needed sorting over the weekend, all the antimalarials that needed to be given had been, all the deliveries had been straightforward and all were happy with their outcomes. The next stop was the clinical room where strange cases or ones the nurses weren't sure about were placed. On the way we passed the hovering man and he was introduced to me by Wilson.

'Nem 'blo hem: Brown Kola.' Brown Kola came from Taepe on the north shore and had heard on the grapevine that the doctor was looking for someone to make him a canoe ... goodness, now that is fast bush telegraph. Then I remembered the strange stop-off we had made at Taepe on our round-island trip some weeks before ... Wilson's idea and unfathomable at the time, still, in fact. Did I want a new canoe back then? Had I said anything about it to anyone? Best not think about it.

'Well Wilson, I do want a new canoe, but it has got to be a bit better than the last one, it has got to be longer, lighter and better at keeping the waves out. I saw one down at the wharf carrying eight full barrels of diesel the other day ... that sort of size, does he think he could do it?' I watched the description going from Wilson to Brown Kola and Brown Kola's eyes got larger and larger as the vision of all those dollars went round in them. While all this was going on a nurse returned from Wilson's store with two cans of fly spray and I excused myself to go and do-in the flies buzzing over the pre-mums, mums and babes. I didn't see why anyone else should get all the good jobs. By the time I had finished the insect genocide and used up all bar half a can, the discussions seemed to be complete.

Brown Kola still looked cheerful so Wilson's description of the Cunard-sized canoe obviously hadn't been too frightening. God, I could hardly wait, a new decent-sized floating canoe which would seat everyone *and* keep the deep out ... fantastic. A few more words from Wilson to Brown Kola and he was away, presumably back to his tiny village on the north shore to eye up and then chop down a forest giant on his land (or a relative's) and then to hack, carve and shape our new vessel. Only when he had gone did I remember to ask of my senior nurse how long this process would take?

'Me no savvy ...' Oh well.

Now the nurses thought nothing of having a ward round interrupted by discussions of future ships for the high seas, but Sarah did and was beginning to give me the 'let's get on with it' look, so I hastily reverted into my ward-round demeanour.

'OK, what's next then Wilson?' What was next was the elderly gentleman in the clinical room who had arrived at the hospital on Friday afternoon just moments after we had left the hospital for the day, and made the huge trek to our house a few minutes away. The nurses had taken his history: sore right shoulder (tripped up a coral shelf on the beach an hour and a half's walk from the nearest road head and then a further hour by truck once one had by chance passed after he had waited five hours for it to do so), examined him: tender immobile right shoulder, and reached the right diagnosis: dislocated right shoulder, but had then come to the wrong plan of treatment. Their plan would have read: Let him wait for three nights and two days 'til the doctors have completed their well deserved weekend off, give him an occasional paracetamol and then get him sorted on Monday morning. It should have read: Go get the doctors immediately as they only live a few minutes away and are in fact employed to cover the hospital twenty-four hours in each and every day and get them to sort him out straight away.

Sarah to Wilson: 'Is he fasting?'

'Yes.'

'He hasn't had any breakfast?'

'Yes.'

Sarah and I mulled this over for a while and decided that he must be fasting and that 'yes' he had not had any breakfast. We looked at each other for confirmation.

Sarah again: 'OK, we will just have to assume it is dislocated as Justin isn't here' (the XR tech having absconded to Honiara on a whim, 'Bloody prat ...' from yours truly), 'let's get some ketamine and IV diazepam ready and we will sort him after the ward round.' I was glad Sarah had such faith; I had personally had great battles with new and hence more easily relocated shoulder dislocations in my time as a casualty officer with all the advantages of XRs to prove only dislocations (and not fracture dislocations) before manipulating them, and then of course I had re-XRed them afterwards to show the shoulder ball sitting neatly in the shallow shoulder socket. Sarah took charge and would have none of those advantages.

We moved on down to the adult male and then the adult female wards where nothing much of interest had come in over the weekend. Next was the paediatric ward were there were some interesting cases. One child of four had had 'PT' for malaria over the last couple of days but had not improved. We spent a few exciting minutes looking for a typhus eschar (scab) and duly found it in his clenched left groin fold. He was put on Chloramphenicol and we hoped would be fit to go in a few days. We would have put him on Chloramphenicol whether we had found evidence of typhus or not as that was the next line of treatment for an unwell child not responding to Chloroquine, but it was still good medicine to try to make a definitive diagnosis, and much more satisfying.

Another little boy of six weeks of age was also presented to us. Cominci was not a happy looking chap. He had a high temperature, negative malaria slide but had nonetheless had his 'PT', but the most impressive thing about him was his left thigh. I vaguely remembered the birth of Cominsi those few weeks before, but because it had been straightforward nothing much had stuck in my mind. A few days after birth he and his mother had been discharged back to their village where he had prospered until a few days before the weekend. He had got a bit miserable and feverish, had undoubtedly seen the local woman who sorted out medical problems without the official medical services knowing anything about it, and had finally made his way to us. The nurses were a bit concerned which was a bit of a worry. Sarah had a good look at him. He had a large, tense, hot, red, hard, tender lump in his left thigh. It was so large that it nearly was his left thigh.

'Blimey,' saith Sarah, 'he's got a massive pyomyositis ... this is never going to respond to antibiotics ... we'll have to drain it ...' Now a six-week old babe is not really the thing one wants to put under an anaesthetic and cut about willy-nilly. This would need some thinking about and some planning. Should we operate in theatre where there was good lighting (goodish anyway), or keep pus out of theatre and de-pus him in the clinical room? And then who should we do first, the dislocated shoulder or Cominci's leg?

'OK ... let's do the shoulder first as that is a clean op, let's do that in the clinical room because we don't really need much light for that, then we will chop Cominci's leg open in theatre ... how does that sound?' from Sarah. I agreed absolutely as this would give me more time to cogitate the thigh. I knew it would be coming my way as Sarah had already bagged the shoulder, and anyway she would argue that back in the UK I had done more surgery than she had. Difficult to argue against. I silently wondered to myself whether we could get all this done before lunch, giving me a good long afternoon to win my fight with the rat trap; the way the nurses were being organised, the prospects looked good.

We were in the clinical room in the early stages of putting the elderly man with his dislocated shoulder asleep when we were disturbed by a ruckus going on the other side of the nurses' station.

'God, what is it this time? Don't put him to sleep yet and I'll have a decko.' I wandered along the covered walkway and through the nurses' station to the steps outside. Down below me was the most awful shouting and screaming. There were at least three people on the back of a pick-up, one of whom was shouting and yelling in what seemed an inebriated manner at the husband and wife with him. There was blood everywhere. What the hell was going on? Wilson was already on the case and was leaning over the back of the pick-up to gather information and staunch the flow of blood. The shouting/yelling elderly man was in a right old strop, waving his arms around and letting all and sundry know that he thought he was particularly hard done by. What a racket. The younger couple, dressed pretty smartly, were doing the cowering/bleeding bit. The shouter was obviously unable to get to them and physically remonstrate because his left tibia was fractured, not that I had XR eyes, but the lower half of his lower leg was on the floor of the truck at about thirty degrees from where it should have been. The younger couple seemed to be bleeding mainly from their elbows and knees. What a shambles. Wilson soon got everything under control, moving all the patients, and then he came up to me to report on what was going on. My mouth was still agape. Anyway, it appeared that 'Dis fella man', the shouter, was indeed very drunk. He had been staggering along one of the beautiful coral roads when who should come along but Mrs and Mrs Alfred Petau, riding sedately along on their newly purchased motorbike. The drunkard, for an as yet poorly understood reason, had lashed out at the bike, or perhaps at the Petaus, and caused a rare road traffic accident. The collision of the drunkard's left leg with the front wheel of the

bike had caused the fracture, about which he was being so vocifer-
ous, and had caused Mr Petau to fly over the handlebars only to
land on all fours on the previously mentioned beautiful coral road,
some of which had sand-papered extensive areas off his hands,
knees and then shoulder and buttocks as he tumbled; some of the
road was actually still embedded in the deeper shreddings of his
limbs and torso. Mrs Alfred Petau was in a similar state except her
injuries were in different places, particularly on her back and legs.
Odd. Wilson explained: she had curled into a ball as she flew over
the handlebars and then over her husband in a rather syzygistic
manner all the better to protect her eighteen-month-old babe she
had in her arms. Anyway it had worked so well that the babe
hadn't even been brought to the hospital but had been left with an
eight-year-old relative in town while the shell-shocked parents were
brought in.

Sarah left the elderly dislocated shoulder (put on the back burner
again), and she and I had a good look at the Petaus' injuries:

'God almighty, what a mess ... this is going to take a bit of
sorting out.' I thought this a slight understatement.

'What do you think we should do? Where do we start? Just look
at all these abrasions and ... and bits of coral and ... well, loss of
tissue, and things,' I finished lamely.

Now what were we to do in the order of things? The old chap
really had waited long enough to have his shoulder done, but there
again would a few more hours' wait harm him while we sorted out
the Petaus and the poor little pyomyositis? Then should we do
pyomyositis first as the babe was in grave danger of septicaemia
and indeed a chat with the angels, or should we do the Petaus as
they were a relatively 'clean' option (not withstanding embedded
bits of road). Sarah saw right through the problem after a minute's
thought.

'OK, what we will do is this: the old chap with the shoulder first
as he should be quick and we have everything drawn up ready to
anaesthetise him, while that is going on we'll get the nurses to ready
theatre, get a few extras sterilized' ('Like what?' 'Scrubbing brushes
of course.' Of course ...) 'and we will go straight into theatre after
the shoulder to clean up the Petaus. While all that is going on we'll
get the nurses to give the little chap with the pyomyositis a large
dose of intramuscular cloxacillin, and when we have finished the
RTA we will incise his thigh in the clinical room as the shoulder will
have recovered from his anaesthetic by then ... what do you
reckon?'

'Er ... shoulder, RTAs, Cominci's thigh ... OK, sounds sensible to me, especially the large dose of antibiotics while the babe waits its turn. Shall we get John Bakila to put a backslab on the shouter while we are busy?' It was agreed. The screen door would have to wait for another day, not just till the afternoon.

Wilson was appraised of our grand plan for the afternoon and set off to arrange things. Sarah and I returned to the clinical room to the long-suffering but uncomplaining gentleman with the poorly shoulder. Within seconds he was snoring the snorey-sleep of those under the influence of ketamine and then Sarah just popped his shoulder back into its correct anatomical position without a by your leave. I couldn't believe it ... all those times I had struggled with shoulders in the past and here was a new girl doing it without a second thought. Ha.

Then it was off to theatre to get started on the road traffic victims, having sent a message to Hilda to give the children their lunch as we wouldn't be back for some time. The Petaus were quite a struggle. After the usual hassle getting started we did Mr Petau first. He went under the ketamine anaesthetic without a murmur and I then found out why Sarah had wanted the scrubbing brushes sterilized. We first cleaned all his damaged skin with iodine and I carefully removed all obvious pieces of coral protruding from his flesh, then Sarah took over with the scrubbing brushes and scrubbed each of those wounds to get all the small pieces of grit and dust out of them as these would be a focus of infection and would prevent healing. I was glad not to be doing that job. As she finished with each wound I followed round and completed my part of the operation by cutting back all the damaged skin and flesh that didn't look viable. This entailed cutting more and more from around each wound until it started to bleed in a healthy manner. Before moving on to the next part of his damaged body we helped one of the scrubbed nurses staunch the flow I had just precipitated, by applying direct pressure before the nurse dressed the wound. It all took some time and made us a bit sweaty. It all seemed to go on and on; each time we seemed to be nearing the end we found one more wound or one more projecting piece of coral or, once, a large piece of coral that had evaded the cleaning then the scrubbing and finally the debridement only to come to light when I was applying pressure to the wound. I took it out from the depths of the wound to find it at least an inch long. What else had we missed?

With the Mr finished to the best of our ability we rushed home to get a bite while Mrs was prepared for theatre and the nursing staff had a welcome break. We trudged back down after a hasty mid afternoon lunch rather fearing the rest of the day's work. But as these things often happen we whipped through Mrs Petau in half the time we had her husband. We were now more experienced and when we got down to it we found her wounds less severe than her husband's; this was probably because she had inadvertently protected herself while trying to protect her child. She didn't respond quite so well to the anaesthetic however and became a gently writhing target, but we got her done.

Next was Cominci. I was dreading this bit. Sarah and I went to recheck the dose of intramuscular ketamine for the fourth time. We asked the nurses to bring Cominci up to the clinical room (the relocated shoulder had taken himself off home, which came as a bit of a shock) where we laid him on the couch looking pale and wan but particularly small. His thigh looked if anything even worse with the skin now shiny and getting dusky: now was definitely the time to be doing.

I went off to scrub in theatre, wondering the while why I was, as we hoped to soon release some very infected pus and me having washed my hands would seem to make little difference, oh well, habits. I was pleased to leave the job of getting the little chap anaesthetised to Sarah ... he really was small. On my return all was ready with Cominci breathing more easily than at any other time. I cleaned his thigh with iodine, draped him leaving the straining upper leg visible and then approached with a scalpel. I put the point of the scalpel near the top of the lump and his skin parted like paper as I drew the knife down the lump. Next I pushed the scalpel further in and was rewarded by a great ooze of pus that kept on coming as I drew the instrument down. Sarah had difficulty keeping up with the flow of pus as she replaced one piece of gauze with another time and again. The leg deflated like a balloon. Pretty wiffy. We scraped all the pus out and left a large piece of gauze inside the wound. Having looked small before the operation Cominci looked tinier yet without a weightlifter's thigh. We hoped he would do and sent him back to his mother in the ward. Sarah and I got changed, then went to write up the notes of the protracted day and then had a bit of a disagreement about whether to go straight home (my idea), or check on the patients (Sarah's idea). Anyway the elderly shoulder had gone so we presumed he was happy with his treatment; both the Petaus were still dopey, but managed a smile: they had after all been given a couple of post-op paracetamol for their pain. The most amazing thing to see was

Master Cominci already suckling. We were very chuffed and set off home with a smile shared between us. I gave the rat trap a kick as we came over the verandah in the dusk; it would have to wait.

The next morning's ward round was swift and sure. Cominci's mother wanted to take him home: we said 'no'. The Petaus were comfortable and talking about trying to get compensation out of the drunkard who now had a sore head as well as a sore leg. He was in the sheepish/defiant stage but we were unconcerned and booked him on the next flight to Honiara to get XRs done and to have his fractured tibia plated by Hermann. It was now only 9.30 am, and my thoughts turned once again to the rat trap. How to broach the subject with my spouse?

'Why don't you nip back home and finish off the screen door while I tie up the loose ends here?'

'Er ...'

'Hey, I tell you what, why don't we go down to Luova with the kids after lunch?'

'Er ...'

'Anyway, there are a couple of things I want to talk to you about.' Oh God.

'Well if you're sure you will be OK here?'

Well, how had that happened? Off to finish the door and then an afternoon on the beach mid week. Cool. I found the rat trap cowering against the side of the house, and as is often the way in my life, having had a break from a problem that was beginning to look insurmountable I immediately bent it to my will and attached it without further ado, giving myself twenty minutes to read in my hammock before Sarah returned from the hospital. This was going to be a pretty good day. But what were the 'things' Sarah wanted to discuss?

LATA HOSPITAL

6th May 1997

Minister of Health
Ministry of Health & Med. Services
P O Box 349
Honiara.

Attention: Permanent Secretary
         : Chief Accountant

Dear Sir

In response to the Minister's letter re: new fibreglass
canoes and/or new OBMs.

We in Temotu Province require neither new canoes or OBMs.
Our canoes are in a good state of repair and we have some
aluminium canoes which should last another couple of decades.
We have just replaced our fleet of OBMs.

Many thanks for considering us but we do not wish to take up
the offer.

Yours faithfully

D. Arathoon.
Director Provincial Health Services
TEMOTU PROVINCE.

Chapter 12

Beach ... Babes

LATA HOSPITAL

29th October 1996.

Clyde Funusui
Accounts Section
Ministry of Health & Med. Services
HONIARA.

Dear Clyde

Many thanks for your prompt reply to querys regarding our
grants. As I said on the telephone I am having struggle
with the budget here and it would greatly assist me if you
would not accept any payments on behalf of Temotu Medical -
Services from other sources (eg. Nursing, X-Ray, Laboratory
in Honiara) with out my knowledge and agreement. If money
can be spent from my budget without my knowledge I may as
well give up.

Thanks again for your help.

Yours sincerely

Dr. David Arathoon.
Director Provincial Health Services
TEMOTU PROVINCE.

cc: PNO/Temotu

cc: Head of Nursing Services - Honiara

cc: Director of X-Ray Department
     Central Hospital.

We seemed to have a lot of things to discuss on the forty-five minute walk to Luova:

'Did I tell you that Barry said his wife could easily ship us out a couple of bicycles? Wouldn't take too long to get here, may cost a bit but would make our trips to the beach a bit easier.' This as I was manfully struggling across the end of the airstrip with one child on my shoulders while the other was beginning to badger me for a ride. Sweat started to drip off my nose and run down my chest; I wiped my face with my hand – there would not need to be much discussion here.

'Great idea – when could we get them by?' – This was definitely not 'the' thing Sarah had wanted to discuss, I was sure of that.

'With a bit of luck only four or five weeks, depending on shipping.'

'Oh good ...'

'Shall I ask him to go ahead then?' We were about to enter the relative shade of some banana and coconut trees, but I was in the process of swapping shoulder-riding children and Meg weighed *a lot* more than Barney.

'Yup – and ask about child seats.' I hefted Meg and surveyed the remaining distance to the trees. 'Let's not worry too much about the expense – what do you think?'

Sarah was sweating as much as me and also looking longingly at the shade. 'I'll speak to Barry this evening.'

And what else? I thought to myself.

A few minutes later, having reached the trees and having persuaded both children that their lower limbs would atrophy unless they were used just a little, Sarah started speaking again – was this it?

'Wilson had a chat to me yesterday.'

'Aha ...'

'You know all the trouble we have been having with the water?' I certainly did. We had been promised that Temotu province had a massive surplus of rain associated with a monsoon where the surplus could become overwhelming. However, for the last four or five weeks we had had very little rain, often going days with none at all and indeed having none for the past two weeks on the trot. This according to Barry was most unusual, but Wilson wouldn't stick his neck out. Barry blamed El Niño, or perhaps it was the lack of El Niño – one or the other. The result was that the water tanks were not being filled from roof capture and were running low. The biggest tank at the hospital had a leak and required topping up with rain regularly and was now nearly empty. Luckily Lata also had a supply of water pumped up every morning from the water source in the bay. Unluckily this being the Third World we had not had any mains water for the same two weeks. Initial enquiries had revealed that the pump was 'bugger up' and needed a spare part sent out from Honiara – or was it the UK? This would all take time. Then we heard that the pump was OK but that there was no diesel to run it – could they borrow a barrel from the electricity generator? No, as this was against the rules. By the time I had thought to lend the pump house a barrel of hospital diesel a ship had come in with plentiful supplies – which was when we found that indeed the pump was 'bugger up' and not just fuel-less. It did indeed require a spare part from Honiara – or was it Australia? In all this time the provincial government had done absolutely nil to help the hospital. I was seething. I had written to the provincial government a couple of times about the lack of water in the hospital but had, as usual, got no reply.

'Well, Wilson was wondering if the hospital truck could do a run to the water source each day – taking the nurses' buckets, so they could at least get some water.' This seemed a reasonable idea but did not really help the hospital much. Wilson had already stopped the patients washing their clothes, and had had a word about washing themselves. The more mobile patients were quite happy to stagger to the sea for a wash. Already we had a problem in theatre – the main hospital tank being so low that the taps in theatre no longer ran – so a nurse had to be dispatched with a bucket and mug to collect some of the precious liquid which was then dribbled parsimoniously over our hands to get us wet, soaped, scrubbed, clean and rinsed before we operated. It was a bit of a shock to know how little we really needed.

'I think that would be fine, when do you think they would like a pick up? ... first thing or last thing? ... do you think Wilson will arrange who will collect the water? ... do you think the nurses will bring their buckets to the hospital or would they expect the truck to go round and collect empties? ... I would be happy for the driver to deliver the full ones but I am not so sure about the empties ... what do you think?'

'I think Wilson has it sussed.'

'OK.'

We moved more easily now with a bit of shade, normally this would be the 'companionable silence' bit with each of us lost in our own thoughts as the pleasure of the beach approached. Today however I felt somewhat on edge, but was determined not to show it. Usually we pootled through life getting on well, never really having to 'have a chat' about anything, never so formal. I tried hard but there was an odd air about (and it wasn't the soup we were gliding through), it wasn't coming in off the sea and a quick glance over my shoulder confirmed it wasn't coming from inland either. The path went over a rise in the ground giving us a glimpse of Tinakula and that also looked its normal rather angry self. It had to be coming from within, but from within me or Sarah? We wandered on. Sarah had something to say. I knew, but had no idea what it could be. She knew I knew but seemed to think that it was so odd or important that she couldn't come at it directly. So I knew she knew that I knew ... my mind was buzzing. Could I have done something heinous? Or worse, something conceived to be heinous which was in fact a minor misdemeanour? Usually heinousness was accepted without a blink, but a minor-misdemeanour-conceived-to-be-worse was met with outrage ... but this was presaged by a certain ... mood. That mood was not apparent today. A spousal glance masquerading as a look at a non-existent parrot showed quietness, a benign inward smile. As if a decision had already been made but the time of pronouncement hadn't quite been reached. Oh God.

I wondered if I should attack in a bid to see off this little chat. 'I'm going to climb Tinakula.'

'Aha ...' Was that it? Just 'Aha'. What about the danger ... what about the eruptions that happened every day, what about the dangerous snakes lurking in the thick jungle, what about the lack of water, what about food, how long would it take, how would I get through the jungle, who would I go with, how would I land on the island??? Not a bit of it.

'I thought I would ask Wilson Yamalo to come with me.'

'Aha.'

'I could hire a canoe and outboard from the hospital ...'

'Hmm.'

'Don't think it would take more than a day or so ... I would try to follow one of the runnels up through the thickest part of the jungle.'

'Sounds good.' This was hopeless; attack had run through non-existent defences and come out the other side with egg on its face. Luova beach was now visible through the trees, brilliant in the sunshine with Malo Island so clear that it looked only yards away. The children had quite forgotten their terminal fatigue and were raring to get onto the sand and into the water. We made sure they had enough screen on and were wearing hats to keep the sun off and let them go. We reached the upturned hull of our canoe and sat against it with a sigh. The beach sloped gently down to the sea, the tide halfway out, or in. The sand was fine and on close inspection a variety of colours from bright red of crushed coral through the deep red and black of volcanic sands and down into the oranges and yellows of sand sand and finally into the stark white of bleached and slowly smashed coral. Everywhere there were chips of shells, opercula and indeed broken shells. Off to the right where Meg was heading now the beach gently curved round out of sight, but we knew it ended at the local toilet beach. Our bit was scoured in that direction which made it clean and the best place for new whole empty shells. Meg began shouting and waving in a beckoning manner in a bid to make me go with her to look for shells.

'In a mo,' I bellowed back, 'I'm just going to have five minutes with Mummy first,' and then to Sarah, 'I don't know why I am assumed to be the best shell hunter in Christendom, but I'll have to cool off first,' realizing too late that of course this would be an ideal opportunity for her to bring up 'the subject'. Oh well, I was still sweating profusely and could always escape if I felt the conversation becoming dangerous. 'Look over there ...' I pointed off to the left along the straight beach at the end of which, about a mile away, was a rocky outcrop that merged with the reef upon which someone was trying to launch his fishing canoe. I could see Sarah looking at this chap wondering why I was pointing out something quite so commonplace. 'No, not him, look there,' and this time I pointed not forty yards away where there was a tiny dugout canoe heading our way propelled by two children, the eldest of whom looked about five. The canoe was not more than five feet long. The two girls in it where glancing at Barney under their eyelashes and insouciantly heading in his direction. He had not noticed. We watched with bated breath. They could not get his attention but could not bring themselves to get any closer so they started messing around and before long had managed to turn the canoe over with much splashing hilarity. The noise level rose as they righted the canoe and gently pushed it backwards and forwards to slosh the water out. Barney stopped mid castle building to watch. He was fascinated, what fun it looked but he couldn't swim and they obviously could, and he didn't know them. Hmm. They carried on trying to entice him to join them and he kept looking. Hmm.

After a few minutes I decided to leave them to it and help Meg with the shell collecting. As I left the shade of the trees I was hit first by the blast of humidity and a second later by the sun, direct and directed off the sand. I didn't have more than fifty yards to go, but had to have a dip just to get there. I decided that later I would use my time by having a quick snorkel. Just me and the ocean. I got up to Meg and admired what she had already found. A quick glance back showed Sarah had the 'how sweeeet' look on her face as she watched Barney and the two girls get closer and closer. I turned to the much more important task of finding undamaged colourful shells.

I joined Meg, much to her satisfaction. It would be a few years yet before she discovered that experiencing pleasure was something that could be done alone, she still being at the stage where her life had to be corroborated from outside. We spent a few minutes in the blazing heat picking up, showing, comparing, keeping and discarding shells. Once I was physically with her it seemed I was nearly superfluous, so I was able to step back and have a real look at her. What on earth was she thinking about? How much of this would a five-year-old girl-child be able to remember? Would it have much of an impact on her later life even if, as a girl, she would remember little of it? She continued pottering about, moving from one good looking shell spot to the next without a worry in the world. She didn't care about water shortages, malaria, meningitis, mosquito screens or anything really. Just the here and now. Bully for you I thought to myself. I manoeuvred myself to get another look at Barney who was now happily playing with the micro-canoe girls. He was also in the now. Lucky people. I had never really thought about our 'horrible' children before and their experience. I had really rather enjoyed the look on the faces of people when we had explained that we were going to the Solomons for a couple of years: 'But what about the children?' 'Oh ... haven't thought about them really ...' and I hadn't. Sarah and I would keep them as safe as seemed sensible and hope that nothing outside our abilities engulfed them. That seemed enough at the time, and indeed now. Why on earth was I spending so much of my mental energy on these two anyway? Enough.

'Megs, I'm going to have a quick snorkel, you can stay here in the sun and get burnt, but I suggest you go back to Mum, or see if you can join Barney with his new friends.'

'OK Dad ...' and she continued with her shell seeking. Daft child.

I went to collect my mask and snorkel. What a treat. Just to float lazily above the reef (as the tide was now receding the coral was in places only inches away from my face), and view all the fish and anemones and sponges and corals out feeding. None of them seemed to have much of a care in the world either. I could feel the sun blazing down through my T-shirt and on the back of my legs, but my mind was taken up with the beauty of the three-dimensional world below me. God it was gorgeous. There had been little wind to stir up the sediment for some weeks (probably due to the lack of rain-weather) and the clarity was fantastic, the water was luke-warm and the colours bright. I suddenly realized that I was in the here and now. Wow, strange. If this was what Meg and Barney were living in the whole time it was great and I need have no worries. However, now that I had allowed my mind to fix on the outside world my viewing was subtly reduced and it was time to get out and see if Sarah wanted a snorkel.

She didn't.

'I've been thinking about Cominci.'

'Aha ...'

'Lovely little chap don't you think?' A babe was a babe to me, but ...

'Aha ...'

'I think I would like another ... baby, that is.'

'Hmm ...' Sarah often joked that she would love to have a coffee-coloured child as they were so beautiful. To her anyway, just a babe to me. I slowly looked up from my lying slouch against the canoe. Oh God, she was serious, she had that mad female look in her eyes when they have made a decision against all that is sensible or thought out or normal or natural but merely dictated by some raging hormone or other. She was serious, oh God. Had she thought about all the potential problems? An elderly multip had increased risks all over the place: risks of the babe being abnormal, risks to her own health, risks in pregnancy, risks in delivery ...

'Jesus ... you can't be serious ...' but one look was enough to put me right. How on earth were we to manage this? I knew the only other doctor in the province, I knew him well, intimately in fact. I had always had my suspicions about his ability in the best of circumstances, but in this? I was pretty sure he wouldn't be up to all the potential hassle in the pregnancy part of it. What about blood tests, dating scans? Had she thought about this at all? How were we to manage the timing to get her on a plane to get her home for the delivery?

'How are we to manage the timing to get you home for the delivery?'

'I won't go back to England for the delivery.'

'All right, how are we going to manage to get you to New Zealand for the delivery, do you think you should go at thirty-six weeks or before? Then you may be stuck there for months, where would you stay, how soon after delivery would you be able to fly? What if something happens? It may take me days to get to you ...'

'I am going to stay here.'

'What?' Had she not listened to my rant about the abilities of the other doctor in the province? Actually she had not as it had been an internal discussion in the aforesaid doctor's limited mind.

'What about Honiara?'

'Nope.' Ha, now we were getting somewhere.

'Be serious ... if the worse comes to the worst it will be ME doing your Caesarean with no assistance, think of that ...' Contented mad hormonal smile.

'Oh, I don't think anything will go wrong.'

My mind was abuzz. Why on earth did she think nothing would go wrong? I wondered if I could wait out this period of insanity, but the look on her face said 'no'. So much for living in the now. This was enough to blast the most fervent Buddhist into reality, or whatever this not-in-the-now was.

'Should we set off back now do you think?' Sarah got up and went to collect our two from their new friends. They were bubbling over with chat about the canoe. I meanwhile had been unable to move from the sand beside our canoe. I was still staring into the troubled middle distance when I became aware of 'Well Dad, can we, can we? Huh, can we?'

'Hmm?'

'Can we get another canoe?'

Jolly good idea.

And I was going to climb Tinakula.

We walked back to Lata, with two of our company now invigorated by their swim and play and chattering away. Sarah and I were quiet. We got back to the hospital to find that the water in all the tanks had completely run out and that our patients had had to take their medicines dry (apart from the TB ward where one of the inmates had shared a green coconut around).

'Oh well Wilson, we had better do a run to the water source this evening, would that be possible?' Of course it was. He thought he had problems ...

As we neared the house Meg and Barney ran ahead to let Hilda know all the excitement surrounding the tiny canoe they had played in.

Sarah said: 'Don't worry, it may take me ages to get pregnant ... think of all the practice we will need ...'

Lata Hospital
Santa Cruz
Temotu Province.

22nd October 1996

Rotary Australia
Northern Donations In kind
John Paskin
44 Pascoe Street
Mit Chelton
Queensland 4058
Australia.

Dear Mr Paskin

A quick note to let you know where the Nurse's uniforms that you donated to the Solomon Islands ended up.

We are the most remote Province in the Solomons and money is always short. Many of our Nurses had only one set of uniform left and so came to work in their own clothes most of the time. Now they have 2 smart sets each and morale has risen visibly. During a recent tour of the Province we managed to distribute uniforms to the nurses manning the clinics on the outlying islands too. It's impossible to describe how delighted they were. The quality of nurses in this country very high and it's right that their dress should reflect this.

So a big thank you to you from all of us here in the Health Division in Temotu.

Yours sincerely

S. Arathoon.
MB BS MRCGP.

Chapter 13

Tinakula

Lata Hospital
Santa Cruz
Temotu Province.

16th July 1996

Permanent Secretary
Ministry of Health & Med. Services
P O Box 349
Honiara.

Dear Madam

I would like same guidance on the payment of overtime and standby claims please. At the moment both these items are being claimed on an overtime claim form and are both being paid at the same rate as overtime. I can't believe this is correct - why should standby payments be as much as overtime?
Any advice you could give me would be most helpful.

On another matter - I am still mystified as to whether non - urgent patients we refer from Temotu to the Central Hospital should pay their own fares a not. Again, any guidance would be most useful.

Many thanks for your help.

Yours faithfully

Dr. David Arathoon.
Director Provincial Health Services
TEMOTU PROVINCE.

We heard the story soon after our arrival in Lata, but with the racket of a straining 15 hp outboard in my left ear I couldn't pinpoint where it had come from. It was told to us to illustrate how safe and child friendly the place was. Some white predecessors of ours had a babe (it was the babe aspect of the story which had brought it to mind now) and it had been arranged for the housegirl to collect the babe from the arms of the doctor's wife at the wharf as she boarded the ship to go on a short tour. The time came, the boat was on time (a minor miracle which rather decreased the story's veracity), Mr White Doctor was busy in the hospital and no housegirl was to be seen. The captain of the ship *Korpuria* could not be persuaded to wait and all preparations were made to leave. The White Doctor's wife leant over the ship's rail and peered into the crowd to look for the face of the housegirl. She called to enquire if anyone knew Mary the housegirl – and a young lad she didn't recognise stepped forward saying he knew Mary. Without a thought she handed the eighteen-month-old down to the teenager asking him to find Mary and place the child in her care. No one in the crowd thought anything of it. At first we could hardly believe it, but by the time we had been in Lata a few months we would have done the same ourselves.

I glanced across to Wilson Yamalo who was sitting on the other side of the outboard with a happy smile on his face – he was looking ahead beyond the bouncing bows of our canoe at our pyramidal smoky destination. At last we were off to climb Tinakula.

Babes had been in my mind for some time. We had had to take Cominci back to theatre and redrain his thigh which had really put the wind up me. He then made such a rapid recovery that he was gone in a few days. Sarah's great announcement re a future babe for ourselves still reverberated – but only for a few months until the discovery of her pregnancy. I couldn't believe it. What were we doing at our age going for another child in the back of beyond with such crappy medical facilities? More to the point, how had such an old multip got pregnant so quickly?

It was all rather academic now. And anyway I was off to Tinakula.

Wilson Yamalo had jumped at the chance to come. After all his father had been onto the mountain with the Australian high commissioner in the sixties – it was difficult to decide whether they had got to the top or not. Wilson's English was nearly perfect, my Pidgin was utterly hopeless outside a medical ward, but he still spoke with all his cultural ties and sometimes the meaning of what he said was obscure, even though his words, accent and pronunciation were perfect. Actually he was a bit of a hero – I couldn't think of anyone else on the globe I would rather be doing this trip with. It was a bit of an adventure.

Having jumped at the chance he then regaled me with stories of 'the white man' who had drowned getting out of a canoe at the very beach we were headed for. I later found out from the Provincial minister of agriculture that the story was true; he had been in the canoe himself. The white man was an English soil scientist who had been doing a survey in the Solomons. The very last island in the very last province he was to visit was Tinakula. He and the minister and a couple of others had hired a canoe and outboard (like us) and had headed to the only accessible beach away from the blasted chaos of the north shore (like us). The seas were a little high but not unusual. As the canoe came in the soil scientist put on his hiking boots and rucksack and got ready to jump into the surf and help haul the canoe ashore. Unfortunately the canoe broached in the surf, everyone fell out, had a bit of a chuckle, grabbed the upturned canoe and swam and pushed it ashore. On arrival there was no sign of Mr Soil, his boots and other scientific accoutrements had dragged him down, never to be seen again. I wasn't overly glad that I knew this as the black line of the 'accessible' beach came into view below the velvet green forest and beside a wave-lashed rock. On the rock stood our old friend the skinny dog who was obviously howling at us, sufficient to lift his front paws off the ground. What with the crashing surf and the churning outboard, we had no idea of his intentions. Then he about-turned and disappeared. We never saw him again.

'What do you think of the waves?' I yelled in Wilson's right ear literally across the outboard. He slowed the craft to assess the rollers as they crashed on the black beach. I could now see one of the problems, and that was that the beach fell away so steeply. Allied to that was the fact that this was the very place we had had such trouble getting around on our last trip to Tinakula with a 15 hp motor – the currents offshore must be pretty dramatic. Wilson revved the engine just to stay in one spot opposite the beach. Even he looked a little worried as we surveyed our target. Then his eyes lit up and he pointed. On the beach stood a little old man and a little old lady with a boy of about twelve. That should make the landing a bit easier. The old man pointed off to his left to what we presumed was the safest place for us to come in and Wilson set off towards it.

'OK,' he said.

'OK,' I said, and went into the bow, kicking off my flip-flops as I went. My job was to jump onto the beach as we ground ashore and pull the boat up – Wilson's was to get us ashore on a wave and not turn us over. I felt anxious as we motored in, watching the couple and boy on the sloping beach waiting to help us. I looked back to Wilson's usually happy smiling face for a bit of encouragement, but he was frowning with concentration which *really* worried me.

Closer and closer.

We were only thirty yards out and there was no sign of a bottom through the crystal clear waters. We seemed to be moving very slowly; I stood to perch myself on the side ready to leap out on the left and then everything happened so quickly I was unable to do anything but leap out, lose my footing and get dragged ashore half under the canoe in the smashing waves. By the time I could work out which way was up and what was happening Wilson was also out and we were all racing the canoe as far up the beach as possible before the next wave swamped it.

While I did my best to recover Wilson chatted to the other visitors. It seemed that they were descendants of one of the families who had been evacuated from Tinakula when it was at its most aggressive. They still owned gardens on the slopes and came every few years to tend them and gather what harvest was available. When I asked Wilson about the boy, he told me that Raymond was 'just a boy' who had leapt into the elderly couple's dugout as they left Nupani Island to paddle the 25-odd miles to Tinakula. He didn't seem to be any sort of relative, and no one else there thought it was odd, so I tried hard not to myself. Once the canoe had been carried to the back of the sand they took us a short distance inland to what had once been the village. This was entirely overgrown, but the outlines of some huts were visible under the foliage. The couple hurried ahead and removed their very few belongings from the best looking and certainly the most waterproof hut. I asked Wilson to tell them that we could use any of the others but they refused outright to relinquish the opportunity to be hospitable. I sat on my trusty purple daysack and we had a conference about how to proceed, all the while chewing nambo and sipping water. I emptied the sack of all but a little water and some food; sleeping bag liner and changes of clothes were to stay behind. It became apparent that Raymond wanted to accompany us and we agreed. The elderly couple thought we were completely mad to attempt the summit, I think they were most worried about the gods up there, and how angry they might be if we disturbed them. Wilson had to pretend they were making a fuss about nothing, as, of course, he was a good Christian ...

The jungle around the decayed village was very thick, but I thought that if we managed to get to one of the runnels we had seen on our way in then we should have an easier time of it. Raymond seemed to know a route off through hidden ways and paths that led towards another shoreline. We followed him. After a few hundred yards of stooping through the jungle Wilson pointed to a particularly insignificant plant, telling me it was a sweet potato. So this wasn't the real jungle at all but someone's garden, well, overgrown garden. We carried on and soon came to a rocky shoreline. Just to the right we could see where a runnel entered the sea; we clambered over to it and found it to be a lovely smooth wide clear passage up the mountain. The runnels had been made by water running off the mountain, gathering together and forming torrents which gouged out the rock lower down where we now were, before entering the sea. This made the bottom of the runnel smooth rock and the sides firm and rocky below the canopy. The slope was about twenty-five degrees; perfect.

We set off, Raymond often flitting ahead, often nipping back to look at an interesting piece of wood. Wilson and I plodded slowly up and up. I was not fit and although we were in the shade of the overhanging trees it was very hot and humid. Strangely we saw few mosquitoes, I suppose because there is no standing water on the island. We could also sit with impunity for our rests as the nasty vicious tiny red biting ants hadn't managed to get a toehold on the island. The forest also looked subtly different, and it was the minister of agriculture who told me on our return that the spreading vine the Americans had introduced in the war as camouflage had also not got to the island. Quite a special place.

Our lovely smooth passage soon began to change as we got higher. The bottom became more v-shaped and the sides steeper and higher. We began to hear a distant clattering which came closer the higher we got. The sides were now no longer solid rock but began to have layers of pumice and gravel and dust in them. The distant clattering was explained when one particular clatter became louder and louder as a stone bounced past us. At the next rest stop we could hear and even see a continuous patter of pebbles falling from the now very steep and unstable looking sides. It did not feel very safe.

'Doctor, me fright . . .' from Wilson. So was I, but I thought I had better hide it.

'Come on Wilson, we'll find a way up the side and into the jungle, it will be better there . . .' Safer but much slower going. Getting out of the runnel proved a tinsy bit difficult. The sides were now about fifteen feet deep and for the most part composed of caustic gritty grey ash. We had a hunt around amongst the falling stones and finally found a dead branch dangling down on the left side. It was too high to reach but I cut a step into the ash with my bush knife, handed the bush knife to Wilson and then boosted him onto the step where he was able to grab the branch. Raymond was next and then as Wilson pulled himself into the forest proper (disappearing immediately) I scrambled onto the step and pushed Raymond into the forest. A heave on the broken branch brought us all together again, weakly smiling at our escape from the trap of the runnel.

Now Wilson came into his own, neatly chopping a way through the jungle, always up, and always steady. We made slow time but it gave me a chance to look at our surroundings. Initially everything was bathed in a nasty psychiatric-hospital green, but gaps soon appeared. The forest also changed slowly the higher we got, soon leaving the last of the coconut trees far behind. The undergrowth became less thick, and the huge trees further apart. The nasty caustic abrasive grey dust came back and before long the whole of the forest was clad in a layer inches deep. It stuck to our sweat and we were soon all brothers of the same colour. The trees changed again from tropical looking giants to smaller species I was sure I recognised from temperate climes. The dismal green light became brighter and brighter and quite suddenly we stepped out of the forest onto an upland grassland. A grey, not a green, grassland admittedly, but grass nonetheless, no more gloomy trees. The grass stretched away ahead, the sun was on our backs, and best of all there was a gentle breeze from right behind, straight from Santa Cruz. Even Wilson smiled.

'OK Wilson?'

'OK.'

It was now my turn to lead up towards the summit that was hidden by the curve of the mountain. As my wife had instructed me I went slowly and deliberately, zigzagging through the greyness. The grey by this time was running into our eyes and chafing at every opportunity, but we were out in the sun and breeze so it didn't seem too bad. Raymond began to fall back, not through lack of fitness but because he had probably listened to the elderly couple and their views on the gods. The slope steepened, the grass became shorter and finally gave way to mosses and other ground hugging plants. All grey. There was a haze around so that it began to feel that we could at any moment tumble right off the mountain. I persuaded myself it was an optical illusion; we had lost the horizon, the sea and sky had blended and it felt as if we were floating. Floating with little to keep us up it had to be said.

Wilson: 'Doctor, me fright . . .' Why did he have to say it just as I was getting nervous? Stupid man. We stopped for a rest and I noticed that we were now standing on rock. Every plant had given up the struggle to exist this high in the nasty grey abrasiveness of the steepening slope. We had to be near the top by now . . . We set off again, Raymond still twenty yards back, in case.

The slope then acutely levelled off and we were there.

It was wonderful. We were standing over 2,700 feet above the hazy sea, a gentle sun on our backs and a breeze to cool us down. I looked over the lip into the heart of the mountain. We were on the highest point of the caldera at the top; right below us the ground was smoking and seemed to be grumbling, while further away the ground became jagged and chaotic where the far side of the crater had slipped into the sea all those years ago. It was very difficult to understand the anatomy of the mountain. The hot steaming interior below us looked enticing. I looked over to Wilson, he was grinning broadly. I wondered if I dare ask him to come with me down into the caldera. We were joined by Raymond who tentatively peeked over the rim.

'Cool eh Wilson?' He had to agree. I thought I had better take some photos and placed Wilson and Raymond in the correct attitudes, then I got Wilson to take a picture of the great white (for white read 'grey') mountain climber. We wandered back to the rim. The rocks below continued to steam. There didn't seem to be anything as interesting as a lake of molten lava, but the broken chaos below beckoned to me.

'Er, Wilson what do you think about—' but I was interrupted by a crescendo of rumbling roaring bawling shrieking noise which overwhelmed us in less than a second.

'Oh fucking hell!' I screamed as the caldera immediately filled with impenetrable grey smoke which rushed upwards at the speed of an express train, blotting out all visibility before we could think. Not that we needed to think as the next thing I realised was that we were all running pell-mell down the south slope of the volcano as it belched behind us. After a few seconds I realized we were out of the noxious cloud and into fresh air, thanks to the southerly breeze. I skidded to a halt and looked back to the top where there was a continuing but now less noisy eruption taking place.

'Wilson ... Wilson ...' I shouted, and below me a now pale grey Wilson shuddered to a halt. 'The wind is blowing it all away, come on let's have another look.' He looked sceptical but could see I was right. We then both bellowed at Raymond to stop but by now we could see his sprinting bounding leaping form had nearly reached the tree line. Each step caused a puff of grey.

Wilson and I gingerly edged back up to the lip. The eruption had all but halted but the grey ash and smoke still streamed out away from us, blown northwards on the breeze. I don't know if that southerly breeze saved our lives, but at the time it felt like it. My inner sceptic struggled a bit with the gods on the heights, but finally gave in and I silently thanked them for merely frightening us stupid. Actually I had been stupid, but we had got away with it. I didn't think I had been physically incontinent but mentally every orifice was drained. Wilson and I gazed steadily at each other. What excellent fun.

'Doctor?'

'Hmm?'

'Then ...' He indicated the swirling smoke. 'Me fright ...'

We stayed only a few minutes more, to get some after shots to go with our 'before the eruption' photos. Wilson bounced back to his normal cheerful self; indeed he bounced right through his normal self and out the other side becoming euphoric, leaping down the dust slopes until we met up with the trees and Raymond again. We found where we had exited from the trees and Wilson insisted that the passage was now much too narrow and blazed away with the bush knife providing Raymond and me with a path wide enough for an elephant. In his heightened state Wilson didn't run out of steam until we came to the lip of the runnel where we had originally come up into the jungle. Here while we had a rest and contemplated the still-dangerous runnel he came back down to earth. We decided we would remain in the jungle, keeping close to the runnel's edge until it looked safer. Going down was so much easier and within minutes of forcing ourselves through the trees we found a place we could jump down into the runnel. Raymond was off and soon disappeared round a corner. Wilson and I were slower but probably more stately as would be expected from famous mountaineers.

We reached the end of the runnel and slowly made our way

Runnel in Tinakula, Wilson Yamalo and Raymond.

back to the ex-village. About 200 yards out Wilson started scrabbling about in the earth, coming up in a few seconds with a sweet potato and a grin. We got back to the camp to find Raymond regaling the elderly couple with his feats. Wilson chatted with them and I lay back to examine the undersides of the leaves above us and grin away at our day. What fun. Wilson soon had a small fire going and he volunteered to make supper. Raymond suggested I follow him to see something. By now I was feeling rather weary and nicely tired and comfortable watching the small amount of activity around me and listening to the inquisitive birds. He became insistent and I went after him wondering what on earth was worth getting up for this late in the day, with the promise of imminent food. My muscles had stiffened from our exertions and I hobbled only a few yards to an open space above the sea. Just here was an engraved stone commemorating the death of the soil scientist. I thanked the boy for showing me and then sank down again on the small plateau overlooking the sea and ran through the day again in my mind. My muscles and mind relaxed so much that I was nearly asleep when Wilson came along to suggest we had a clean-up before supper. He and I went to have a swim at the steeply sloping beach and emerged pink and brown respectively. Both refreshed and now famished.

Supper passed in an exhausted blur, Wilson and I soon took ourselves off to the best hut with the dying light and chose the two better wooden cots which the elderly couple had obviously recently been using. Within seconds Wilson was snoring and shaking the rotten timbers. I slowly slipped off into a doze and then a progressively deeper and deeper sleep.

I was rudely jerked from my slumber and checked my watch: 3 am. What on earth had woken me? I looked across at Wilson in the moonlight chinking through the decaying walls ... there was a strange feeling in the air made worse by Wilson suddenly tossing and turning in his sleep. Perhaps his disrupted sleep had woken me? I lay back and composed myself for oblivion again. Just as I was drifting down and through there was the most enormous earthquake. I was suddenly very awake and had to grab hold of the hut support beside me to prevent myself falling off the cot. The quake was accompanied by a dreadful groaning and grinding and a slow waving of the very earth itself. I broke into a chilly sweat and hung on for dear life. It went on for so long that I was able to realize that even if the hut fell down it was so rotten we could come to no harm. To this day I think the crater gods were having the last word.

The next morning Wilson denied all knowledge of the earthquake.

We had a small breakfast and helped by the others took the canoe to the water's edge. Wilson ran through our respective jobs which would get us as safely as possible away from the black beach into the deteriorating weather beyond. We were all to run the canoe into the waves and on the word of Wilson, I was to jump in and start paddling as fast as I could. Wilson would nonchalantly step into the canoe and start the outboard with one pull and we would all live happily ever after. All went better than expected until the motor refused to start. Wilson pulled and pulled and never a sign of a firing cylinder. I was only just able to hold my own against the sea and we balanced precariously offshore under the anxious eyes of those still safely on the beach. I started to sweat and worry again. Wilson was in the middle of suggesting that he strip the engine ('What ... *here???*'), when he noticed that he had forgotten to insert the safety cord which was attached to his wrist and was supposed to stop the engine should he fall overboard. He sheepishly plugged it in and the dear old motor started first pull. We waved goodbye to our friends and headed south towards Santa Cruz.

We were more than halfway back when I found myself on my knees bailing like fury as the weather worsened and the waves got bigger. From the bouncing bows I looked past a grinning Wilson to find the volcano had disappeared behind a dark veil of rain that was inexorably heading our way. I changed my focus to the handy-man ... he met my eye.

'Wilson.'

He raised his eyebrows to indicate he could hear me.

I indicated the swirling veil behind him: 'Me fright ...' He pretended not to hear so I would have to repeat myself louder towards him as he leant over to hear. 'I said "Me FRIGHT".' Wilson glanced nonchalantly behind us and turned back with a smiling shake of the head. It would be all right, he indicated with as few facial muscle movements as was possible.

Soon after we were in the lee of Malo Island and able to converse in a normal shout against the outboard.

We pulled in at the Lata wharf and I left a still cheerful Wilson to the packing up and putting away while he chatted to his friends. I took the back way straight up the hill to the hospital before turning on to the road to our house, rehearsing all the while our adventures in my mind. I didn't want to sound too boastful, but on the other hand I didn't want it to sound like a walk in the park. It had to be sufficiently understated to cause the greatest impression on my wife without being frightening or too insouciant. I was just smiling to myself again when I looked up and who should I see but Sarah coming out of the hospital (at the weekend?) with a rather grim look on her face.

She was mumbling to herself: 'Bloody man ... what a *stupid* thing to do ... idiot ...', then she caught sight of me: 'Oh, are you back already?'

'Er ...'

'You'll never believe what has happened ...'

'Er ...'

'You remember that chap on the motorbike?' I raised my eyebrows in the custom fashion, 'You know, Mr Petau ... well he has really and truly got up my nose this time ... and at the weekend, what a prat' and she lapsed into a glowering tight-lipped silence.

'Er ...'

'I can't believe he would do that after all the time and effort last time ... idiot ...'

'Er ...'

'All that time as an in-patient when he could have been running his store ... all that sympathy I invested in him ... Ha.' This time I waited in respectful silence. After all, I had been out gallivanting while Sarah had been working over the weekend; there was little I could say. We had reached the short drive to our house and Sarah came to a halt and turned to me. 'Mr Alfred Petau went and fell off his motorbike again, and this time there was no one else involved except some bottles of beer, we are going to have to sort him out again ...'

'Oh, right.' We turned to walk to the foot of the verandah.

'By the way, how was Tinakula?'

'Yeah, it was OK.'

Lata Hospital
Temotu Province.

26th April 1996

John Melelao.
Hospital Clerk
Lata Hospital.

Dear John

I have recieved the proposed salary increment 1996 and agree with it. It seems that the staff have not had an increment for many years.

As far as I can see, once everyone has passed their incremental dates the cost will be SI $21.48/day, or SI $473/month.

Yours sincerely

Dr. David Arathoon.
Director Provincial Health Services
TEMOTU PROVINCE.

Chapter 14

Bikes, Boobies and Break-ins

Touring Officers: Dr Sarah Arathoon
                         N/A Nancy Faka (Lata to Tikopia only)

Ship: Southern Cross - collecting clergy for a
            conference, hence only brief stops at each port.

Date: 18 - 24 May 1997.

Leave Lata 18/5/97

Utupua 19/5/97

N/A Alfred Nyiene involved in a delivery throughout visit
4 patients seen including an ante natal mother who had
travelled by OBM from Vanikoro and who accompanied us back
to Lata on the ship. Vaccines delivered.

Vanikoro 19 - 20/5/97

Stay here prolonged by engine trouble.
N/A John Kae recently taken over from N/A Alfred Wale who
went with us as far as the Duffs, his new posting.
4 patients seen.
Vaccines delivered
Request for kerosene, petrol, a tape measure, a pulse timer
and batteries for the autoscope received.

Tikopia 21/5/97

12 patients seen including the relief nurse who has been
unwell for some time and accompanies us back to Lata on
the ship.

Clinic building still bodly in need of repair - doors not
working, no running water, mosquito netting badly torn
ceiling panels missing. New battery need for radio.

Drop N/A Nancy Faka off here following completion of a refreshe:
cours in Lata.

Anuta   22/5/97

VHW David?   - Has many problems with gaining cooperation
of chiefs on Anuta with the result that medical care on this
island is substandard. Suggest he comes to Lata for help and
advice as soon as possible.
13 patients seen - 1 accompanies us back to Lata to see
visiting Rehab team and 2 to follow on next ship.

Vaccinate several children.

Duffs 23/5/97

N/A Alfred Wale leaves the ship here to take up his new posting.

VHW Stephen?   - Been doing relief work.
10 patients seen - including 2 to come to Lata on next ship -
one to see visiting surgeon and one for TB investigations.

Alfred Wale declines offer of vaccines as no kerosene for
fridge.

Manuopo 23/5/97

N/O Selwyn Hou & staff in attendence.
See 40 patients in only 2 hours - very unsatifactory for patients,
doctor and nursing staff - Includes a patients to come to Lata
to see visiting surgeon, 3 to come for investigations, 1 to go to
Honiara to see the visiting ENT team and a married couple
to   the infertility clinic in Honiara.

Manuopo is short of STD medicines.
Vaccines delivered.

Return Lata 24/5/97.

Dr. S. Arathoon.

30/5/97

We had had a bit of a problem, and it had not just been with Mr Petau. I had the idea that we should get some chickens – mainly for fun but also to eat their eggs, and indeed to eat them. Mr Alan Taro (whose gentle wife had been given an MBE by the Queen) owned a store in town and told me he could get hold of a small flock of chickens. I had hurried home and asked John-the-gardener to help build a chicken house which he and I then did in a most satisfactory manner using all local materials (i.e. wood) and not a piece of roofing iron or wire in sight. Meg wanted me to make sure the chickens had a room for home schooling and so we built an annexe as well. The house looked fantastic when finished, green and lovely as only coconut fronds can be. I was pleased with the effort, but unbeknownst to me so were the pack of feral dogs who had been out of sight but had kept a sneaky slinky watchful eye on proceedings.

The day came when the house was ready and Meg and I collected a cardboard box stuffed with very white chickens from the Taros' store. We chucked some grain into the house and the birds accepted their new quarters happily. I spent a few languorous hours on the verandah in my hammock watching them pecking about in the garden. The pack of feral dogs also kept a salivating eye on the doomed chooks. They must have been encamped below the garden in the coconuts, occasionally sending one of their filthy ilk up to glance round into the garden to make sure the idiot whiteman was still grinning in ignorance.

Mr Petau had by this time given his trouble but had survived and even made it home – in fact much quicker than the first time round. We didn't know if this was because he felt such a fool falling off his motorbike while drunk, or just for falling off his motorbike again.

His cleaning-up procedure had been interesting to say the least, mainly because I had volunteered to do it on my own with only one nurse to assist. We wheeled him down to theatre on a trolley and Mary gave him a bit of IV ketamine, diazepam and pethidine while I scrubbed up. Then it was to work just repeating what had been done the first time. Right at the start I noticed he had scraped the recently healed scar tissue right off his elbows and knees. And buttocks. He was murmuring a bit in his drugged-up state and I asked Mary to give him some more diazepam. I started cutting away at the non-viable tissue to get back to some good bleeding flesh, cutting away at each site and leaving Mary to follow behind with pressure. I had just got halfway through the first limb when he started murmuring again and this time flexing and extending his limbs in time to whatever rather exciting dream he was having.

'I think we could give him another shot of ketamine Mary – oh go on – give him some more diazepam as well.'

She did.

It made no difference. He really started squirming about and soon moved from the pre-thrashing stage right into the very middle of the thrashing stage. He had yet more of everything except pethidine but it only seemed to spur him onto the epileptic-camel phase (with verbal accompaniment). By now I was forcibly grappling with Mr Petau. He had morphed into a frenzied camelid determined to fling himself to the bloodied floor of the operating room. I had gone wild and become a quivering whitey gripping both sides of the trolley with the camel directly below me. I had my snarling face two inches from his.

'Get back on you bastard ... sorry Mary.' He declined and his lower half slid onto the floor, from where the only limb I had managed to get to had its pressure released and began to bleed profusely.

'Shit – Mary, give me a hand – I said "GIVE ME A HAND"' above the roaring bawling storming racket from the camelid. We managed to get Mr Petau back onto the trolley and wheeled him straight back to his bed on the ward. I was covered in blood and spilt iodine, and not happy. Mr Petau's wounds slowly stopped bleeding and his camel noises descended into a rumbling grumble and then a snore. I left the nurses to it. The staring nurses and shocked patients looked appalled.

'Just cover all his injuries and leave him.' I went back to get out of my theatre gowns and counted how many vials were scattered on the floor of the battleground. He had had five times as much diazepam, and three times as much ketamine and pethidine than would normally be good for him. He should have been dead.

Three days later he left hospital and walked home arm in arm with his wife. Perhaps his liver had been in training and had gobbled all the drugs we had given him without even looking up. Amazing what a bit of excess alcohol can do. The human body really is incredible.

A couple of weeks later Barry's cat had given birth and the children had badgered us into accepting a pair of kittens when they were big enough. Meg and Barney visited the happy, soon to be broken, family of puss-cats most days. The kittens were to be called Billy and Muffin, and were to join two other pets we had recently obtained who lived out by the back door next to the hermit crab who had swapped his outgrown shell for an empty medicine bottle. These two were called 'Duck' and 'Ling' and as a pastime shat contentedly on our back step. Two days before the kittens were due to come to us the chooks arrived and settled in.

The first night I put the chickens in their brand new house I said to Sarah, 'I hope this is strong enough to keep the dogs out.' Ha ha ha. In the morning the chooks were all lined up at the door and trooped out blinking into the sunshine when I let them out. I was chuffed. I had been lulled ... The next day we were due to get the kittens and all was well in our pacific world.

During the second and final chook night I was awakened by a scuffling followed by a squawking ... I knew instantly what was going on and leapt out of bed, grabbed a torch, ran onto the verandah and vaulted naked into the garden – the torch playing its beam over half a dozen evil looking curs exiting the now flattened chicken house, each with a chicken in its thin bloodied jaw. They all ran off sniggering through the feathers of their prey. All? Not quite – one was stuck, thrashing around in the pile of coconut fronds that the chicken house had become. I had a flash of an idea, ran back to the verandah and extracted a six-foot piece of wood from under it. I hared back to the eyes I could see glinting through the fronds. At least the eyes had the grace to look dismayed as I dropped the torch and double handedly brought the heavy piece of wood smashing down onto the skull that owned them.

Actually the eyes had conveyed a message back to the brain: 'MOVE' and the brain had relayed the message to all four limbs and the heavy branch missed the eyes, skull, brain, body and every hair of the evil brute by at most two millimetres. I quivered with rage: 'OH BUGGER ...'

This rage was increased when Ling was eaten by the evil curs three nights later. I started lacing tins of tuna with ketamine instead of chloroquine and putting them all round the garden.

Sarah said, 'How do you know the pikininis won't eat it?' So I went all round the garden and collected them up, leaving only three tins out overnight and carefully bringing them all in in the mornings. The tins emptied. The feral dogs seemed immune. I was exasperated.

I was still incensed some days later when Sarah called me out of my murderous reverie: 'Come on, let's get down to the airstrip – Barry thought our bikes may be coming in today.'

'Mum, Mum, can Billy and Muffin come as well?'

'No Megs, it's too far for them, they would only get lost – leave them with Hilda.' We set off on the ten-minute walk to the airstrip. Outside the hospital we were spotted by Wilson Lyno who said he had a patient he thought I might like to see.

'You go on down and I will meet you down there in a few minutes,' I said to Sarah.

'What's wrong with this chap, Wilson?' It seemed that he was a man from Taepe, the mysterious village on the north coast, with the lone dog and friends which Wilson had made us stop at on our clinic-visiting round island trip. The village also rang another dull bell in my mind ...

'Dis fella man' had managed to cut his left knee with an axe (ding ding) while building a canoe (clang). I knew who I would see even before I peered into the gloom of the clinical room. There was Brown Kola looking sorry for himself with a grubby bandage around his left knee. I clapped him on the back in greeting.

'Ah, Mr Kola, working hard on my canoe I see.' He looked sheepish.

'Let's have a look.' Wilson removed the dirty piece of linen to reveal a neatly incised, surprisingly clean axe wound through a quarter of the patellar tendon.

'Don't worry Mr Kola, you'll be back chopping away at my canoe in no time. Wilson, could you just clean it up a bit, put in a couple of stitches and send him on his way? Thanks.' I think Brown Kola had been looking forward to a couple of restful days recuperating in hospital. His eyes said it all as I left him.

As I wandered out of the hospital into the glare I looked up to see an elderly man coming up the coral road with a paddle over his shoulder – and on each end of the paddle sat a white ball of happy looking-around fluff. Baby Booby birds. I looked behind me and then back to make sure my mind wasn't playing tricks – it wasn't. I stopped the gentleman. He said he was from Nupani and had paddled to Santa Cruz (? 60 miles) to see if anyone would like to buy his pet birds. I would. He wouldn't let me buy the paddle – had to get home I suppose. The birds cost $15 each. I took them home and left them on the verandah with Hilda who looked a bit sceptical. Back to the airstrip just as Brian brought the plane in.

'Where have you been – what took so long in the hospital?'

'Oh, it was a bit of a complicated case and took longer than I hoped ...'

Barry had come down and we were all excited to see two very large cardboard boxes hefted out of the hold. Barry put them on the back of his tractor and we headed back home.

'What on earth are those?' from Sarah as we drove up the short drive.

'Oh a couple of young Boobies I bought – didn't I mention them?'

She stared at me.

'To make up for Ling?'

While Barry kindly put our bikes together and fitted the child seats I nailed two pieces of wood to two nearby trees, well up out of reach of feral dogs, and placed Betsy and Belinda, our new Boobies, on them. They looked around, and a little worried. I nipped into the kitchen and cut some slices of fish from our supper. Betsy and Belinda looked even more worried. I opened Betsy's beak and crammed a couple of slices down her gullet, then did the same with Belinda. They both feigned choking and shook their heads, nearly falling from the perches in the process, but began to look at home. They started to preen. I left them to it.

That first day with the bikes we went to 'Alan Taro's beach', a beautiful deserted beach down towards Venga. There was something odd going on in the sea and the eddies and rips and swirls made it too difficult to snorkel amongst the coral stacks. After a few too many coral grazes I gave up and sat in the shade and just existed. Gentle warmth, happy children and drowsiness.

Later we slowly pedalled home.

'You know how het up you were about the chickens and the duck?'

'Ya.'

'Well, I've been wondering ...'

'Ahh ...'

'I wonder if it's time we had a bit of a holiday?' What a great idea.

'What a great idea – any thoughts on where?'

'How about Rennel and Bellona?'

'Sounds great ... I wonder if we are eligible yet ... I wonder how long it will take to find out ... I wonder if we can get flights ... I wonder how much it would cost ... I wonder ...'

'I'll sort it out.'

'Er, right.'

We arrived home to find a distraught Hilda. In broad daylight the dogs had taken Muffin.

Lata Hospital
Santa Cruz
Temotu Province.

6th May 1997

Editor
BMJ
BMA House
Taristock Sq
London WCIH 95R
ENGLAND.

Dear Sir

I am glad to see that David Bergers account of the vicious
fish out here in the Solomons has elicited some response.
I found the commentary by John Rees rather condemning in
that he considered it 'wrong' not to fly the patient.
Having worked here for over a year in an even more remote
Province I can only applaud Dr. Berger in his treatment of the
patient and requesting comments on his actions. There are
so many variables out here in the Solomons that I can safely
say that no one form of treatment (or in this case transport)
should ever be condemned. Sudden changes in the weather,
aircraft fuel loads, the patience of the aircraft captain
(and the other passengers), time of day (the small aircraft
here are often unable to land at night) the state of the
Provincial Health budget etc etc etc. All these and many other
factors have to be taken into account when we make similar
decisions every week. The patient survived, so the decision
was correct. If the patient had not survived then the decision
not to fly him needs review, but may still have been correct.

Yours faithfully

D. Aratheon
Director of Provincial Health Services
Temotu Province
SOLOMON ISLANDS.

Conflict of interest: A filler article in the BMJ, written
by David Berger encouraged me to contact him and resulted
in my current post.

1. Berger D. A fish induced pneumothorax: dilemmas in the
    remote management of a sucking chest wound (with commentary
    by J Rees) BMJ 1996, 313:1617-8 (21 - 28 December).

2. Henman D, Finlayson F, letter to BMJ 1997; 7088 (19 April)

    Word Count: 207

Published!

Chapter 15

Laggards, Legs and Leave

Lata Hospital
Santa Cruz
Temotu Provinc.

30th April 1997

President
Paramedical Association
Lata Hospital
Temotu Province.

Dear Sir

Many thanks for forwarding to me a copy of the minutes of your last meeting held on 24th April 1997.

As some of the points discussed involve me and the budget of the Health Service. Let me make a few comments:

(1). Re memo sent by DPHS to all Departments concerning paying for passages to go on Annual Leave.

    a). Life is not fair.

    b). My actions are governed by General Orders. I have little lee way within the orders, but I am prepared to exercise the little I have.

    c). Shipping problems - no one is asking you to wait around for the next ship, using up your leave. If you wish to travel by sea, then continue working until the next ship arrives and none of your annual leave will have been used up.

    d). Purchase of new truck and OBMs. I am not sure you really want me to comment on this. The truck and OBMs are to be used for the good people of Temotu, whom we all serve. Against this we have the rather selfish wants of a group of people who wish to have their airfares paid to go on annual leave. Perhaps it is better for 17,000 people to be a little better off, rather than 11 families to be able to fly on their annual leave, paid for out of the coffers of Medical Health?

        A quick calculation shows that it will cost Temotu Health approximately $32,000 to send you and your families on annual leave by air. If your consciouses can cope with that, then I am a little at a loss what to say. All that money (except the seafares) has been put to good use, and if I remember correctly all those who wanted to travel by air last year did so, although they had to pay for most of the fare themselves.

    e). Discussing 'such matters' with ALL heads of Department. Having been to many meetings I can honestly say that decision making is best made outside them. I have not gone outside General Orders in this decision as I am sure you will all agree.

2). Meetings with **Departmental Heads**. I am always prepared to meet with Departmental Heads. My only **criteria** are: Adequate forwarning, a printed agenda and good time keeping.

3). Other matters

b). Need for Hospital Secretary

I agree. I have requested that the position be reinstated and filled, but as usual have had no reply from Permanent-Secretary, MIMS Honiara.

c). Casual Labourers

I am willing to pay casual labourers and always have done. I will do so as long as it is justified before they are taken on.

d). 'Ben's problem' The Paramedical Association meeting is not the forum to bring up this problem. However, as ist has been brought up, I will inform the Association of a few facts. I have watched Mr. Suilua for the last year. He is the laziest and most in-effective worker in the whole of the Health Service of Temotu. I have begged Health Education in Honiara to remove him from the Province so that he can undergo further training or disciplinary action, and so that we can get an effective Health Educator. I no longer consider him to be employed in this Province, but as you can imagine this will have little effect on Health Education in the Province. (As for giving Mr. Suilua a new OBM to use.... is this a joke?)

e). Transport to water source. There will be one trip by Medical truck to the water source on each day the water does not come up to Lata. Perhaps the Province has been paying airfares for its employees annual leave, instead of investing money in a decent pump?

Many thanks again for informing me of the out come of your meeting.

Yours faithfully

Dr. David Arathoon.
Director Provincial Health Services
TEMOTU PROVINCE.

I was feeling a bit odd.

On a ward round trying to concentrate. Rather difficult. Bit achy. Perhaps a lack of coffee, but unlikely.

'Ya, that sounds like a good idea.'

Hmm. When did this start? Last night? – No, felt fine reading stories to Meg and Barney and then reading to self.

'What? Yep – that sounds like a good idea.' Sarah gives me a strange look.

'I said, "Have you done an XR on this chap's leg?"'gazing at a very nasty infected foot – a consequence of being a fisherman in a Third World country, therefore being barefoot and stoical, stepping on a fish bone, putting up with the agonizing pain day and night for three weeks before seeing a friend who recommended that although they were a bit odd up at the hospital it may be worth a visit as 'who knows ... ?'. Of course I knew all this, but the fact of knowing it in a recess of my mind and using that information sensibly when I felt strange were two different things.

'Oh, sorry, I was thinking about the last case. Yeah, I X-rayed the lower leg, no obvious osteomyelitis and I will do an I and D after the ward round.' 'Der,' I felt like saying.

'That OK with you Dr Maybel?' said Sarah to our Tikopian shadow who had started accompanying us on all our ward rounds since the boredom of the TB ward had got to her. She smiled, hung her head, flushed slightly and shifted her feet before nodding. She understood not a word of English, but invariably her advice, or agreement, was spot on. And her feet were enormous. Worth her place on the ward round for that fact alone. And the fact that she had some medical experience in that her grandfather had vomited his life's blood up in front of her ... to be absolutely precise *on* the front of her.

I mentally and physically retreated to the back of the ward round retinue, getting a surprised look from John Bakila. Sarah knew what she was doing, whereas currently I didn't seem to. Let me have a think – could it be the thought of going on holiday? Unlikely to explain the aching. What about the thought of my beloved giving birth in a Third World hospital whose director wasn't entirely happy with the situation? Could explain the aching *and* the sweating *and* light-headedness *and* poor concentration.

'Yes I think so ...'

'Er ... never mind.' Another strange look.

That was it then. Not my fault at all that I felt so strange – all Sarah's fault for making me make her pregnant out in sunny Santa

Cruz. I felt better immediately – but only for a few minutes until I was asked to make a decision: 'Er ... I don't know.' Then I also noticed I had a pain in my left groin. I looked round to make sure I wasn't being observed and carefully pressed my hand to my left inguinal area. Ow – a painful lump the squeezing of which caused a flush of extra sweating and more light-headedness. Bloody hell, what on earth was going on?

I thought I had better make a decision. I said to John Bakila, 'John, could we get Ishmael ready for that I and D now?' He looked at me askance – minor operations happened after ward rounds, not during them; however, as a glance showed a devil-may-care glint in my eyes, he quietly and efficiently cut out a nurse, and I followed them back to the clinical room. The warm room smelt a bit iffy, but Ishmael was smiling through his face-sweating agony with his grossly swollen left leg raised up off the bed. He had obviously been given two paracetamol tablets at dawn four hours ago, and knew he couldn't possibly be in as much pain as he seemed to be. Hence the rictus smile and sheen of sweat.

'Er – John, could you help me here?' I was gazing rather unsightedly at the chart recommending doses of ketamine for different weights. I knew Ishmael's weight, and knew that I could work out the dose required if I really had to ... but John was there and he was totally capable, so I thought he could do it for me.

'IM or IV?' he asked.

'Ah ... you decide.'

'We usually do IV for short procedures ...' I looked back at him blankly. 'Let's do an IV then.' he said.

Ishmael was readied while I leant against the wall of the clinical room, gazing down with interest at my feet and flip-flops. They really did seem interesting. Funny how the motes of dust moved just so in the shaft of sunlight on my feet.

'OK doctor.'

'Great John, great ... er, have you got a trolley ready?' He gave me another odd look and then looked down to the now not so sterile trolley I was leaning on, having heaved myself away from the wall.'Ah ... don't worry John, his foot is full of ... you know, what's it called ... er – pus that's it, so if the trolley isn't entirely sterile it doesn't matter – OK let's go.' John gave the ketamine IV and Ishmael dropped off swiftly and began a non-camelid snore. We all smiled at each other. I carried on smiling. This was going well. Great in fact. I looked up. John and the nurse were still looking at me. Expectantly. Now what? John caught my eye and gently inclined his head glancing to Ishmael and then back to me. I did a 'What?' uplift of my eyebrows in the best Solomon Island fashion and John did the same inclination of his head and eyes followed by what must have seemed to him to be bluntness close to rudeness:

'Doctor, would you like to do the I and D now?'

Ah yes, the I and D, that's what all this was about. I reached out to pick up the scalpel only to have my hand's journey interrupted by John's hands holding out a pair of gloves for me to don. 'Ah yes, gloves.' I smiled weakly and put them on, gazed a bit more at the sleeping patient, gazed a bit more at the grotesque foot and then felt the handle of a scalpel being placed in my hand. Ah yes, the I and D. John subtly painted the sole of Ishmael's foot with iodine to indicate that I should proceed. I bent at the waist, squinted, decided the best place to start and put the scalpel point against the leather-thick sole at the apex of the swelling. Nothing happened. I pushed a bit, still nothing; I pushed a bit more – still nothing. This foot looked as if it would pop if someone blew on it, but it wouldn't succumb to my scalpel. I straightened to get more leverage – just as well as with the next effort the scalpel decided that it was time to get on with his short life and do something, jagged through the quarter inch of homespun leather under Ishmael's forefoot and let out a jet of high pressure green fishy pus. This shot past where my face had just been and didn't stop till it hit the far wall of the clinical room. The stench was indescribable. It was appalling. John Bakila backed out of the door looking green. The pus slowly dripped down the wall to the floor, the foot deflated and I was sure a smile crossed Ishmael's anaesthetized face. The smell in the small clinical room was beyond endurance. It was as if a large fish, suffering the very terminal stages of Clostridium Difficile poisoning, had excreted out of Ishmael's foot. Bad as it was I was seeing, or in this case smelling, the whole event from two removes. I bent down, peered into the foot, dripped a bit of sweat off my nose onto floor/pus and patient and started to clean the cavity out. There was another half pint of loculated creamy pus inside but I scraped it all out and packed it with a bit of gauze soaked in water. John was still outside but the poor nurse was cornered at the back of the room, unable to force a passage through the miasma to the safety of the outside world. I finished up, asked John to keep an eye on Ishmael and went to join the ward round.

I found them at the far end of the hospital at the paediatric ward. As I limped past Glenson, our eight-year-old with a fractured femur, I tickled him – he couldn't get away as his left leg was nailed

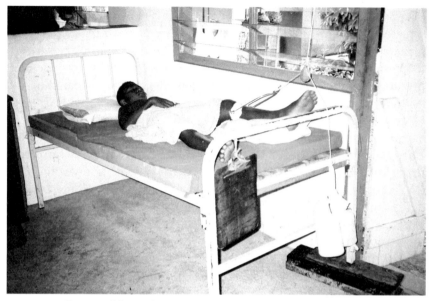

Fractured femur in traction, note pulley from *Bucephalus*.

to a piece of traction apparatus and he was confined to his bed. The
traction consisted of a cord attached to his proximal tibia which
ran up to a pulley and then down to a plastic juice container with
just the exact amount of water in to give the desired effect. He
giggled, which alerted the ward round to my presence. Maybel
looked as though she had been interrupted in mid-consultation, but
Sarah just looked worried.

'Where have you been?'

'Oh, John and I have just sorted Ishmael out.'

'Was that the horrific stench that came past a few minutes ago?'

'Yup.'

'Er . . . why are you limping?'

'Dunno.'

'What's wrong with your leg?'

'Er . . . dunno,' glancing down at my left leg. Just above the flip-
flops and the dust motes was a leg I didn't wholly recognize. When
had it started to swell? When had my mosquito bites decided to
blow up? And more to the point – what were those red lines track-
ing up from both sides of my ankle towards the rest of me?

'*You've been scratching your mossie bites.*'

'No, don't think so.' Sickly smile.

'Let's have a look.' Sarah led me out into the sun under the covered walkway beside the paediatric ward. 'Your bites are infected – no wonder you have been stranger than usual. Let's get some cloxacillin down you and you had better go home.'

'Should I have some coffee?' She gave me yet another strange look of hopelessness and asked one of the girls to give me 'Cloxacillin 500 milligrams stat' and sent me on my way. It didn't seem that long since I had walked down the slope from our home to the hospital with Sarah for the morning ward round, but time had become somewhat elastic over the last hour or so, and the slope had become a rather tiring hill. The heat seemed to be worse and the soup somewhat thickened. I wasn't struggling mentally, in fact everything seemed delightful; but physically I was sweating, limping, groaning and occasionally stopping to get my energy back. I made a detour to chat to Betsy and Belinda who were already losing their baby fluff and getting their scrubby ugly teenage feathers – birds' acne I thought as I chatted to them. They both had a gleam in their eyes which was due to the fact that they thought I had fish on me. I considered nipping up to the house to get some – looked at the enormous distance of thirty yards there and back and decided against.

I hobbled up to the verandah and the kitten came out to see why I was sitting on the bench – I told him I was just enjoying the view. He wanted to know why I wasn't at the hospital working. I told him I had been sent home by Sarah to get the lunch ready. At 11 o'clock? He didn't believe me. Daft animal.

I hobbled through my fine mesh door and into the kitchen. Hilda was very surprised to see me, but unlike the cat too polite to demand what I was up to. I put the kettle on and got some coffee out. Hilda gave me the look normally reserved for alcoholics.

'Ah ... I'm just ... ah. Just going to have a read in my hammock Hilda. The kids OK this morning at kindy?' She agreed they had been fine when she dropped them off. I had been meaning to have a word about her 'dropping' Barney off. There was no reason why he couldn't walk the short distance to the kindy – she didn't have to carry him – even if it rained. I wondered if I could get this concept across in my current lofty position but decided against. I picked up my coffee, grabbed Patrick O'Brian for company and went to my hammock on the verandah.

Sarah woke me three hours later. I felt great, although the sharpness of the colour of everything was diminished. My aching had gone and even my inane grin seemed to have slipped. My coffee was undrunk; Patrick O'Brian had not been consulted.

'You look better.'

'God, that was a great sleep. I dreamt we were on a desert island about three yards across – Betsy was in a coconut tree above us and volunteered to fly us to safety. We couldn't decide whether we wanted to go or not and she got fed up and died of old age at our feet – weird eh?'

'Pretty weird.'

'How was the rest of the ward round?'

'Good, that bloke Ishmael woke feeling much better. We've had a few more patients come in but nothing special, some malaria, little chap with probable scrub typhus and a young man with pneumonia … looks like it's going to—' at which the heavens opened and vast quantities of water fell on everything; Belinda and Betsy could just be seen through the curtain of water revelling and preening, cleaning and shaking.

'Hilda's going to get wet,' Sarah shouted across to me from the bench above the roaring of the rain. I smiled back, not wanting to have to scream my agreement, but at the same time imagining all the feral dogs scattering for shelter. I hoped they wouldn't find any. We sat on in companionable silence watching God give his regular demonstration of power. It even felt a little chilly with the temperature dropping momentarily to 26 or 27 degrees centigrade. I was getting damp as the wind blew the spray off the coral of our garden under the eves of the verandah. The sensation of coolness was worth savouring.

Hilda of course was much cleverer than we gave her credit for and only came home as the downpour started to relapse into a drizzle. Sarah came across to examine my leg which had been well elevated while I was sleeping. 'Time you had your next dose of cloxacillin … did I tell you I have looked into staying on both Rennell and Bellona?'

'Nope.'

'Well I was lucky and managed to get through on the phone to a lady in Honiara who told me all about the caves you can stay in on Bellona, which I have to say sounds strange, but even odder, the chap she recommended for our stay on Rennell is an MP.'

'Huh?'

'Yeah, he seems to have some sort of lodge on the large lake in the middle which he lets to tourists.'

'Sounds great, if somewhat weird.'

'Anyway, I have given her some dates and she says she will get back to us; now I suppose we had better breach the subject with the Ministry of Health ... I wonder if they think we have been here long enough to justify giving us leave? I wonder what our contracts say about it?'

'Dunno.'

'You remember that horrendous stench you sent down to me courtesy of Ishmael?' I nodded. 'I felt sure just before it arrived that I would have to go off for a honk' (Sarah's morning sickness was more the any-time-of-day-vomiting kind rather than the simple nausea) 'but it seemed to cure me for a while and I got through the whole ward round before nipping home to chuck up – you were snoring – and then returned to see the new patients and phone Honiara.'

'Oh good' – she did actually look tinged with greenness now I could look at her without the visual vividness brought on by my fever.'You OK?'

'Hang on ...' and she swallowed a few times. 'Yeah, OK – what about you?'

'I feel great,' at which I got up out of my hammock, stood up – began to grey-out and had to sit down again, tensed my calf and thigh muscles, got my eyesight back and had another attempt at standing.

'See: completely fine.' What a pair. We both went to stand at the edge of the verandah by the steps with Hilda approaching in the brightening sunshine as the last raindrops fell and steam started to rise over the land. Her umbrella was still up, Barney was well protected tied to her back with a papa, and Meg had her own umbrella. They were all soaked from the knees down and spattered with mud from the ricochets.

'Hey, it looks as though we are going to go on holiday – waddya think of that?' I greeted them.

'How's Billy?' replied Barney.

'Look at this,' replied Meg, holding up a drawing.

'We're going to sleep in caves and ... and ...' but they had both disappeared into the kitchen with Hilda for a biscuit, carrying Billy and chatting merrily in Pidjin.

'Oh well, 'spose we could cycle down to Luova for a swim ...' but a look at Sarah's colour and a personal knowledge of my leg ruled it out – '... or we could have a cup of tea.'

So we did.

28th April 1997

The Provincial Secretary
Lata
Temotu Province.

Dear Sir

RE: THOMAS YANDE

I have made enquiries into dismissal of workers under the
Labour Act. Please find below my findings.

Labour Act - Chapt. 75 (Part VI of this Act)

Section 65

An employer shall not dismiss a worker employed by him without notice - EXCEPT in the following circumstances:-

Subsections

        A. Where the worker is guilty of misconduct,
           whether in the course of his duties or not
           inconsistent with the fulfillment of the
           express or implied conditions of his agreement.

        B. For wilful disobedience to lawful orders
           given by the employer.

        C. For lack of the skill which the worker
           expressly or implicitly warrants himself
           or herself to possess.

        D. For habitual or substantial neglect of his
           duties.

        E. Absence from work without leave from the
           employer or absence from work without other
           reasonable cause.

As you can see, any one of these conditions is enough for a
worker to be dismissed without notice. You will also note
that Thomas Yande's misconduct fulfills subsections A, B, C,
D and E.

I hope this information is helpful to the service and disciplinary
committee when or if, they ever meet to discuss this matter.

Yours faithfully

Dr. David Arathoon.
Director Provincial Health Services
TEMOTU PROVINCE.

cc: Thomas Yande

Chapter 16

Food: Fish Guts, Foxes and Frights

LATA HOSPITAL

22nd April 1997

Mr. James Keni
Statistic Section
Ministry of Health & Med. Services
P O Box 349
Honiara.

Dear Sir

My Hospital Clerk has been trying to contact you for the last
3 months to try to get your advice regarding our Hospital computer.
He has tried each and every day of the week and each and every hour
of the working day regularly with absolutely no luck. Are you
still employed by MHMS? If so how is it that you seem to spend
most, if not all of your time, out of the office? I would be must
grateful if you could phone my Clerk (John Melelao) on 53043 soonest.

Many thanks.

Yours faithfully

Dr. David Arathoon.
Director Provincial Health Services
TEMOTU PROVINCE.

6/8/97 .... Reply form PS ....

cc: PS/MHMS

'Well, that wasn't too bad.' I wiped my greasy fingers and lips on a piece of loo roll. 'Not sure if the children would have liked it though ...' We had just eaten our supper which consisted of a local delicacy: curried flying fox. I had heard that some locals ate the large slowly flapping visitors who one could see most evenings heading out of their roosts on Malo Island towards the gardens inland on Santa Cruz. Initially we thought it rather sweet, but became aware that not everyone liked to see all their hard work and soft fruit ravished by airborne hairy smiling mammals. The people of Malo were quite content to let them roost there during the day as long as they spent their night-time working day next door on Santa Cruz feasting away. I had asked Wilson Lyno how they were captured before being despatched and then cooked. Apparently they weren't 'caught' so much as blown out of the sky with a 22 rifle, skinned and then always curried. Yum. After mulling this unlikely story over for a couple of weeks I finally plucked up courage to ask Wilson if he would take me out next time he went hunting flying foxes. He agreed.

Actually the next time Wilson went out evening hunting he was the guest of Samuel our hospital pharmacist, who owned both a 22 rifle and a telescopic sight. Wilson had mentioned me to Samuel and he had agreed to me going.

I was told to meet them at Luova, the nearest bit of Santa Cruz to Malo Island and I had been a bit surprised when Wilson had informed me that 'We should be there at half past five, English time.' On contemplation I realized that food was at stake – hence the insistence on English time. Also if we all arrived the statutory one and a half hours late it would be pitch black, the flying foxes would all have gorged and would be invisibly discussing the busy events of their night-day.

I cycled down to Luova and was most surprised to find both the others there waiting in the shade beside the beach. The day still seemed in its prime, but we knew that all of a sudden night would fall. So did our hairy foxy prey. Before long we spied black lazy silhouettes breaking up from the trees on Malo and then going back to roost – the quarry awoke. I was still wondering how on earth I could possibly hit a high-flying beast, telescopic sight or no. It became apparent that I would be given a shot or two after Samuel and Wilson had had theirs. The rifle was lovely, light and well oiled – *very* unlike the Premier's gun which I had seen slung over his shoulder a few days before. This was in an appalling state of rusty neglect and was being carried by what looked like a tramp in rags, up the road to the Provincial farm. The tramp turned out to be Father Ini Lapli, dressed down from his normal duties as premier, on his way up to the farm for a bit of pigeon blasting.

Wilson and Samuel were getting excited as the first prehistoric shapes started on their way to Santa Cruz. Surely they would be miles high by the time they passed us? Some were, but others were still a bit groggy from their day-night's sleep and just managed to stagger to the trees above our heads. Samuel lined up the nearest. It was so close that I could see its smiling rather lap-dog expression as it looked down at us the wrong way through a telescopic lens. A loud *crack* rang out and I unconsciously closed my eyes. So did our foxy-friend who continued to blink down. Samuel had missed completely and was not happy: with his gun, with me for being witness and most of all with Reynard who continued to grin. Some of the nearby foxes heard the shot and decided to wake up fully and get up to the gardens on the plateau and start breakfast. Our closest friend was so engrossed watching the hopping-mad Samuel cursing under his breath and reloading, that he forgot all the old wives' tales about his predecessors who had been lazy and stopped on the way to the gardens and were never seen again. He was lined up again and the crack of the rifle was the last earthly sensation he could have been aware of as his head, brain and presumably soul should he have one, were unceremoniously removed by a piece of supersonic lead. He fell at our feet. Samuel was most excited and picked him up for me to admire. Ex-foxy was jumping with fleas who were only too aware that something terminal had happened to their rich warm red home and were already looking for new abodes. I hastily put the corpse in Samuel's shoulder bag.

Then it was Wilson's turn, and as expected he was coolness personified – two shots, two meals.

Now it was my go. 22 rifles always surprise me; a heck of a cracking sound associated with no kick-back. Samuel insisted I have a go at a high-flying fox, as it was the nearest. My first shot passed harmlessly through his port wing – eliciting not a flicker of interest on his foxy-face, as he was concentrating on his breakfast which would start with pawpaw. I could see the neat round blue hole in his leathery wing through the telescopic lens as I watched him flapping to join his friends. I wanted a more stationary target next time. Wilson spotted another of the lazy sub-species who had stopped for a rest having crossed the whole mile from Malo. He was some distance off and looked a bit stupid – not like someone cogitating the universe and all its mysteries, more like someone reading *Hello* magazine. The telescopic sight brought him closer, but he still looked an ignoramus.

'Er Wilson – what happens if I do hit him? Won't he just fall into the sea?'

'By Samuel go lookim.'

'Okey-doke.' I aimed squarely at Mr Stupid's mid-resting-torso and pulled the trigger: *crack* – distant look of surprise on foxy-face as he fell off his perch with a wounded left wing. I must have hit his humerus as only one wing seemed to be working – and that not very effectively as he was certainly earth-bound. Actually water-bound. His right wing managed to get in a few beats which served to take his face, body and parasites further from us. Splash. Samuel was away, running through the shallows. Looking over his shoulder Foxy saw him coming and started paddling with his one good wing – he started turning in large circles which was certainly enough to put off his capture for a few minutes as Samuel ran after him neglecting to take the hypoteneuse for some time. Even Wilson smiled. The end was never in doubt and a quick grab, followed by a pull and twist of his flea-ey neck and our latest victory was added to Samuel's wet shoulder bag.

Dark was now definitely coming on and I said I had better be off. Wilson and Samuel thought they would stay on to get a little more kaikai. Samuel very generously said he would bring me up two 'birds', skinned, gutted and ready for curry. I hoped he would remove the indigestible-looking wings. He did. Hilda showed us how to cook them and as both children refused to sample this fare (having seen rather anthropomorphic pictures of certainly flea-less fruit bats in a book, and ' ... they look like Lara' our dog back in the UK) Sarah and I had a whole fox each. Interesting. Strong flavour. Best curried, I could see.

'Well better than the fish guts old Andreas ate anyway.' Sarah and I collapsed in laughter at the reminder of Andreas. He had been brought into the hospital in a very poorly state with many very weird signs and symptoms. He had vomiting and diarrhoea with abdominal cramps. He had pain in his teeth (!), blurred vision and areas of numbness in odd places. Even his heart was beating irregularly. He was very unwell. He didn't have either of our usual fallbacks of malaria or scrub typhus and he remained in the same state for the first few days. He was given chloroquine: he got no better. He was given chloramphenicol: he got no better. We expended a great deal of brain power fruitlessly trying to diagnose his rather strange symptoms with the idea of making a difference to him or naming his disease – or even both. However he got no worse and was hanging on in there and maybe even improving. In the end we rechecked his story. He was a fisherman and had taken advantage of the stir caused by the near miss of a recent cyclone (which had also caused all the odd rips and pulls we had experienced down at the Taros' beach, not that we realized at the time) to go out on the reef and managed to catch a very large fish. This fish was deemed large enough to provide the basis for a banquet for twenty people at a wedding ceremony. The stipulation made to Andreas was that the fish should be prepared: i.e. gutted. Andreas was a sensible sort of chap and realized that the guts he removed would make a jolly nice meal for himself. He ate the lot and subsequently found himself under our gentle and baffled care. This was not simple food poisoning as one would expect in someone who was mad enough to eat fish guts; there was something else going on. As he slowly began to improve we found the diagnosis, late it has to be said, but it would have made no difference to his treatment in our Third World. An old mildewy medical book in the hospital revealed 'ciguatera poisoning'.

Ciguatera toxin is a heat stable poison found in fish in tropical climes (an Aussie would have diagnosed it immediately). It bio accumulates and the larger the predator the more poison it contains. Most of the poison is stashed in the guts of the fish and does it no harm. The toxin originates in tiny organisms called dinoflagellates which are released when there is disruption of a coral reef, e.g. after a ship strike or a nasty piece of weather has smashed up a part of the reef as in our case. It does indeed cause a very strange array of symptoms easily confused with MS. There is no specific treatment except support. Luckily our use of antimalarials and chloramphenicol had done Andreas no harm. He was well enough to go home a couple of days after our flash of inspiration. I let Wilson tell him that he may have symptoms for years if not decades, and he should be careful having intercourse with his wife as it could be passed to her. I would love to have been a fly on the wall at that discharge talk ...

The ex-foxy corpses remained on the table looking at us as we mused about Andreas. We both smiled again.

'I wonder ...'

'What?'

'Well, you know that fright I gave myself the other night?'

'Yeah.'

'I wonder if that profusion of those monsters was also something to do with the bad weather we had recently, like Andreas' poisoning?'

'Don't know, we don't know if they are normally there at night even if there hasn't been bad weather … you would have to go back in a few weeks and have another go and see if they are just as many.'

'Thanks.' I wasn't keen to repeat my experiment which had given me such a fright. A couple of weeks before in a fit of enquiry I had decided to go on a night snorkel down at Luova. This required the use of a waterproof torch which Wilson was able to supply. Sarah wondered if I would be 'all right' on my own as she had to stay at home to look after the children. I scoffed at her. Ha.

However, as I cycled across the end of the airfield in the true starlit darkness of the tropics I had a prickling of doubt. My waterproof torch lit my way down through the tree-lined track to the beautiful beach at Luova. Didn't look quite so attractive viewed from my lone eyes with absolutely no one around. Oh well. I leant my bike against a tree, started down the strand, hesitated a moment and turned back to pick up a thin branch to take with me. I sometimes carried a piece of wood when snorkelling with Meg so that I could point things out to her as she held on to my shoulder. This saved a great deal of time as otherwise every time I saw anything interesting we both had to bring our heads out of the water, unplug our snorkels, cough and snort, discuss what/where/why and both plunge our heads back under only for our drifting to have changed our orientation, or indeed for the said sight to have gone off for lunch.

I felt a little more confident with the stripped branch in my right hand to accompany the torch in my left hand. The tide was about halfway out when I reached the sea. I entered ankle deep, pulled down my goggles and placed the snorkel into my mouth. One deep breath and I slowly slid into the water horizontally. Initially the visibility was poor. This wasn't entirely due to the candle-power-lacking torch but also due to the slow mixing of fresh water oozing through the beach into the salty Coral Sea. This caused waves of distortion a bit like those seen in a warming pan of water where there is a slow change of density. This lulled me into a false sense of security. The reef when it appeared looked darker than it should have even when seen at night. I swam a little closer. The whole reef as far as I could see was covered in dark irregular shaped patches. I swam closer still …

'Oh shit!'

I shot to the surface coughing and spluttering, pulse rate rocketing.

'Bloody Hell ... Jesus.' I was scared. What on earth were those monsters? How to find out? What to do? I mulled it over a while, treading water and gazing at the stars. I had better have another look. I screwed up my courage and gazed from the safety of the surface. Big black ugly spiky horrible things. They would need a closer perusal. Head back out, few quick morale boosting breaths and back down (slowly) to have another look.

The reef as far as my eyes would let me see was covered in Crown-of-Thorns starfish. I had only seen one before; it now seemed obvious that it had been left behind by its colleagues at dawn as they all shrank back into their dark lairs. They have to be the ugliest life form dreamt up, so far. Also they were *eating* my coral. Where had they all come from? Were there possibly enough cracks and hollows for all these vampire-monsters to live in out of sight during the day? Now I was getting angry. They had purposely frightened the life out of me *and* they were eating the precious coral. God. They deserved everything they got. Back to the surface, gentle hyperventilation (against all the rules, but it helps) and back down. I went wild: stabbing, crushing, smashing, hitting and generally venting my anger. In a short while the water was full of bits of starfish, the larger parts drifting slowly to the seabed, the smaller just hazing the water. Soon I was exhausted and oxygen-less (hyperventilation notwithstanding). I found myself staring at the glittering undersurface of the sea from a distance of about fifteen metres. More pulse racing and fear ... a push for the surface, stick dropped. At last a huge gasp. Phew.

I neglected to tell Sarah about my hypoxic episode, but certainly let her know about the rest of the adventure.

'God they are bastards, but at least there are a few dozen which will no longer eat our reef.' Or frighten me ...

'I wonder ...'

'What?'

'I wonder if they are related to earthworms?'

'Huh?'

'Well you know, every time you cut an earthworm in half it grows into two new ones ...'

'Oh thanks.'

The children were in bed, Hilda had gone home, our fruit bats were now skeletons, the desktop fan was on and we were both content. Content with a little underlying anxiety due to living in Lata for eight months continually 'on call', slightly out of our depths medically and away from home. Actually more away from house as our bungalow here in the warm evening soup was home.

'Shall we leave the washing up for Hilda in the morning?'

'Hmm? Did I tell you that I had a reply from the ministry about our request for leave?'

'No.'

'Well the reply was that they would think about it and get back to us.'

'Ah ... when are our flights booked for?'

'Two or three weeks' time I think.'

'We'll never get a reply by then.'

'I know, but let's go anyway. I can't wait.'

'Nor me.' My background anxiety immediately fell away.

We did finally get a reply from the ministry. It was 'No'. However that was two months after we had returned from Rennell and Bellona, which was fine by us.

LATA HOSPITAL

18th April 1997

Senior Accountant
Ministry of Health & Med. Services
P O Box 349
Honiara.

Dear Sir

Todate we have not received Wages or Service Grants for the
months of: Dec 1996, Jan/Feb/March/April 1997. Please could
you give me some idea when we may expect these monies? The
situation here in Temotu is likely to become desperate quite
soon.

Many thanks.

Yours faithfully

Dr. David Arathoon.
Director Provincial Health Services
TEMOTU PROVINCE.

cc: PS/MHMS
cc: PS/Temotu
cc: SIBC/Honiara

Chapter 17

Holiday

MINISTRY OF HEALTH AND MEDICAL SERVICES

TEMOTU PROVINCE

TENDER NOTICE

15/04/97

The OBMs listed below are for sale by closed bid tender. They
are for sale on a 'where is' 'as is' basis. They can be viewed
at the Hospital from the 24th April and bids have to be into
the Director of Provincial Health Services by the 5th of May.
A decision on the tenders will be made by 7th May and the OBMs
purchased may be taken when the whole price has been received

	No.			Tanks	Faults
$1,800	1.	Johnson 25 HP	–	No tank	Clamps
$1,500	2.	Evan Rude 25 HP	–	Tank	Needs Power packs
$1,000	3.	Yamaha 25 HP	–	Tank	No faults
$2,500	4.	Evan Rude 25 HP	–	Tank	No faults
$500	5.	Yamaha 15 HP	–	Tank	Minor faults
$800	6.	Yamaha 15 HP	–	Tank	Minor faults
$800	7.	Yamaha 15 HP	–	No Tank	~~Some faults~~ No faults
$600	8.	Yamaha 15 HP	–	No tank	Needs new Exhaust and pump. minor faults

David Arathoon.

D. Arathoon.
Director Provincial Health Services
TEMOTU PROVINCE.

The province of Rennell and Bellona consists of two uplifted coral islands which look like oblong soup plates when seen from the air. Rennell is the largest such island in the world and has a massive shallow lake taking up most of its eastern end. This province was where we were going to spend our week's leave.

We had a pretty hectic time in the lead up to our holiday – the hospital seemed busier than usual. First of all we had a couple of old biddies who came in within a few days of each other. They were of a similar age and had exactly the same problem: difficulty swallowing, or dysphagia to us medics. Agnes came in first and was the more poorly of the two. She hadn't been able to get solids down for some time and was now having significant problems with liquids. She had sensibly tried custom treatments but when none of them worked she came to us. Her few grubby clothes certainly looked loose on her. Phoebe on the other hand was somewhat younger and had only just got to the problem-with-liquids stage having manfully mushed all her solids for some weeks. Both of course were keen Betel-chewers which may have explained their problems. Agnes and Phoebe never met each other and both were in and out of the hospital within days. I persuaded our XR technician (he of the permanent limp) that Agnes needed a barium swallow so that we could get pictures of her gullet as that was probably where her problem lay. He was somewhat reluctant, which I couldn't understand – he had the machine to take the pictures and even some barium, but he was not keen. I spoke to Wilson. He sorted it. It became apparent later that Justin had never done a barium swallow before but was unable to say so as he would have lost face. The pictures he took were grand from a technical point of view, but not from the point of view of either patient. Both showed the classical chewed-apple-core look of a nasty oesophageal cancer. Interestingly enough the XRs of each were virtually interchangeable, although clinically they were at different stages of the disease. Both declined further assessment in Honiara (where I knew they would be subject to having a tube rammed through the tumour ... I didn't mention it to either as I didn't want to put them off) and happily went back to their villages with some paracetamol tablets (to be crushed and mixed with water) to die an unfortunate death of starvation and finally thirst. I think they both made the right decision.

Some months later I mentioned this oddity to Hermann Oberli. He agreed that seeing two relatively rare cancers within days of each other was odd and then came out with a two-word German phrase which meant, 'Whenever you come across something rare or unusual another will happen along very quickly.' Very precise language, German.

Also in our last-week-before-holiday we had some problems with Hilda. She had become a little withdrawn and reticent, and a few days before our departure she came to Sarah in tears as she had been thrown out of the Jehovah's Witness church. After much sobbing and gnashing of teeth Sarah managed to put a coherent story together. Hilda's eldest daughter was called Wendy. She had left Temotu for Honiara some months before in the search for a job, staying with wantoks the while. Being a caring mother, and not wanting her daughter seduced by the dim lights of Honiara, Hilda had written to Wendy explaining nearly in words of one syllable that she had found her a secretarial job in Lata. This was not quite a lie (Jehovah forbid) as it was only hinted at. Wendy came home, realized she had been duped and found herself at a loss, with lots of time on her hands and not enough cash to return to Honiara. So she started a relationship with the young Customs man. He does not belong to THE church, but some other Christian sect. Wendy's 'relationship' consisted of snatched words with this chap. Hilda found out about it and was not happy. Hence the reticence and withdrawal. When Hilda heard that Wendy had gone completely off her head and was currently not only talking to the young Customs man but doing so *in his office* with the door open she decided action would have to be taken. Like any other self-respecting-twice-divorced member of Jehovah's church would do when a daughter was making a disgusting public fool of herself, she took a large stick from her garden and beat them both with it. Jolly sensible action I thought. The upshot of all this was that on the strength of a thirty-minute chat with a bachelor, and what Wendy considered a public humiliation by her mother, the two 'lovers' were to be wed. A bride-price had been agreed ($3500 – not a lot but the going price for a girl from Malo island), Wendy had been excommunicated from THE church for the atrocious crime of marrying a non- (or different-) believer, and unfortunately our lovely housegirl had also been temporarily thrown out of THE church for being such a sinner as to beat her child (. . . in public). Poor old Hilda. Sarah and I really tried hard to understand, but it was difficult to keep straight faces. The only silver lining around Hilda's thundercloud, she informed us, was that she would now be allowed a piece of birthday cake if a birthday perchance occurred before she was permitted re-entry to God's bosom.

*

Fourth day before holiday:

Eric the nurse: 'Doctor, would you have a look at this middle-aged lady for me please?'

Doctor: 'Certainly Eric, how old is she?'

Eric the nurse: 'Oh, twenty-eight or twenty-nine I think.'

Doctor: (crestfallen) 'Oh ... OK ...'

On the penultimate ward round we were presented with an elderly man of forty years who had arrived the evening before having been vomiting blood for two weeks. He had the grey pallor of death upon him, and he duly died before the next ward round. I thought he had stomach cancer with liver secondaries, but Sarah thought he had a hepatoma with bleeding oesophageal varices (like varicose veins in the gullet). Of course we never found out what he died of. On that same round we managed to discharge a young man of nineteen years. He had been an inpatient for ten days, initially coming in very unwell: he had a high fever, jaundice, a cough, myalgia and weakness such that he was bed bound. He became progressively worse under our care and treatment. In the end I had the now notorious 'chat' with his parents viz 'I think he is about to die.' That did the trick – or it may have been the custom medicine we allowed them to perform on the ward which consisted of making the sign of the cross on his chest, arms and forehead with the ash from an unidentified burnt leaf. We were pretty desperate. He then slowly picked up. After discussion with Sarah my discharge summary read: 'PUO (pyrexia of unknown origin), ? Hepatitis B, ? Atypical pneumonia, ? Scrub typhus, ? Dengue fever (?? All of them)'.

'Oh well, I suppose we ruled out malaria.'

Which was something. We had been badly caught out by a patient sent to us from the Reef island clinic, another male of nineteen years, Damian, who we really didn't want as all his so-called symptoms sounded rather psychological when they were relayed to us on one of the radio calls. We had decided that psychological problems would be better sorted out with the patient surrounded by what he knew and by his wantoks. He was sent over by canoe anyway. He had been admitted and I had rather cursorily investigated him as his symptoms were very non-specific, and he seemed very well. When all my investigations came back negative I was able to give him the good news (he seemed disappointed) and I made sure he was sent back to his wantoks as soon as possible. This caused a problem I did not need in our pre-holiday week when a few days after his discharge and boat trip home his sputum results came back from the lab. None of the nurses admitted to sending off his sputum to be examined for tuberculous bacteria (probably to save my blushes), but there they were teeming away in his lungs, now miles away on the Reef islands. I asked for Damian to be returned, but this took some days as a nurse had to be sent to his village and he was found to have gone off with some friends on a fishing trip. Luckily, we got him back and onto the TB ward a couple of days before our departure so we could initiate his six months of treatment. Damian's face was a mixture of 'I told-you-so' and pleasure at the thought of six months of leisure and food. The nurses remained professional throughout ...

The day of our departure for hols arrived in an excited Arathoon household. The children weren't sure why they were excited as their lives already resembled a continuous holiday but they joined in. Sarah's nausea at any time of day had turned into nausea-at-any-time-of-day with occasional vomiting thrown in just to cheer her up. She HATES vomiting. We had done our last pre-holiday round at the hospital and were assured by Wilson that having been in charge of the hospital for eighteen months with no doctor he was quite capable for all of eight days. Barry came to pick us up in the TDA tractor and trailer, Lynne helped us load our few things (most volume taken up by snorkels and masks) and Jake and Amy had walked all the way from the other side of Graciosa Bay to wave us off. This was full-on excitement. As I was about to close the front door and join everyone else on the back of the trailer Mr Brown Kola appeared as if from the blue. One moment my mind was on what was to come, next moment I was face to face with Mr Kola on the verandah.

'Me cut canoe finis.' The canoe was ready ... HOORAY ...

'Oh thank you Mr Kola, where is it?'

'Lo der,' pointing towards the wharf. Perhaps I could nip down to the wharf before the plane came, to run my eye over *Bucephalus*.

'Who is that?' from Sarah.

'I think I may have to nip down to the wharf?'

'What on earth for?' It was getting more and more difficult to converse over the roar from Barry's tractor so I had left Mr Kola on the verandah to put my case to my spouse. She was not impressed, merely glancing at her watch. I went back to Mr Kola.

Over the diesel tractor racket I shouted 'Canoe lo wharf?' pointing in the general direction of the sea. He gave me an odd look.

Then he in turn pointed: 'Canoe long Taepe.' Taepe was indeed in the same direction as the wharf but was fifteen miles further away and not much good to me there.

'It's not much good to me there is it? You need to paddle her over and I will pay you once it is at the wharf.' He gave me a strange look, but seemed to agree. I went back to the trailer and jumped on. 'Straight to the airstrip please Barry, don't worry about the wharf.' Wife gives me a pleasant smile. I give her a pleasant smile.

We arrived at the airstrip on Bellona having admired its gentle shape from above. The airport buildings consisted of a small grove of trees next to the smooth grass airstrip. We wandered off the plane hoping against hope that John Tay or one of his wantoks would be there to meet us. As we were the only whities on the plane we need not have worried. We put our luggage down and a gentle middle-aged man and his rather good-looking wife and daughters approached and introduced themselves as the Tay family. They took all our bags and helped us onto the back of a tractor and trailer, a few interested bystanders jumping on for the fun of it. John Tay spoke excellent English in a quiet manner so conversation was limited until we reached the edge of the island where the grassy road petered out to nothingness at the vertical edge of a cliff. We all got out and suddenly I had a wash of anxiety. Who knew where we were? Were we about to be robbed and beaten at the edge of the world? Of course I need not have worried. Just round a corner were some immaculate steps leading down the cliff to our accommodation right beside the crashing sea.

The accommodation consisted of a pair of caves protected from the sea by a large rock. The children were to sleep in one cave and we were to have the other. The sun was blazing down by now so the contrast with the interior of the caves was marked. John Tay had carefully thought out the problem of dripping condensation and each bed had a coconut leaf roof or awning constructed above it. It was fantastic. We were left to settle in which consisted of upending our bags and going to examine the cleverly constructed cold water shower. The family uttered a universal sigh and although it was only the middle of the afternoon we were all soon snoring away. The Tay family arrived carrying platters heaped with fabulous local food cooked by Nita, John's wife. John said his wife wanted to know if we would like crayfish as well?

'Oh all right then.' We ate and ate, crayfish, fishfish, slimy cabbage, rice, and taro. What a feast. John stayed with us silently sitting listening to the crashing waves and watching the sun set.

'What do you think of the sunset?' he asked me. I was pretty taken aback. Here was a man who not only lived in the Third World but also saw this sunset nearly every day. Surely he would not be able to appreciate its beauty. But he did. He seemed to be in a trance as he asked me, and only slowly tore his eyes away from the sight when I hadn't answered for some time. I was nearly lost for words.

'It's beautiful,' I said. He smiled his enigmatic smile and looked back west.

'It's God's,' he said. I was truly dumbstruck.

The next day John showed us a small hole behind Barney's bed which we all crawled though into another cavern, aptly named 'Bat Cave'. By the light of a dying torch John pointed out the bats we had seen the night before wheeling around above our heads. They looked somewhat grumpy at being woken at the start of their day's night. The amazing thing was that Barney was totally unperturbed by the thought of hordes of bats flinging themselves around and under his bed in the twilight. Our second day on Bellona was spent doing little else. Sarah and I did wander along the cliff a few scores of yards. Meg and Barney did wander down to the shore to look for opercula once the tide was out, but most of our collective time was spent resting, reading and dozing. A perfect place to recharge. Very well fed and recharged we were taken back to the airstrip on our final Bellonic morning. Our gentle hosts seemed sad to see us go, particularly our pikinini. We were each weighed with our luggage on a set of scales which were unhooked from their upside-down position on the largest of the trees in the departure grove. The departure official remained sitting cross-legged on the ground throughout our formalities and slowly waved us off as we boarded the plane. The overriding impression of Bellona was that of a gentle place.

We set flight to Rennell and landed at a hot dusty coral strip with the sun an hour from its zenith. We waited and waited. There was indeed a solid state airport building, but we didn't stay inside as the tin roof caused the furnace inside to be hotter than the furnace outside. As a family we joined the small crowd in the moving and diminishing shade of the building. There were debates about possible transport to the other side of the island which we wished to get to. Most of the other passengers only wanted to go halfway. There was talk of a tractor and trailer being provided and we saw a couple coming and going lethargically in the heat. Finally after a couple of hours the recognizable noise of a tractor at speed and under load broke through the haze. A plume of black smoke indicated that it was coming from the direction we all wanted to go in. It drew up in front of the terminal building and of all things a pair of whities stiffly disembarked from the otherwise empty trailer. Rather disconcertingly they wished us luck. Our group went over to the tractor and someone chatted to the driver. He was indeed going back, but wanted to have a bite to eat and a drink first. He suggested we all boarded while he did so. It became apparent that there were a lot of us. Indeed there were twenty-seven people and all their produce packed on to the trailer when our driver returned. We were all hot and sticky. At the start of the journey we sat carefully on the piles of taro and mangoes and pineapples on the floor of the trailer. As we bumped along the load shifted slowly and gradually until after a hot humid hour we were sitting on the floor of the trailer and the produce was on top of us, hemming us in, preventing movement. The children being lighter were still on top of the fruit and vegetables. I turned round to see how my pregnant wife was getting on in the opposite rear corner. She looked overheated, greasy with sweat and to top it all green about the gills. I raised my eyebrows in inquisition. In reply she leant over the side of the trailer and vomited profusely. Oh dear.

After another hour we reached what we were informed was the halfway point at a shaded beach. All our fellow prisoners offloaded themselves and all their cargo leaving the vehicle mercifully empty.

We carried on much more comfortably and in much more shade. Even Sarah's vomiting stopped and we were all able to communicate finally as we were no longer on different layers of the trailer. In fact we were alone at the back with only our baggage. After a couple more hours of diminishing glare and heat and humidity we finally arrived at our 'tourist' destination. This was a lovely airy clean wooden building built out over the lake on stilts. We were met by Martin-the-MP who spoke immaculate English and dressed in very western clothes, the impression being he only omitted a tie as he was away from parliament. He showed us round our accommodation which had views across the lake with the sun beginning to set in the distance. We had a small supper and dropped into bed for yet another deep deep sleep, with Martin's words in our ears that he would take us on a tour of the lake the next day.

The next day dawned beautiful and clear. Martin arrived by motor boat to take us off after breakfast. He was on time, give or take, which made the whole place seem even more surreal. Our first stop was a net Martin said he had set out after our arrival the day before. He pulled it up and disentangled a couple of dozen tilapia, who spent the rest of the morning flapping in the bilges. Then it was off to his village to get more fuel. He was obviously a big man here and was greeted by the villagers as someone who had once been a bit naughty but who had done well. How this was conveyed to us I have no idea, but Sarah and I both felt the same when we discussed the day later. As we drifted away from the village and a few waving old biddies Martin pointed down into the crystal water to show us a complete aircraft lying right below us. Wow. Sarah and I looked at each other.

'Martin ... do you think we could have a snorkel down to that aeroplane?' He was in no rush and agreed. We left the children in his care, took deep breaths and headed down the ten feet to the top of the Catalina. It seemed whole and complete, even sitting upright on the bottom of the lake. Neither of us felt like staying down too long, the whole thing was a bit unsettling actually. Martin told us that no one was killed when the plane crash-landed, coming to rest on a reef out in the lake. Many years after the war, 1992 in fact, the Catalina was bodily lifted from the reef by a cyclone and dumped thirty yards offshore from Martin's village. It now provided quite good fishing.

On across the lake to 'Bird Island' which consisted of a collection of tiny coral islets upon which hundreds of Boobies, frigate birds and others nested. Wonderful views of wheeling birds overhead with their young peering cautiously over the nests at a bunch of whities below. Then on down to the far eastern corner of the lake where the Catalina base had been during the war. The base had completely reverted to forest and even with the eye of local knowledge supplied by Martin it was impossible to make out exactly where it had been. However ... this was now the site of THE provincial guest house. Work had started on it some years ago and it even had a roof. No work had been done on it for eighteen months and it was beginning to look a little dilapidated. We came ashore for a rest and a bit of quiet after the background blur of the outboard. Martin retrieved the tilapia from the bottom of the boat and joined us lying on the grass beside the lake under the cool trees. We all became drowsy. Out of the blue and I am sure unplanned a local middle-aged lady appeared from the forest and greeted Martin. She turned out to be one of his sisters-in-law and she cooked us a scrumptious lunch using the suffocated tilapia and bits and bobs she found in the forest within a stone's throw of where we sat. All done over a tiny fire lit and cooked on within seconds. She was amazing. After lunch we all had a quick swim to cool down followed by yet another doze. The sister-in-law was gone by the time we awoke.

In the afternoon we carried on our tour of the lake, now along the north shore. Here Martin showed us the 'Octopus Cave'. Initially this looked rather uninteresting, but it soon opened out into a large cave, with a continuation of the lake as its floor. There were enough gaps overhead to provide attractive shafts of sunlight which travelled unhindered to the base of the pool. Martin explained it used to be a tambu (or taboo) place until a local lad and seven of his friends pitched up outside, each in his own canoe. Mightily tempted, the giant octopus tore out of his lair and grabbed all the canoes, at which and without a by-your-leave, the eight boys chopped off all his tentacles with stone axes (it must have been some time ago ...), removing them to their villages to eat, returning only to chop up and carry off the head and beaky bit. This was the story Martin had been told as a boy, and we knew of no reason not to believe it. He had never in his life swum here, let alone snorkelled which we now persuaded him to do. When he shot out of the water and back into the boat after fifty-three seconds he was grey and shaking and not just from the cold. However ... I have to say that when I dived down at the furthest point in the cave and saw a large sump disappearing off into the cliffs I had to agree that perhaps the octopus may have a brood down there still, so I joined them all in a hasty retreat.

The last site of interest was another mile along the edge of the lake and was said to be an underground stream which joined the lake to the sea outside. It looked like an overgrown bay to us, and Sarah and I gave each other knowing looks when Martin informed us about the place. How on earth did he know that there was a stream there? The answer was that local fishermen had caught mamoola fish on the seaward side which contained tilapia in their guts. They only seemed to be caught opposite this bay, and neither they nor we could think of a better explanation. An underground stream it had to be.

We got back to Martin's over-water wooden tourist house tired but happy. Again we slept well and the morning trek back to the airport was much easier with the sun hidden in clouds, a gentle breeze and only six locals and no produce with us in the trailer, which arrived on time and took the correct amount of time to get to the airport without breakdowns or punctures. The plane was on time, there was no turbulence and Sarah didn't vomit for a full twenty-four hours. Heaven.

Wilson had looked after the hospital perfectly. Little had happened in the time we had been away: the water tank at our house had been mended and was leaking worse than ever; the generator was on the blink and the electrics in Lata town were up the spout; the bakery had run out of flour; fisheries had run out of fish; the shops had run out of beer; the hospital computer had broken down and been sent to Honiara (never to be seen again ...); there was no fuel in the hospital but that didn't matter as the hospital truck had also broken down. The mains water had stopped running again; there had been no rain since we had left. Ah me ... time for a supply ship to visit. It was due but had broken down in Honiara and had been postponed for an indefinite period.

Back to real life.

MEMORANDUM

TO: Director
Provincial Health Services
LATA
Temotu Province

NO: F.06/5/2(VI)

DATE: 30.7.97

Tel. No.

Your ref:

LATA WATER PROBLEM

Your letter of 29th July 1997 refers.

Firstly, I would greatly apologise for the continuous water problem faced by the residence of Lata Township. We can't do much at moment because of lack of proper needed resources but I hope that with your past period of stay in Lata, you should by now understand that situation we all faced particularly to the financial crisis in the country hence, affecting the Services to the Provinces. It should also be understood that Solomon Islands is still in the category of a third World Country and not fully civilised as United Kingdom where budgetry funds are readily available for all services. On that instance, we are unable to solve our problem on our own but to seek assistance from Honiara.

Temotu Province operates and relies mainly on the monthly grants from the Central Government. Such grants are not normally being paid to our expectations either and we are now in arrears since May 1997, when this accute water problem started. Thus, it greatly affected our own efforts in trying to alleviate our problematical situation.

We are handicapped from readily available resources; i.e. finance and materials. The Province has no vehicle fleet of her own to fetch water from the main source which is about 8 kilometres away from Lata and the tank you did mentioned in your letter cannot just walk on it's own from Lata to the source, refill itself and walk back by itself with the 800 gallons of water to Lata Hospital.

On finance, as per my paragraph three, it is impossible to hire private vehicles as Central Government cannot even afford to pay us the monthly grants on time for our services. There is also no good size of a truck with the current fleets of vehicles on the Santa Cruz roads that can be on lend to us for your 800 gallons tank.

Since the accute water problem started in May, I tried to seek immediate assistance from Central Governing bodies in Honiara but nothing so far received. Our appeals had gone to; the National Disaster Council, the Ministry of Transport and Communications to lend us their Water Carrier - their respond was negative, the Ministry of Provincial Government from whom we are still waiting their shipment of water tanks for Lata residences and the current two Temotuan sitting members of Parliament if they could also help out to our approaches to the Ministries concerned.

We had also approached the Malirgi Management for their truck to carry your tank to fetch water for the Hospital but given excuse that their vehicle was too old and could not carry that 800 gallons of water from the source to Lata. The Works Foreman of the Road and Bridges Section currently deployed to Santa Cruz had also been approached if they could lend us their dump truck but also excused on their road construction task which must be done within the time and programme given.

...../2

In such a situation, I suggest that common sense should be used and while the parent authority (Province) cannot immediately ratify the problem, our own Divisions should help and render self help approach to such emergency situations. The Medical has 3 vehicles, a Pick-Up and one Hilux. Why not allow them for that purpose? A minimal approach could otherwise ease the problem which is much better than just to wait and bark on and on, waiting for spoon feeding.

It must also be realised that Medical Services in Temotu had been recentra- lised in the past. Funds for it's services comes in direct to it's Lata Bank account and not via the Provincial budget. Therefore, if funds are in the Hospital account, then release payments to that emergency requirement for Lata Hospital. Do try and be operational in emergency ocassions.

Lastly, my good Doctor, I had sensed your letter as a personal attack, questioning the integrity of my office. The letter should not be copied to Public Notice Boards as it should have been a matter for your office, your mother Ministry and my office to sort out. It is degrading to some extend and I will not entertain anymore letters from your goodself to me on that manner. I repeat, <u>no more letters of that nature</u>.

Be further reminded that I will be closely watching out for such motives.

S P MEIOKO
Provincial Secretary
<u>Temotu Province</u>

cc: CNO/Temotu
cc: President/Temotu
cc: PS/MHMS
cc: PS/MPG
cc: PS/MTWC
cc: Director/NDC

Chapter 18

Canine Corpses and Contraception

LATA HOSPITAL

4th August 1997

Provincial Secretary
Temotu Province.

Dear Simon Peter

Very many thanks for your letter regarding the water problem in
Lata. I am only sorry it took a publicly displayed letter to
cause you to write. However, now you have informed me of some
of the facts I can now concentrate on trying to solve the hospitals
water problems within our own resources. Far from being a personal
attack upon your goodself, that letter was a cry for help. It is
amazing how far a little dissemination of information will go
in relieving peoples worries and fears.

Again, many thanks for your informative missive.

Yours sincerely

Dr. David Arathoon.
Director Provincial Health Services
TEMOTU PROVINCE.

The new canoe was ready. It was huge. It was beautiful. It completely overwhelmed the original and when Lynne offered to buy our old one I was initially uncertain what she was talking about. Of course she could buy it. I would have given it to her if she had made that request. Brown Kola had kindly delivered the new boat to Luova and it had been manhandled out of the water and into the shade of the trees by excited locals. It weighed a lot. On the advice of my friend the Bishop I had hired a local teacher (another Tikopian) to put an outrigger on and to make a mast and sail. I made a few fruitless journeys to Luova before my visit coincided with that of the teacher. He turned out to be a tall, wild-haired, huge-footed artisan who certainly knew his boat business. He and a silent smiling plump young man introduced to me as 'Moffat' carefully cut out and attached a beautiful outrigger to complement the ship. This all took some days presumably because the teacher was otherwise engaged on a lesser job, but Meg and I were present when the boat was finally launched with its outrigger attached. When it had initially been carried out of the water, eight or so various men and boys had been required to move it. On its even heavier return the teacher and smiling Moffat, being Tikopian, carried it themselves. It was as stable as a raft and Meg and I spent some time jumping in and out of it and splashing, much to their amusement.

I decided to get it straight out of the water, turn it upside down and get it dry again so I could paint it bright yellow from a can of paint Barry had kindly bought me for this purpose on his last trip to Honiara.

*

Bishop Lazarus blessing Tepukes.

An aside:

Barney: 'Dad ... why is the boat called "Blue-syphilis"?'

Me: 'Barnes – it's "Bucephalus" and he was a famous horse that Alexander the Great rode into all his battles – he was large and sturdy.'

Barney: 'What's "sturdy"?'

Me: 'Well, someone you can rely on ... anyway Alexander's horse was called "Bucephalus", and I thought that would make a fine name for a canoe, that we can rely on ... what do you think?'

Long scrutiny.

Barney: 'I think it should be called "Yellow-syphilis ..."'

Lynne had also been in Honiara, they both having trips courtesy of the VSA. While there she had investigated two canine problems – one for her and one for me. Mine involved her going to an Australian vet to pick up some 'Fox-pro' which I had ordered having been told it was an absolutely lethal dog poison. I couldn't wait to try it. While at the vet she had got advice on her own problem: the pubertal, randy pooch that she owned. The vet had given her written instructions for castration of her dog accompanied by simple line drawings done there and then in his office, and sufficient ketamine to put her mutt under long enough for me to follow the dots and extract his manhood. I was sceptical having experienced old Scabby face under the influence of drugs, but I was more than willing to give it a try.

On the allotted afternoon we adjourned to Lynne's house and invited Adam, the original man but soon a dog-with-no-descendants, into the bathroom, the floor having been scrubbed with Dettol so we could say it was clean. The stupid inquisitive dog followed us and looked round the bathroom door. Ha – he was caught by the scruff of the neck and pulled into the middle of the floor. By now he had sensed something was amiss and gazed round fearfully at the crowd of us around him. Lynne had already weighed him and I gave him the maximum recommended dose for his size – plus a sufficiency for luck. He soon became drowsy much to the excitement of the children who were determined to watch the de-bollocking. Sarah and Lynne stood by with cameras to record every detail. Adam sat, then he slipped forward with his nose on his front paws, then he grinned and finally slowly collapsed onto his right side with tongue lolling and excited children squeaking.

'OK Lynne, let's get him onto his back a bit while I put some gloves on and ... oh ... right ... um ...' The moronic dog had now vomited profusely all over the Dettolled floor. I glanced around. What to do? I went back into the sitting room, moved some of her furniture around, went back to the bathroom, grabbed him by his back legs and dragged him into the outer doorway of the sitting room where the light was good. His tongue continued to loll and he continued to grin. He was still breathing – just – and had a smear of vomit leading from his right ear back into the bathroom.

'OK, let's try again; Lynne could you unfold the instructions and put something on them to stop them blowing away – yup – put the picture on the other side next to the instruments.'

I reread the sparse instructions and Sarah and I contemplated the drawings for another few minutes. Then I incised where shown and faithfully followed all the instructions – the light was good and either through beginner's luck or skill the operation site remained blood-free with obvious anatomy. Within fifteen minutes we were back where we started, looking down at an unconscious dog that now had a single row of sutures on his scrotum instead of scrotal contents. The children were a bit let down that nothing exciting had happened. We threw his testicles into the bin to prevent him committing auto-cannibalism on waking.

'Well, keep an eye on him Lynne, give him a bit of water when he wakes, and er ... well ... let us know how he gets on?'

The children went back to the care of Hilda while Sarah and I headed back up the hill to the hospital to see a little boy of ten who had fallen out of a tree – we had no other details and I silently hoped it wasn't another cervical spine injury. Something relatively major

Lynne and ball-less pooch.

must have happened for us to be called back. We found Adrian in the clinical room looking a bit sheepish, but not with the strange angulated neck of the severely damaged. He looked pale. John Bakila told us that Adrian had been climbing a tree near his family's home, had slipped and fallen onto the house causing quite a bit of damage to the corner of the building, and as we could see, to his left arm.

Adrian's upper arm was covered with many too many dressings. In the bin I could see the huge pile of blood-soaked rags he had come in with and now he had a huge pile of clean dressings on, also pretty bloodstained. Again I tried to explain to our staff that if they wanted to stop bleeding, direct pressure through a minimum of dressings worked best. I could see the dulled look of those beyond persuasion. *Everyone* knew that if one dressing became blood soaked you just kept on adding more until the bleeding was staunched. Sarah gently removed Adrian's dressings to reveal a very large ragged dirty tear taking up most of his inner upper arm. It did not look very fresh and enquiry confirmed the wound was two days' old. Yuk. He still had decent pulses and working fingers and nerves beyond the wound, which was good. He needed to go to theatre via XR so we could clean up the wound and hopefully rule out a fracture. Knowing how long all this would take to get ready, we popped back home for a quick cup of tea and to ask Hilda if she could stay on for a bit to look after the children. On the way up our garden path I pointed out to Sarah that our vegetable patch now sported some rather fine melons, some pawpaw trees had appeared as if from nowhere, and best of all the limes looked nearly ready – we would soon be able to make lime-on juice cordial from our very own fruit. How all this had happened so quickly neither of us could explain. John-the-gardener only ever seemed to cut the grass, but he must behave like the cattle in a Gary Larson cartoon and get all his planting and weeding done when he knew we couldn't see.

Hilda was only too pleased to stay at our house looking after Meg and Barney. We had a cup of tea, and soon Sarah was commiserating with her about her daughter Wendy, and the devil and all her woes. As the tears began to flow I made 'going-back-to-the-hospital' movements with my fingers behind Hilda's back – Sarah raised her eyebrows indicating she would be along shortly once Hilda was in a fit state. The tears had turned into sobs and very nearly bellows by the time I got to the end of the garden path. A flicker of movement in the Limon tree caused me to look round. A thin green snake was whipping through the branches – surely I had time to have a closer look? I took a pace towards the tree, looked at my watch – decided against – took a step towards the hospital – remembered how few snakes I had seen on dry land in the Solomons (none) – two steps towards the Limon tree – no snake to be seen, and so a hurried walk back to Adrian and his ripped arm.

The XR did not show a fracture and Adrian was already on a trolley. John Bakila pushed him into theatre while I got changed into greens. Adrian used his good arm to transfer to the operating table, John put a butterfly cannula into the back of Adrian's right hand and I started to scrub. One of the nurses had gone out for a bucket of water and she carefully poured water onto my hands over the sink.

'John, when do you think the province are going to do something about the water?' John looked busy, but a half-cocked single eyebrow informed me that 'never' was probably when. He pulled the overhead theatre light to shine on Adrian's left arm. It looked dimmer than usual, but I could see that two of the four bulbs were still working. 'What about those bulbs we ordered three months ago John, any sign of them?'

'No more yet.' God. Still, two bulbs were better than none, and I suppose having any sort of theatre light was something. John slowly injected the ketamine, then the pethidine and finally the diazepam into the butterfly. I was always amazed that the diazepam worked, as we only mixed it with plain sterile water much against all western-ized instructions and it never seemed to clog a cannula. Adrian drifted off nicely. I was now clean and dressed in gown, hat and mask. John looked after the top end and another nurse undressed the wound again. I leant forward – actually it didn't smell foul at all. I daubed all that I could see with iodine tincture and then gowned-up the patient leaving only the iodined wound visible. Next I carefully felt along its length with my index finger. About two thirds of the way up the wound I felt something hard that shouldn't have been there. I couldn't get a grip of it and asked for a pair of heavy forceps. The hard thing was still difficult to get hold of but in the end I got a good purchase. It seemed well embedded. After trying unsuccessfully from various directions I tried pulling along the length of the tear. Just as Sarah came into theatre I extracted a bloody piece of grey rotting wood from the wound. It kept on coming and coming and only stopped when its entire seven inch length was out. We all looked shocked – how had something this big not been obvious? The extrac-tion was followed not by a jet of arterial lifeblood spurting all over the floor, but by a gentle bright drip. Phew. I continued exploring the wound and found further pieces of building in place, but none as spectacular as the first.

*

Ten years before: Essex: November evening: casualty department:

'See doc – vere's vis fing roigh tere,' pointing at the inside of his left wrist, 'dunno wot it is, mate.' Nor did I. He had been involved in a road traffic accident eight years before and sustained nasty injuries to his left wrist (due to being tough and not needing a seat belt) requiring two separate complex plastic surgery operations to give him some use of his hand. I felt the lump. It was hard. Something looked as if it was trying to escape. I asked a nurse for some forceps and a blade, made a small incision without local anaesthetic (well, he was 'ard) and gripped the 'fing' and pulled out an inch-long piece of windscreen. I put a sticky plaster over the wound, washed the piece of glass and sellotaped it to his casualty card.

'Ooh – fanks doc' and he was away.

Adrian started to wake soon after we had packed his wound with nice sterile saline-soaked gauze. I decided against stitching the wound immediately as it was two days old and had contained a significant amount of house. Suturing and asking such a wound to heal by first intent was froward to say the least. I decided to request the wound to give of its best, for after three days of open discharging and rest I would take Adrian, his left upper arm and wound (but minus the bits of house) back to theatre and then stitch it, hoping all the small bits of debris I was sure to have missed had had time to make themselves scarce. We didn't even write him up for antibiotics as everything smelt so good. In the Third World a sniff is as good as an agar plate back in the UK.

'Blimey – I thought that was going to turn into a major cock-up, what would we have done if there had been a fracture? What if he had had a durn great splinter stuck in an artery – that could have been interesting. What if …?'

'What if?'

'Yeah. What's this tree by the way?' We were finally walking back home and opposite the library was a scrawny tree with what looked like new buds on it.

'Dunno. Better ask Barry.'

'I think I am going to give that Fox-pro a go tonight.'

'You had better be monumentally careful – if it's as lethal as the vet made out and one of the pikinini gets hold of it, we are done for.'

'Hmm, I think I will only put two plates out – near the house and only for a few hours. Think that would be OK?' Sarah cocked an eyebrow in reply.

Fox-pro was innocuous looking stuff. Designed to be attractive to foxes in Australia it looked like pretend tofu-meat. It had quite a strong odour – not pleasant but probably sufficient to entice four-legged mammals that spent their leisure time nuzzling the faeces of other canines.

'Let's hope *this* works, because if it doesn't I think I will give up.' I had warned by mouth everyone in the hospital about what was going on, I had put notices up around the station and generally let it be known that this was the week for everyone to keep their pet dogs in overnight. Most I spoke to seemed disinterested.

It worked all right.

The next morning walking along the verandah on my way to work I thought I could spy the back leg of one of my mongrel cur enemies poking out from under the steps. I grabbed a stick and crept along hoping to surprise him with a terminal blow both to his ego and his skull. He didn't move; I inched along. At last more of him came into view and I could now see that the blaggard was fast asleep on his back with his legs in the air. Oh no he wasn't, he was lying on his back with his legs in the air – DEAD.

'Yee-haw.' The rest of the family rushed out to see what all the fuss was about. We all went and examined the slowly swelling corpse. He seemed to have a piece of custom rope tied round his neck to the steps – had the thought of being outwitted by the whiteman caused him to hang himself from our verandah steps? I was mystified until John-the-gardener mooched up the path to tell us that what little Fox-pro had been eaten last night had been extremely successful. He knew of three other dogs that had died, and he knew that the owner of 'our' corpse had dragged him to our house as a protest. John suggested he drag Rover into the undergrowth and incinerate him as he indicated that the smell would soon be bad.

I was so pleased with my work that I grinned all the way to work. Four bastards in one night, and not a sign of a dead child. I couldn't wait to tell Wilson. He was on the steps of the nursing station looking more lugubrious than usual. Perhaps John-the-gardener had told him about the canine carnage on his way past the hospital.

'Wilson, Wilson, you know that dog poison I told you I was going to put out last night? Well it worked an absolute treat – four of the damned things are dead.'

'Savvy dog blo' me?'

'Ya,' a pup, the latest Lyno household acquisition.

'Him die finis.'

LATA HOSPITAL

15th September 1997

Dentist & On call Surgeon
Central Hospital
Honiara.

Dear Doctors and Dentist

Re: Patrick POSA
Age Approx 38 Yrs

This man fell from a ship last night in the Reef Islands and
was then hit in the face with a propellar from on OBM. He had
no LOC & didn't seem to inhale any sea water. He has had no
difficulty breathing but has pain in his jaw and neck. The
facial wound bled quite profusely.

O/E   Conscious and alert
       V. Swollen, brused face/jaw/neck
       Extensive lacerations of lips (through and through)
       Mandible obviously fractured as severely distorted and
       the left moves independently to the right.

       P 68. BP 130/80   RR 26   T 37.1 °C

       HS - Normal

       Chest - Clear

       Abdo - nad

Plan   IV up   NBM
       Hb 107
       WBC 20.8

No XR facilities as our XR technician has absconded without
permission.

Yours faithfully

Dr. David Arathoon.
Director Provincial Health Services
Temotu Province.

B: I have also put him on
cloxacillin IV and flagyl PR

Chapter 19

Nets and a Nitwit

LATA HOSPITAL

8th April 1997

Chief Health Planning Officer (Ag)
Ministry of Health & Med. Services
P O Box 349
Honiara.

Dear Sir

Many thanks for your request for our five (5) years Health plan
here in Temotu Province.

I have to admit I was a bit confused by your request. You donot
state what sort of data you require and the information you wish
us to read and make appropriate comments on is meaningless.
We have many problems here in Temotu which tend to prevent us
thinking as long term as five (5) years:

1. Service and Wages Grant:

   Currently more than four (4) months overdue. Difficult to
   make any meaningful plans when we are unsure from one month
   to another if we will have any money in our account.

2. Communications

   a). Verbal/Written: I have had a singular lack of success
   when asking MHMS for any advice. Letters tend to go
   unanswered and faxes forgotten. We do have more luck
   dealing with Hospital consultant, but they can be
   extremely difficult to track down.

   b). Shipping: Since the privatization of the shipping lines
   we have had great difficulties obtaining such basics
   as fuel for OBMs and the hospital truck, as well as
   patients rations.

3. Nursing Staff

   For at least the last year we have been lacking our full
   quota of nursing staff. This makes the day to day running
   of the hospital sometimes very difficult and has meant the
   closure of Health clinics from time to time.

4. Doctors

Temotu is considered a poor place to work by the Central -
Medical Profession.   That is the only reason to explain the
lack of a full-time Doctor in the Province for the 18 months
before March 1996. That would also explain why Doctors refuse
to do locums here to cover the expatriate Doctors leave.

However there are a few projects which the Province should be
able to achieve in the next five (5) years.

1. Malaria

It is generally agreed that the rate of decrease in malaria
in Temotu is not as great as in the rest of the country.
Steps have already been taken to combat this.

We are considering an eradication programme on the Duff
islands. This may be completed this year.

2. Health Education

This most important subject has been covered extremely poorly
by our previous Health Education Officer. He is supposed
to be replaced and things can then only improve.

3. Medical Cover

It is essential that when the Expatriate Doctors leave in
early 1998 that at least one of the positions is covered
immediately.

I hope this very unexciting plan is of some use to you.

Yours sincerely

Dr. David Arathoon.
Director Provincial Health Services
TEMOTU PROVINCE.

Hammocks definitely had their advantages. However, it now seemed to me that they may be outweighed by what seemed to be major drawbacks. The drawbacks revolved around time. Time and peace. And leisure. Time to think and cogitate. Time to contemplate people: Yachties, Birdman, Butterflyman etc. Time to think about life and the universe. Why is it that people in the First World join gyms? They join gyms to fill time, to get fitter to stay alive longer to spend more time ... at the gym. They could be at home cogitating, but no, they are in the gym being mindless and winding up their endorphins to 'feel better'. Better than what? Better than they deserve with their empty lives full of pastimes which fill time and avoid thought. Thought is dangerous.

What is it all for? What are we up to? Why? – more to the point. The hammock enables me to see that there isn't a reason. We are not here 'for' something or someone. We are here by chance. Chance started and runs the universe. We are lucky in that we can use hammocks to discover these things, but actually most of us spend most of our lives filling our time with mindlessness. We shop, we go to the gym, we go to church and we neglect hammocks. Not that it matters of course. Chance sorts everything out in time. The hammock says: 'Do as you would be done by.' That just about covers it really. Murder, adultery, theft of camels etc., etc. Simpleness.

Even lying in the arms of the hammock however did not stop me feeling extreme anger at Birdman. I thought back to his arrival. Like most of our visitors he suddenly appeared as if preordained. I slitted my eyes in concentration, reached for my coffee and gently swung the hammock on the verandah to aid my memory. Yup, at first he had come across as a smiling pleasant young chap, somewhat hirsute it has to be said, but that in itself was not enough to engender quite the anger I felt for him. In the end it became obvious he was a taker and not a giver. He accepted our offer of accommodation and hence food with alacrity. His mission was to get out to Vanikoro Island to murder specimens of a non-descript 'White eye' bird he had heard was to be found there. He wanted samples to take back to the UK. All this was excusable and mostly something to be encouraged. He wanted to increase the knowledge of mankind by killing a few non-descript birds and then describing them. One of the problems was that his visit followed that of John Tennant, or 'Butterflyman'. He was resourceful in a different way. He refused to be housed by us, and was only persuaded with difficulty to share our food. He was also after non-descript organisms, in his case butterflies, and particularly 'little blue jobbies' as he would call them. He had all the right contacts in the Natural History Museum, and was a great, quiet, efficient enthusiast. Within a day of his arrival I had been bitten by the butterfly murdering bug and cut a nine-foot length of bamboo, re-bent a thick wire coat-hanger, cut and stitched up an old mosquito net (actually it was brand new, but my mind's eye lay happier on the lie) and made my own butterfly net. I had to make a smaller trial-sized model first to make sure the large one would work. It did. I gave the prototype to Meg and she and her brother spent many a happy hour pursuing very descript bright coloured butterflies around the garden dressed in their underpants and a hat. The butterflies soon learnt that the approach of noisy, shrieking, laughing, arguing, mad-looking, net-wielding pre-humans meant flittering flight was required urgently. The outcome was that the corpse-count was much lower than the fun-count.

Most evenings I would see the prototype-net lying outside and would tell Meg to bring it in, in case a pikinini was overwhelmed by desire for such a magnificent object. 'If you leave it out, someone will steal it.'

One day someone did. Meg came to me and asked if I had seen her net. No. Where have you looked? Everywhere. So I looked everywhere as well. No net. Had she brought it in last night? Unsure. That meant she hadn't.

'Seems like someone has stolen it then doesn't it?' Lots of tears, then more tears when Barney found out. Could I make another? I could, but not right now. Off to Hilda for sympathy.

'I told her, I told her,' I said to Sarah.

'I think she has learnt her lesson now. Do you think you could make her another?'

'Of course, but not right now.' Right now I was off with John-the-butterflyman to hunt butterflies. We were due to be out all day. Sarah said she would cover the hospital and Wilson Yamalo said he would drop us off on the road up to the provincial farm which Butterflyman thought looked like a likely place to perform Lepidoptera-cide. We set off with the orb of the sun still low in the horizon. Tinakula seemed more upset than usual and plumes of smoke and ash streamed from her summit continuously. I took this to be a good omen, due to my lack of understanding of volcanoes. But of course it wasn't. Sitting in the back of the bumpy truck I felt like a guilty schoolboy on the skive. The day was still mild, the sun was out, the volcano was performing, what more could one ask for? What we should have asked for were some butterflies. Within an hour of being dropped off we were tired, dusty and thirsty. The local Lepidoptera were obviously all off at a convention because they certainly weren't near the road to the farm. We trudged on and on and on and soon added 'hungry' to our repertoire of sensations. Butterflyman did not see anything new. He kept his arm in with a few swishes of his net followed by a torsal crush which separated the life from its butterfly, the physical half of which ended up in a labelled envelope, the metaphysical half returning to its maker.

We decided to stop for lunch under an old tree overhanging the white-hot-reflective coral road. Lunch was a tin of tuna ... each. John's idea of bliss. The afternoon was a mirror image of the morning in that we walked and walked, strove and strove but very few butterflies did we see, let alone kill. Only Tinakula changed; she became less angry and her outpourings dwindled to nil. Her evil eye had done its job on us and she could not see the point in using up more energy than was strictly necessary. It was all a tremendous let down. I felt terrible that our island had proved such a poor killing ground, and John felt bad about dragging me away from my 'important work' at the hospital. Finally, and not a moment too soon, I saw Wilson Yamalo driving along looking for us. We had virtually walked back to Lata by then, but the thought of being driven the last mile was luxury. Wilson stopped and I leapt into the back, putting a hand out to help Butterflyman with his gear.

'I think I'll walk the last bit home thanks. You know it's looking possible the little blighters will come out again.' He was desperate so I waved to him through the dust, a large and now forlorn figure.

Not forlorn by suppertime when he reappeared, clean, tidy and grinning.

'Just after you left' (of course ...) 'I followed a small track off the road leading to a garden. On the right side I came across a tree with *these* on it.' John opened an envelope and tipped out three very small and decidedly blue, undistinguished butterflies. He was very pleased with himself.

'I'm sure they are non-descript, they look similar to some I have seen in the British Museum, but to my eye they are a new species.' A new species. My mind flew with the idea. A new species. Here on Santa Cruz. A new species. A bad thought crossed my mind. I tried to look nonchalant, but Sarah caught me looking into the middle distance across the bay, grinning and holding the single female non-descript little blue jobby. A NEW SPECIES. She also got a glimpse of my bad thought before I could shut it back up.

'I suppose you want to go back with John tomorrow morning to that small tree on the way to someone's vegetable garden, hey?'

'Well ...'

'I wonder what the poor overworked, heavily pregnant locum would say? The one on maternity leave?'

'Well ...'

John grinned.

We did set off the next morning. Before the time of the ward round we had found the path and the tree, and there they were, all fluttering round still. John was very pleased. He swished two or three times and caught another couple. In total that made four males and one female. After each swish of the net the remainder would rise up and then gently settle back to whatever they considered best on a Wednesday morning, on that particular tree. John had shown me the difference between males and females, and let on that he really needed more of the type with similar sex chromosomes. He was getting edgy looking through his flock to try and spot another female. I gazed wistfully.

Then:

'Ooh John ... isn't that another female?' and I drew back my bamboo/coat-hanger/mosquito-net net ready to swish and strike.

'Aah ... let's just have a—' but it was too late; I swished and struck and caught three of the little blue jobbies. John was crestfallen as he had seen the female float up to the top of the tree.

'Sorry John ...'

'Well ... not to, er, worry ... well, let's have a look at the blokes you have caught.' He turned the flicked-over net and suddenly went still. His hands were only metaphorically shaking but his voice was physically. 'You've caught a female,' he said with very nearly an exclamation mark. And so I had. John gently crushed the life out of her and her male colleagues and we lifted them out of the net and gazed in rhapsody. I had never realized that I could feel so good, so elevated, so excited and cheerful by causing the death of another creature – but I surely did.

We set off home for a coffee and a chat, and met Sarah coming up the path. She could see how pleased we were, and as I had only been skiving a few hours she was pleased in her turn. She did have one difficult question, 'How can you tell it's a female?' I graciously let John explain.

'I forgot to say, John Bakila says that a yachtie came in this morning asking if someone could have a look at his pregnant wife.'

'What did you say?'

'I said of course ... but don't worry, *I* will see her this afternoon.'

'Don't forget about the charge ...' I had always tried to invite ourselves on board whenever a yachtie came to town, and considered a look round their yacht payment for any services rendered.

'Well ...' Sarah didn't like to ask.

She didn't have to; having examined a rather pretty Iranian lady, wife of the American yachtie, we were invited to supper on their boat at a seldom used anchorage near the airstrip. The pretty Iranian was very westernized and was in the early stages of her first untroubled pregnancy. She was fine. She didn't wear many clothes from the Santa Cruz point of view, but there were sufficient to be fine by me.

We cycled down at dusk, with both children on best behaviour, and were met at the corally shore by a dinghy containing Mr American-yachtie. Actually he was pretty civilized too and came across very polite and generous. They had prepared an amazing meal for us from their dried and frozen foods. This included a succulent steak and *real* potatoes. We had wine and even ice cream. Best of all we were shown round their neat boat, having everything explained to us as we went. It became obvious that they were getting as much out of our company as we were getting from theirs. It seemed romantic to sail the Pacific waves as a happy pair, but it seemed that they also required some outside input, perhaps just to remind themselves how lucky they were. I think we did too.

Our evening finished with both Sarah and even-less-clad-pretty-Iranian-lady jumping into the sea for a cooling dip. Neither of them had had a drop of alcohol, but they both seemed happy. As Sarah swam ashore to our bikes the children and I were carefully rowed back. I was somewhat tipsy and had a bit of difficulty getting Meg into the child seat, but then we were away. The mosquitoes had all gone to bed and the stars shone brightly on our meandering way back along the airstrip.

'Do you remember that massive yacht?'

'Oh God, yeah.' It had been an abomination: sixty-five feet of first-class catamaran, bathrooms for each cabin, on-board desalination plant sufficient to provide tons of fresh water a day. Enough to make sure that all visitors washed the salt off their legs with hot clean water on boarding. Or perhaps it was just us? The ship was on its maiden voyage and was shaking down well. There was an Aussie skipper and a Brit chef with a wife who cleaned and waited on table.

It was overwhelming. The family who owned the ship were friendly enough but one could tell from their chatter that they had been cocooned and insulated by the ship from every port they had visited. They could have been sailing round the Isle of Wight ...

'Or that mad Aussie couple?'

'Yeah ... amazing.' They had appeared from their anchorage quite far down the bay, again in an unusual place, and I had bumped into him laughing and chatting with some locals near to the market. At the time I thought he must be an unusual chap as our locals were sensibly wary of outsiders and certainly didn't chat and laugh at the drop of a hat. He was a real character and put everyone he met at ease. Soon I had managed to wangle a look round the yacht he shared with his wife, accompanied again by an evening meal. We had an uproarious time, he, his wife, Sarah and I and our two squeezed onto the back deck of his small yacht. He plied us with homemade beer and wine (me, I should say, as Sarah was not a drinker), and they gave us a lovely meal cooked from ingredients they had bought from our market and from fish they had caught themselves. Horace and his wife were about fifty years old and had decided never to have children. It was surprising then to see them interact with our two. They weren't all over them and they didn't ignore them. They treated them like a nephew and niece, and kept them entertained without visible excess or stress. Very unusual. We left with a goody bag filled with jars of home-made jams and home-preserved fruit. We had arranged for the hospital truck to collect us at 9 pm, which was just as well as other-wise we would have been there all night. They were gone by the morning and we were a little sad.

My mind came back to Birdman and I could feel my anger grow again when I remembered the next time I saw him. I was on tour and contemplating Quentin Crewe. I had sent him an ancient adze head made of giant clam as a very early Christmas present. Not only had he received it but had written back to thank me for it. I still felt enormously important to have such a pen pal. Mr Crewe told me that he had placed the adze upon his mantelpiece where he could see it easily, and more importantly from where he could get it down to appreciate its workmanship and texture. He had a way with words I could never attain, but I completely understood his sentiment. These adze heads were to be found on the outer islands where they had been dropped either at the end of their useful lives or when the newfangled metal ones began to be used. Some were quite crude and often stained with betel juice, but now and again one would be found that was a beauty. I had asked the locals to look out for them so that next time I came on tour I could buy some more. This was the next time, and having contemplated Quentin Crewe my mind naturally turned to whether or not anyone on Vanikoro had found me some more adzes. The very last thing I was expecting to see was Birdman. He had come out from Vanikoro in a canoe before we docked and the first I knew about him was seeing him striding along the side deck, huge grin on face and huge rucksack on back.

Poking out of the top of the rucksack was an object I recognised ... Grrrr.

'Hey, great to see you, you'll never guess ...'

'What the hell is that?'

' ... I did finally get to see that White-eye and ...'

'Sure, sure, BUT WHAT IS THAT?'

'Oh this is the butterfly net, I thought it may come in useful out here on Vanikoro ... anyway, I saw a few to begin with but the ...'

'I know what it is ... why have you got it?'

'*You know*, I borrowed it to come on the tour, anyway I finally got the local chief to say I could kill a few and ...'

'Look: that net went missing from our house. We all spent many hours looking for it and both children were *very* upset that it had gone ...'

'Oh, I thought I had asked Sarah ...'

' ... AND we led the children to believe that local pikininis must have taken it.'

'Oh, I thought I had asked Sarah if I could borrow it.'

'Well she spent a long time looking for it and even longer consoling Meg and Barney.'

'Oh ... sorry ...'

'Hmm, well at least I haven't got round to making another yet, but I think I will just take it back now if that's OK,' and I did, drawing it not too carefully out of his rucksack.

'So you see I did manage to get a couple,' at which he held up a dead, rather sorry-looking bird which was impaled on what looked like an ice cream stick.

He was incorrigible.

1st April 1997

Under Secretary Health Care
Ministry of Health & Med. Services
P O Box 349
HONIARA.

Dear Lester

Many thanks for arranging for 3 Doctors to cover our annual leave
in Feb/March this year. Unfortunately not one of them actually
arrived in the Province and again we were Doctorless for an
extended period. Thanks again for trying.

Yours sincerely

Dr. David Arathoon.
Director Provincial Health Services
TEMOTU PROVINCE.

cc: Dr. Obed Alemaena

Chapter 20

Anuta

TEMOTU PROVINCE

LATA
SANTA CRUZ
SOLOMON ISLANDS

The Islands on:
Ndeni (Santa Cruz)
Tinakula
Reef Islands
Pileni
Matema
Nupani
Nukapu
Nifiloli
Duff Islands
Utupua
Vanikoro
Tikopia
Anuta
Fataka

In reply please quote reference no.   F: 01/1/1   DATE: 18 June 1997

Provincial Police Commander
LATA
Temotu Province

Dear Sir,

UNLAWFUL GAMBLING IN GOVERNMENT PREMISES

It has been of great concern that while your office and
mine are trying to stop unlawful gambling in Government
owned premises at Lata Township, our Public officers are
doing things the opposite. They actively continue to engage
themselves in unlawful gamblings in Government premises
while the Public expects them to uphold law and order.

Reliable sources had reported that our Public/Police officers
continuously do gambling at QXX in Lata at nights, mostly
disturbing neighbours who raised concerns and uneasy feelings
about the situation. Related problems had also been reported
and in particular, one usual gambler had unlawfully committed
sexual intercourse with a married woman, occupant of the
said quarter.

Such a situation will certainly bring in more problems and
disturbances if it is allowed to continue. Thus, the purpose
of this letter is to seek cooperation from your high esteemed
office again in trying to curb the situation, expecting
the uniformed men in leading the role in stopping such unlawful
games from continuing. At the sametime, all Heads of Divisions
should do the same. Render assistance, speak to the staffs
under our direct control and advise them not to engage themselves in unlawful gamblings at Government Quarters.

Yours in the name of good law enforcements,

S. P. MEIOKO
Provincial Secretary
TEMOTU PROVINCE

cc: All Divisional Heads → PNO
cc: DPS/Temotu
cc: Occupant/Q38 - Mr. Palusi
cc: Commissioner of Police/Honiara

On that very tour I had finally made it to the fabled Anuta – it was worth the wait. Prior to that we had spent a couple of days at Tikopia; this was useful because I needed time to get the water tank up and attached to the gutter from the back of Nancy's clinic. All the doubters were somewhat shocked to see the beautiful new water tank come off the ship and be carried ceremoniously and cheerfully by the local lads, from the beach to the oversized clinic. I had brought some of my tools with me from Lata as well as Wilson Yamalo, and between us we got the thing erected. The local cheerleaders were led by Charlie, number two chief's grandson, who took an avid interest in the whole thing.

At the end of the first day, just as Yamalo, Lyno, John Bakila and I were settling onto our uncomfortable slatted beds at the clinic (we thought that they would be more comfortable than the bunks on the ship – we were wrong) Charlie reappeared looking for me. He wanted to know if I would like to go night fishing with him. I wasn't quite sure what he meant at first. I knew the Tikopians were renowned for their nocturnal hunt of the garfish from their customized dugout outriggers, each fitted with a stand amidships upon which stood a pressure paraffin lamp to attract the garfish. This was not what we were going to do. Charlie showed me his 'fishing tackle'. It was a very crude harpoon-gun consisting of a three-foot piece of iron 'bar' (used to strengthen concrete) which had been sharpened at one end. The propulsion was provided by a thick length of rubber tied together to form a loop. At one point on the loop was tied a piece of wood approximately six inches long and rounded to fit comfortably into the palm of a hand. The gun was cocked by placing the opposite side of the loop from the handle against the blunt end of the bar, stretching the rubber and gripping the handle against the bar nearer the pointy end. It was extremely basic but looked powerful and could be used one handed. Charlie suggested I have a go on dry land in our room. I gripped, stretched and aimed – everyone else in the room took cover – I chose a piece of my bed and let go of the bar, retaining the handle – THWACK – the bar was well embedded. It took me a few minutes to release it. Wilson Lyno suggested I didn't try again indoors. This was going to be fun.

Night had fallen. Charlie took back his fishing tackle and led me to his grandfather's hut where he picked up a couple of dead waterproof torches and a couple of his young friends. Charlie obviously had no spare batteries, but wasn't to be fazed. We all went down to his personal canoe, got in and silently paddled out to a tourist yacht anchored out near the reef. Charlie jumped aboard which took the American couple a little by surprise, but having had the full frontal charm exerted on them they popped below to get a few sets of batteries. I am not sure what Charlie told them but they may have got the erroneous impression that they had been invited fishing with us. While they faffed about getting waterproof jackets on (?) and getting their dinghy over the side we slipped away, careful not to use our torches until we were a long way off. We could hear them for the next twenty minutes or so above the surf, calling out to Charlie before they got bored and returned home. I wore my snorkel, mask and a pair of fins; Charlie and his mates only had masks. At one point I persuaded Charlie to try the snorkel as it seemed to me a lot more efficient to keep one's face under the water looking for prey while breathing through a snorkel, rather than having to lift one's face (and hence eyes) every thirty seconds or so to take a breath. He kindly went through the motions, but soon reverted to the simpler tried and tested system he was used to.

The water was warm, the surf murmuring, the stars glinting, the garfish-men quietly chatting, the torches playing over the beauty of the reef. What a great way to spend an hour of one's life.

I followed Charlie through the water. When he got excited and pointed I made my greatest efforts to see what he was trying to show me – usually to no avail. Then when he dived along the path of his pointing finger I followed him down. He would cock the fishing tool at the surface, gently glide down and down, aim carefully at a rather bright part of the reef and fire. Suddenly that part of the reef transmogrified into a bright fish – more often than not sporting a three-foot length of bar from its eye. Occasionally I would spot a more dozy fish before Charlie and draw his attention to it, and occasionally he went down – torch in one hand, gun in the other – and brought it back up to me to extract from the bar. The fish were placed in the bottom of the canoe, which was keeping pace with us, propelled by the lazy hanging arm of one of the other boys in the water.

The canoe quickly filled with fish – and some things even better. Charlie's eyes seemed to be able to penetrate every nook and cranny – and if perchance a crayfish had backed into one in an attempt to avoid the torch beam – Charlie would shoot down, grip the outcrop of coral and have a good look under and into it. Then he would slowly bring up his rubber powered harpoon gun and dispatch the cray. Yum.

I did not see one Crown-of-Thorns starfish, thank God.

After an hour or so I was shivering with cold, I had severe nipple rub from the salt water and my T-shirt and Charlie decided it was time to call it a night. He gathered us all together and we swam towards shore pushing the canoe along, all in high spirits. While we had been out a small wind had got up and the surf had changed from a gentle murmur into not quite a roaring but certainly a loud grumbling. I was very pleased to see that in all the excitement Charlie and his friends lost control of the canoe and it broached in the surf. They were *not* happy ... They righted the canoe in a flash, bailed her in another embarrassed flash and we collected at least half of the very dead fish which had taken the opportunity to escape. We did however collect all the crayfish. Some of the escapees sank without trace and some drifted beyond the range of our torches. It was a strange end to the evening.

I was whacked, sweaty and soaked when I got back to the clinic to find all my colleagues gently snoring away. My slats suddenly looked pretty damn comfy and I slept the sleep of the dead all night, drying out the while.

The next day we were due to leave for the remote island of Anuta. At what seemed like first light Charlie reappeared and said I had been invited for breakfast at his grandfather's home – number two chief. I put on my best (and at this stage also my worst) shorts and T-shirt and followed Charlie along the narrow sandy paths to the number two chief's hut. I bent double to enter and was warmly greeted by the chief and his wife and extended family. Breakfast consisted of a huge pile of grilled crayfish, most of whom I recognised, slippery cabbage and sticky rice. All washed down with fresh water. A feast. I felt very distinguished sitting with such important people but actually I had been invited for another reason altogether. The family wanted my opinion on one of the male relatives. The poor chap was wheeled in and asked to open his mouth. Most of the right side of his tongue and pharynx were taken up with a huge fungating smelly cancer. He grinned away but must have been in some pain. Tikopians don't seem to understand physical pain. From the look of his blackened teeth he had been an avid chewer of betel nut all his life, and unfortunately all the noxious carcinogens within the natural betel nut were going to cause his demise sooner rather than later. Through Charlie I asked what they would like me to do. I could take him back to Lata; perhaps get him on a plane to Honiara. It was not impossible that he could get palliative radiotherapy in Australia. Actually what he and they wanted was for him to stay on Tikopia – perhaps I could leave some paracetamol behind in the unlikely event he felt any pain later? Somehow I got myself into the position of promising more; I would make phone enquiries of consultants in Honiara and send 'some medicine'. In the event, having spoken to the chief dentist (who must have got sick of the sight of oral cancer) I sent a few pills of methotrexate, a nasty chemotherapeutic agent. Whether the man was still alive when they arrived I would never find out. Not a pleasant way to go.

Having had my fill physically and concurrently been drained mentally, I wandered back to the oversized clinic to observe the latest inoculations. We had paraffin-powered fridges in an attempt to keep the old cold chain rattling along, and from one of these John Bakila was quietly and efficiently jabbing all the babes and children presented to him by Nancy the local nurse. He looked quite content if somewhat incongruous with a frangipani flower tucked behind his right ear. Wilson Lyno was sorting out a few patients – yet more cases of Tikopian tuberculosis to bring back to Lata for six months' free food and lodging. And treatment. As seemed so often to be the case I felt surplus to requirements and didn't take much persuading by Yamalo that we should circumnavigate the caldera that the island consisted of. Nancy soon found a couple of young boys to show us the way. I took my net and caught a few butterflies – the butterfly fauna of Tikopia was quite well described so it was rather a desultory hunt in the heat of the day. We wandered along the southern low-lying side of the island taking many interweaving sandy paths between large shady trees until we reached a large rocky outcrop: 'Tevetekoro' apparently. Just beyond was the sandy bar which separated the fresh-ish water in the caldera from the sea. We jumped over the incomplete canal which had been cut through this in readiness for the annual release of water and fish. The eastern and northern inner slopes of the caldera got steeper and steeper; the butterfly net generously morphed into a climbing aid. Yamalo and the boys went up like mountain goats leaving the sweating panting dripping white doctor in their wake. They kindly consented to stop at the very top where there were views all around: to the sea and ship to the north and the caldera lake, sandy bar, rocky outcrop, reef and then the endless sea to the south. After five minutes of dripping and puffing I did finally manage to raise my head and get up from my collapsed seating position to enjoy the vista. Magnificent.

But also moving: we could see a small line leaving the huge clinic heading back to the shore in readiness to re-board the ship. Yamalo suggested we get a move on. I wondered what the chances of being left behind were, but decided not to challenge the thought. We all ran helter-skelter down to the beach, back to the clinic to pick up our belongings and tools and finally out to the ship by the last boat. Charlie and his friends and relatives said goodbye, our young guides came down to the beach to do the same and just as the ship pulled away from the shore and the descending sun, Nancy came into the water's edge to wave. I felt moved and a bit 'swallowy' but I was not sure why.

The sun set rapidly and we had a swift supper of rice and fish on board. Then it was a collapse into our bunks until the early dawn.

When the early cartographers went to Tikopia they at least could measure the place in units of kilometres or miles, but when they got to Anuta they were reduced to yards and metres. And inches. It was tiny. It also didn't look too glamorous in the cloudy morning murk and drizzle. It really was small. An ex-volcano like Tikopia, but this time a volcanic plug with a bit of surrounding flat land for gardens, as opposed to Tikopia's huge water-filled crater with surrounding gardens. As we got nearer to the island the weather began to lift a little and the drizzle gradually drew to a close. I went with Wilson Lyno, John Bakila and the cooled vaccines in the first canoe ashore. A proportion of the population meeting us on the coralline strand were dressed in traditional Tapa cloth clothes and looked romantic if somewhat chilled. We set up our clinic under the tree where Sarah had famously had her public consultation with a foreigner – in this case a Tongan national with a well-muscled torso and pretty much shaven head. He wanted something for his 'spots' and Sarah dismissed him by saying that his acne would improve 'when he grew up'. At that time she did not know that he was a wanted runaway from Tonga having stolen a motor boat and headed off into the wide blue Pacific Ocean, run out of fuel/food/water/sense and drifted for some time before the miracle of bumping softly into Anuta. He had left Tonga precipitously as he had been accused of murder. The general consensus was that he was probably guilty but that Polynesian hospitality forbade the elders giving him up. Sarah was pleasantly shocked when this was whispered to her later by our nurses. All the Anutans were very impressed by the white female doctor.

I held a clinic under the famous tree for a few hours, seeing patients, helping John Bakila with the inoculations, and gradually sorting the sheepish non-TB sufferers from the goatee-TB sufferers. The whole time, in my peripheral vision, I was aware of a plump smiling very un-sick looking young man trying to catch my eye. After a while I thought that he must think that he knew me. A little while later I realized I knew him, but couldn't for the life of me place his face and large frame. As I kept my eyes averted from him it niggled away at me and I got more and more frustrated with myself the longer the clinic went on. I began to worry what I would say to him once the clinic was over and he came over to say hello. The penultimate patient saved the day. He was a more complicated case and I had to concentrate. As soon as he was replaced by the last patient my now empty mind was filled with Moffat's name, for it was he. He had helped the teacher build the outrigger for *Bucephalus* back at Luova on Santa Cruz. I smiled at him and saw his face break in half with a huge reciprocal smile. 'How are you Moffat? Let me see this last chap and I will be with you.'

He was indescribably chuffed at being recognized and I in turn was immensely relieved to remember his name. Very unlike me. It was a strange feeling to be recognized on a tiny island in the middle of the watery wastes of the south Pacific. Moffat came over and shook my hand, continuously grinning away. My Pidgin was execrable and his near silence was due to poor English but we communicated well enough. He indicated that as the clinic was over, would I like to come along with him? – you bet. We headed inland along more sandy, shaded paths very reminiscent of the day before. As we walked I suddenly had a sensation of déjà vu. I stopped and looked about me. Ahead lay a straight sandy path, and when I turned round there was the same gently concave sandy path behind. There was quite a lot of detritus on the path: leaves and coconut husks and bits and bobs. It wasn't déjà vu; it was an unswept Tika dart pitch. Moffat confirmed my feelings and I felt very pleased to have recognized it, and now to have seen both the pitches on the planet.

About halfway up the pitch on the right side heading towards the lump of the volcanic plug we came to a lean-to amongst the trees. Under this sat a middle-aged topless woman fiddling about. Moffat introduced us as we joined her and it slowly became clear that this was his mother. I could see where he got his smile from, although hers was desecrated by natural betel nut blackness. Moffat wanted to know if I would like something to eat. I was getting very hungry and accepted his hospitality, thinking we would have to return to the 'village' to do so, although we had only just sat down with his mother under the three-foot-high lean-to. But no – she leant forward, lifted a dried coconut husk from a few embers which had not until then been in evidence, blew on the embers, put back the husk at which the small fire sprang to life. Next she reached down beside her and lifted a banana leaf and took three small fish from a pile. The small fish were still twitching with freshness and were neither scaled nor gutted but simply placed on the coconut husk fire. After a few minutes they were each carefully lifted by the tail with a bony finger and thumb and turned over with an accompanying smile from mum. A few minutes more and Moffat and I were each handed a banana leaf plate upon which lay a grilled reef fish. The skin and scales had blackened and come away from the flesh. The guts and contents stayed put and we ate by hand with relish. This was without doubt the most delicious fish I had ever eaten.

Still is.

After our meal Moffat really did need to return to his house for an undisclosed, or in fact, poorly understood reason. He knew I wanted to carry on exploring the island and handed me over to the care of a group of young boys who had nothing better to do. In fact they had lots of better things to do: climbing trees, chasing each other and playing with puppies to name a few, but they gladly gave up their time to get close to the whiteman and practise their rudimentary English. I was put in the special care of another Moffat, younger and absolutely no relation to *Bucephalus*-Moffat. He took his duties seriously and stayed at my side pointing out occasional butterflies while his friends raced back and forth. A very pleasant gang. After a few minutes they had a conflab and seemed to come to some conclusion. Moffat approached and asked if I would like a green coconut to drink. On seeing me agree one of the other boys shot up a nearby, alarmingly leaning coconut tree and within seconds was right at the top chucking down nuts. The whole point of this demonstration was so they could bring up the subject of the Tongan refugee. They had the most amazing and important piece of information to impart about this probable killer:

'*He couldn't climb a coconut tree.*'

They fell about with laughter when they realized I had grasped their meaning. They couldn't believe it. Nor could I. How could he have survived? I wondered. This in turn brought up the subject of trees and land and belongings. On Santa Cruz each damp patch of reef, each square inch of land and every last soaring forest giant is owned by someone or someone's family, whereas on Anuta all the coconut trees are held in common ownership. This perfection of communism seemed to work well. I was unable to understand what happened with the land and gardens, but it looked like families owned patches of gardens. We slowly wound our way up through the trees to emerge onto the fertile windswept plug at the top. Most of the boys stopped to pick flowers and sit and make flower-crowns for all. There were glorious views all around and within a few paces back and forth we could see in every direction to the merging of the sea and sky. Off to what I took to be the east of us I could just make out a white line in the blue sea where waves were crashing on the uninhabited islands of Fatutaka. Wilson Lyno had told me that the Anutans paddled the fifteen-odd miles across to the islands at certain times of the year to gather seabirds' eggs to eat, young seabirds as pets and to fish the reef. It looked an awfully long way in a small dugout, out-riggered or not.

We spent thirty minutes or so on the top of the plug, generally lazing around, catching a few butterflies and chatting in a non-verbal manner. The youths I was with were very relaxed and of mixed ages, all boys. It was fascinating to watch a large sixteen-year-old helping a ten-year-old with his flower weaving. They took pride in wearing their flowers. They seemed to wear them for their own gratification, not as some sort of western peacock show for the other sex. The way of life they lived did not seem onerous. There was no sign of women (or indeed anyone) working themselves into an early grave by slaving away in the gardens. They all seemed well fed, in fact pretty chubby as a general rule. Apparently Polynesians have great ability to lay down fat when there is an excess; this allowed them to survive voyages of huge distances in sea-going sailing canoes, reach new destinations (like Anuta), and still be in good enough nick to garden, fish, eat and reproduce. Although I was not there long enough to be certain, their life seemed good. They didn't have access to our western medicines, having refused all offers of a clinic, but their attitude to life completely made up for this. They seemed happy, self possessed and entirely self reliant. I think it might be because they were not overly 'educated' in our western fashion they were able to live so well. They were educated in what was important to them: fishing, gardening and family life. Perhaps they are luckier than we?

Moffat the younger decided it was now time to go. No one wore a watch or showed any interest in 'the time', but now was obviously the time to return to the village. He took me back an entirely different route, much steeper and past the holes dug into the earth which contained fermenting food covered in banana leaves which would stay put until an emergency. This food would remain edible for years, so Moffat informed me. Having turned back a couple of leaves on top of one of the ten-gallon holes I decided that it would take a pretty severe emergency to make me sample this fare. The landscape was made up of steep slopes with a patchwork of gardens, fruit trees and a very few stunted forest 'giants'. Timber is one of the most valuable commodities on the island. I was surrounded and caressed by butterflies and birdsong on the way down, and this time managed to appreciate it in a damp non-puffing way.

I think that even old Eve wouldn't have bothered Adam with a scrawny apple if she had had the good sense to have lived here.

We arrived back at the scattered leaf huts nearer the shore and Moffat led me to Moffat's house. This was as simple and strangely elegant as all the rest, nestling on the soft sand with soft outlines over a rigid frame of wood. *Bucephalus*-Moffat crawled out and met me with a smile dismissing non-*Bucephalus*-Moffat with a twitch of an eyebrow. He led me back into his home, crawling on hands and knees through the entrance. Inside it was quite gloomy, but I could see that there were a few people at the far end, and in the middle was a young, plump, pretty woman who turned out to be Ruth, Moffat's wife. She had prepared a repast for the family of which I was invited to partake. The reason Moffat had left me in the capable hands of the gang was so he could tell Ruth to get cracking with lunch. Ruth and Moffat had a chubby (very chubby) babe who gurgled and watched from the arms of an aunt from the back of the hut. I made all the correct sounds regarding the first-born of any couple and the babe was brought forward to be examined. More compliments along the lines of 'Isn't he fat?' Pleasure all round.

The floor of the hut was soft sand, very like the sand immediately outside the door in fact. The few timbers of the roof were supported by a couple of posts only, and the wind- and weather-proofing was provided by woven leaf sections tied to the timbers with vines. There were no windows and it took a few minutes for my eyes to adjust to the murk.

I was asked to sit on a Pandanus mat, and a huge amount of starch in various forms and flavours (actually lack of flavours) was presented and eaten with our fingers. The pièce de résistance was a huge purple cerebral-looking 'pudding' which Ruth seemed most proud of. Even in the murk the purple-ness shone forth and it was only with an effort that I managed a smile while chewing. The flies

Anuta: L to R: Moffat's hands, Ruth's fan, 'the' pudding, Ruth.

liked the pud, as they had liked all the other food, but Ruth 'roused' them with her fan.

I had had the most amazing day. I'd even seen some patients and felt I had learned something from these self-sufficient people. I thanked my host and hostess and returned to the clinic tree where the nurses were packing up ready to go. I noticed John Bakila again had a flower behind his ear. I would have to gently pull his leg about going native.

John: 'Flower blo' you, hem good tumas,' pointing at my flower crown.

Me: 'Ah ... yes, thank you John, yours looks good too ...'

We gathered everything together and headed to the shore. I noticed that all the canoes on the beach were covered by leaves and wondered why. I lifted the cover on a few and found the most fantastic pieces of art. The simple dugouts had extra pieces lashed to them with vine-string. So even if the original trunk was missing a large part, it was still used and the defect filled with another piece of wood, cut to the correct size, shape and thickness, holes drilled through it, and the whole lashed together. The boats also had simple ornamentation and were more angular than any others I had

Polynesian child.

seen. Beautiful, unique, and most interesting to me. I pointed all this out to Wilson Lyno, then when he showed little interest Wilson Yamalo. He, being a handyman, should have known better, but he was just as accepting as his namesake and could not bring himself to show much interest. Think of the time, think of the trouble taken ... Oh never mind.

We got into the last canoe back to our ship, and when I turned to wave goodbye I found all the Anutans had gone – off to get on with their lives.

How odd it felt to have made such a small impact on people who had made such a large impact on me.

Solomon Islanders are born survivors

SIR — I, for one, am not surprised at how the Tikopians and Anutans in the Solomon Islands survived a cyclone of such savagery (report, Jan. 6). These people are Polynesians — not pathetic, pampered, institutionally weak Westerners — and have a centuries-long knowledge that allows them to survive.

They build houses, the roofs and walls of which blow away in a high wind, leaving the precious wooden frame intact. Of course, the result then looks "destroyed". As a former director of provincial health services for Temotu Province in the Solomon Islands I note that my old Western-built medical clinic took a battering.

They keep a store of fermented food underground, they use their noddles and retreat to caves during the worst of the tempest.

They also have powerful chiefs and family ties, are not grasping or avaricious and are happy.

The communities are much nearer perfection than anything our great Western civilisation has yet dreamt up. They appear to have little — only food, water and shelter — but are happy with their lot. They are tough and stoical, rather than whingeing, moaning or complaining unlike we Westerners and their fellow Solomon islanders whom we have infected with our ideals in Honiara.

They are part of their immediate environment, not squatting uncertainly on their patch of the world. They manipulate their populations to remain sustainable. Of course they have illness and diseases, but their attitude to them is far more advanced than ours. They are amazing.

Dr David Arathoon
Ilchester, Somerset

End?

It was Christmas Eve and I was lying awake in bed. Sarah and the foetus were quietly asleep beside me. Black black black. It was absolutely pitch black. Why wasn't I asleep? I wondered if I was asleep. I shut my eyes to check, then opened them. Black either way. I stared at where the ceiling would be should there be a photon of light pollution to show it. I let my mind go free ... to wander.

What a strange life. What a strange year we had had. What amazing people we had met and got to know. All our real life local friends, and in some cases foes. The Wilsons: Lyno and Yamalo. John Bakila and the nurses. The Bishop and his powerful wife. The patients on the wards ... the TB patients. The local politicians, the provincial workers, the chiefs on the islands. The Moffats. The amazing bunch of old crones literally dressed in rags carrying lanterns and singing carols at the end of our verandah a couple of hours ago. The whities: the 'chooks' – the Peace Corps. Jake and Amy gently asleep down the corridor having helped Meg and Barney with their stockings for the morning. Barry who had helped us settle and was full of care and friendship; his replacement Ashley who had arrived full of energy and ideas. Lynne. The other real and unreal people we had met and got to know: Sassoon and Graves and particularly W.H.R. Rivers. Quentin Crewe and his weird emerging friendship with my father. La Compte de la Perouse and the New Caledonian French. Dillon and Bligh. Stephen Maturin and Jack Aubrey.

All the lone dogs. The bloody local curs. The pigs. The reef fish. The turtles. Our multitude of pets, now sadly mostly deceased including Betsy with her bilateral panophthalmitis of unknown cause.

And the name of the tree at the end of our drive with the massive display of bright red flowers? Barry had let us know its local name before he left: 'Christmas tree'.

I wondered: is this real life?

Not Quite ...

This is how it happened:

2 am: 'Where are you going?'

'Just to the sitting room to read.'

'Hmm,' suspiciously.

6.30 am: 'Do you think you should phone Lynne?' (to come and child-mind).

'Wadaya mean? Are you nearly there?'

'I think so.'

'Oh God ... do you think you could walk to the hospital? ... No? ... Cycle?'

'Er ... I don't think so – you had better get the hospital truck.'

'Oh God ...'

6.40 am: Phone Lynne and hospital while getting dressed, cycle to hospital, tell staff to get hold of Yvonne the midwife, pick up hospital truck, drive home. Find wife sitting on edge of bath:

'Er ... I don't think I can get to the truck.'

'WHAT?? ...'

'I think it's coming.'

'Quick, can you get to the bedroom?'

'Yup,' stagger, stagger.

Lynne arrives and phones to divert Yvonne to us, then waits in sitting room.

Lie wife on bedroom floor on a papa, rip off wife's knickers (those were the days ...).

'You're right – it's coming.'

'Oh God ...' and out she popped, 8 lbs and 10 oz of squished purple ugliness – just like our other two at the same stage. Completely by chance Sarah seemed to have a set of everything a reluctant midwife may require right to hand. Ros squawks, children wake, placenta delivers itself, Ros cleaned and dried, Lynne brings the other two to examine mother and new sibling. Not very interesting and go off for an early breakfast. Get wife off floor and cleaned up. Wander through to Lynne for congratulations and tea.

Forty minutes later Yvonne arrives: 'I dreamt you would have a BBA,' says she. A 'born before arrival'. Bit late Yvonne ...

Then Hilda arrived.

That's what you get.

Bucephalus with precious cargo: Sarah, Ros, Mary, Hilda.

Mathias and family with Sarah and Ros.